RESPONDING TO
DEFENSE DEPENDENCE

RESPONDING TO DEFENSE DEPENDENCE

Policy Ideas and the American
Defense Industrial Base

ERIK R. PAGES

Foreword by Theodore H. Moran

Westport, Connecticut
London

Library of Congress Cataloging-in-Publication Data

Pages, Erik R.
   Responding to defense dependence : policy ideas and the American
defense industrial base / Erik R. Pages ; foreword by Theodore H. Moran.
      p.   cm.
   Includes bibliographical references and index.
   ISBN 0–275–95313–0 (alk. paper)
   1. Defense industries—United States.   2. Military-industrial
complex—United States.   3. Industrial policy—United States.
4. National security—United States.   I. Title.
HD9743.U6P33   1996
338.4'7632'0973—dc20   95–11275

British Library Cataloguing in Publication Data is available.

Library of Congress Catalog Card Number: 95–11275
ISBN: 0–275–95313–0

First published in 1996

Praeger Publishers, 88 Post Road West, Westport, CT 06881
An imprint of Greenwood Publishing Group, Inc.

Printed in the United States of America

The paper used in this book complies with the
Permanent Paper Standard issued by the National
Information Standards Organization (Z39.48–1984).

10 9 8 7 6 5 4 3 2 1

Contents

Illustrations

Abbreviations

ABMA	American Bearing Manufacturers Association
AEA	American Electronics Association
AFBMA	Anti-Friction Bearing Manufacturers Association
ALESA	American League of Exports and Security Assistance
AMT	Association for Manufacturing Technology
ARPA	Advanced Research Projects Agency
ATP	Advanced Technology Program
ATV	advanced television
CBO	Congressional Budget Office
CEA	Council of Economic Advisors
CECC	Consumer Electronics Capital Corporation
CED	Committee for Economic Development
CNC	computer numerical control
CTI	Critical Technologies Institute
DARPA	Defense Advanced Research Projects Agency
DIB	defense industrial base
DoD	Department of Defense
DPA	Defense Production Act
DRAM	dynamic random access memory
DSB	Defense Science Board
EC	European Community
EIA	Electronic Industries Association
EPROM	erasable programmable read-only memory
EFA	European Fighter Aircraft
EMPB	Emergency Mobilization Preparedness Board
FAR	Federal Acquisition Regulations
FCC	Federal Communications Commission

GAO	General Accounting Office
GATT	General Agreement on Tariffs and Trade
GNP	Gross National Product
HDTV	high-definition television
IC	integrated circuit
IMIP	Industrial Modernization Incentives Program
IP	industrial policy
IR	international relations
ITC	International Trade Commission
JCS	Joint Chiefs of Staff
JDA	Japanese Defense Agency
JLC	Joint Logistics Commanders
M&A	mergers and acquisitions
MANTECH	Manufacturing Technology (Pentagon program)
MCTC	Microelectronics and Computer Technology Corporation
MITI	Ministry of Trade and Industry (Japan)
MOS	metal oxide semiconductor
MOU	memorandum of understanding
NADIBO	North American Defense Industrial Base Organization
NC	numerical control
NCID	National Committee for Industrial Defense
NCMS	National Center for Manufacturing Sciences
NIC	newly industrializing country
NIST	National Institute for Standards and Technology
NMTBA	National Machine Tool Builders Association
NREN	National Research and Education Network
NSC	National Security Council
OMB	Office of Management and Budget
OSD	Office of the Secretary of Defense
R&D	research and development
RSI	Rationalization, Standardization, and Interoperability
SCSG	Semiconductor Congressional Support Group
SIA	Semiconductor Industry Association
SRC	Semiconductor Research Corporation
TRP	Technology Reinvestment Project
USTR	United States Trade Representative
VHSIC	Very High Speed Integrated Circuit
VRA	Voluntary Restraint Agreement

Foreword

What is the appropriate role for the government to play in managing the health and vitality of the defense industrial base in an era of declining defense budgets? The United States has traditionally been less autarkic in its defense industrial base policies than either its allies or its rivals. American leaders have also been less willing to utilize industrial policy measures to support the defense industrial base. In the late 1980s, however, fundamental questions began to emerge about whether market forces alone could be relied upon to provide the United States with the kinds of capabilities and capacities the nation would need to meet the threats of the future. The growing challenge from abroad to the competitiveness of a broad array of U.S. industries suggested to many that a more interventionist approach might be needed in sectors where the United States was becoming dependent on external sources of supply. But public sector intervention always carries with it the possibility of misallocation of economic resources and the injection of political favoritism in the picking of winners and losers.

The decline of U.S. defense budgets and the increasing globalization of U.S. industries, including defense industries, has brought a new urgency to the problem of foreign dependence. At the same time, increasing sophistication in the analytical community—especially the emergence of strategic trade theory and the rigorous appreciation that concentration among external suppliers can constitute a genuine national security threat—has raised the level of debate. These are the analytical and policy trends that Erik R. Pages captures with unprecedented clarity.

Responding to Defense Dependence traces the evolution of concern about America's growing dependence on foreign sources of supply for vital inputs to the U.S. defense industry. Dr. Pages examines the U.S. response, as policymakers struggled between laissez-faire and various forms of industrial policy. The task has been to find the right balance between simply letting the market work on its own and engaging in the more blatant forms of public sector intervention.

The research draws from detailed case studies of some of the industries that most frequently are included in the roster of concern for national security. The author combines an in-depth analysis of four key industrial sectors—machine tools, semiconductor manufacturing, ball bearings, and high-definition television—with a close examination of how new analytical concepts such as "strategic trade policy" influenced the debate. The research integrates detailed empirical analysis of the most important cases with a refreshingly accessible explanation of the new and rather complicated analytical techniques.

One of the most remarkable findings is that policymakers in Washington actually show evidence of moving along a learning curve, benefitting from previous mistakes (like the disastrous price maintenance structures deriving from the 1986 Semiconductor Agreement) and deciding to eschew trade protection as an appealing policy tool. The challenge for the future will be to find a middle way to support critical industries with resorting to trade restraints or opening the door to pork-barrel subsidies.

This study will be valuable to a broad range of audiences. It offers a rare combination of economic analysis, international relations theory, and intensive examination of the policy process. It provides a detailed analysis of the industrial policy debate and the reasons for its successes and failures. It links international relations theory to new literatures on policy ideas, agenda setting, and the monopolization of the policy debate. It constitutes the first book-length study of U.S. defense industrial base policy and the issue of defense dependence.

Responding to Defense Dependence could not be more timely, and the importance of the questions it addresses will only grow more weighty over time. There are lessons here for the analytic community, for the policy community, and for the business community.

Theodore H. Moran
Karl F. Landegger Professor of International Business Diplomacy
School of Foreign Service
Georgetown University

Preface

My interest in the topic of this study—the American defense industrial base—stems from direct personal experience. While working as a Congressional staff member during the mid-1980s, I was contacted on several occasions by local firms who supplied parts and subcomponents to the U.S. Department of Defense. These companies had recently lost their contracts to overseas firms who had obtained the U.S. work through various bilateral cooperative arrangements.

As I investigated the business' complaints, I immersed myself in the world and jargon of the U.S. defense industrial base. What I found was both interesting and startling. Most of my contacts in the Defense Department and the Congress acknowledged that defense dependence was growing. They even acknowledged that these trends could prove to be dangerous in the future. But, for a variety of reasons, few efforts were made to address the issue of defense dependence. The local impact was direct and clear. The affected companies lost contracts, and, in several cases, went out of business. The national impact—on overall U.S. national security—was less clear. This book represents my attempt to understand these impacts and to explain the evolution of American defense industrial base policy.

In addition to examining this a fascinating empirical puzzle, this research effort has tremendously broadened my own perspectives on both international relations theory and political science in general. While trained in international relations theory and national security policy, I was forced to broaden my research interests to the topics of industrial policy, trade theory, science and technology policy, and a host of other issue-areas. concepts. As such, I can point to myself as a living embodiment of the shift from the concept of national security to one of economic security.

I would like to acknowledge the encouragement, advice, and support of Joseph Lepgold and Theodore H. Moran. Dr. Lepgold has proved to be both a supportive mentor and a good friend. He has provided helpful editorial comments and invaluable guidance on how to think about thorny theoretical problems. Dr. Moran has been a source of deep knowledge on both theoretical and substantive grounds. His enthusiasm and expertise provided the spark and inspiration I needed at a time when I felt that this project would never be completed. His outstanding work in melding rigorous academic research with substantive policy recommendations remains a model for all scholars.

I would like to further acknowledge the valuable help of various colleagues who have commented on parts of the manuscript or who served as intellectual sounding boards as these ideas were developed. Particular thanks go to Drs. Andrew Bennett and Robert Lieber of Georgetown University. My former colleagues at Business Executives for National Security (BENS), particularly Stanley Weiss, Tyrus Cobb and Bob Gaskin, provided me with both a stimulating intellectual environment and countless other types of support. My experiences with the talented staff and members of BENS contributed immeasurably to the development of the arguments presented in this book.

Moving to more personal acknowledgements, I thank my wife, Krista, who, in international relations parlance, compelled me to finish and deterred me from quitting. Our daugther, Madeline, joined us at the end of this effort, and has brought us immeasureable joy. My mother, Bente Pages, provided me with a loving environment and support in all of my endeavors—even when she questioned them. However, most importantly, I want to dedicate this work to my father, Richard Etienne Pages, who sadly passed away before this study could be completed. While I can never recreate his intellectual curiosity, cheerful demeanor, and passion for excellence, I hope that some of his qualities shine through in this work. His unconditional support for this effort helped steer me through some very difficult times, and my only regret is that he cannot join me to celebrate its long awaited completion.

1

Sounding the Alarm: Recognizing Defense Dependence

In 1980, a House Armed Services Committee report reached the following conclusion:

> There has been a serious decline in the nation's defense industrial capability that places our national security in jeopardy. An alarming erosion of crucial industrial elements, coupled with a mushrooming dependence on foreign sources for critical materials is endangering our defense posture at its very foundation.[1]

This congressional report was one of the first official recognitions of serious deficiencies in the American defense industrial base (DIB).[2] A number of factors contributed to the committee's alarm, but growing foreign dependence raised the most concern. The United States had relied on its superior industrial might to prevail in previous conflicts, especially in World Wars I and II. By the 1980s, as more and more weapons systems became dependent on foreign parts or technology, observers feared that this industrial strength might not be available to support U.S. troops in future contingencies. Among the industries considered to be affected by dependence were microelectronics, ferroalloys, machine tools, ball bearings, industrial fasteners, and advanced ceramics.[3] For example, import shares in the machine tool and anti-friction bearing industries rose in the 1980s to respective levels of at least 50 and 80 percent.[4]

This research seeks to explain U.S. government responses to this turn of events. It does so by testing the utility of realist approaches in explaining American defense industrial base policy in the 1980s. It examines the importance of relative gains considerations in influencing U.S. policymakers' perceptions of the competitiveness of the American industrial base. This study further examines methods for integrating realism's emphasis on relative gains with concepts derived from the literature on agenda setting and the impact of policy ideas. In particular, it introduces concepts from the literature on policy learning as a means to help explain changes in U.S.

defense industrial base policy. The intended result is a more complete and nuanced explanation for government responses to dependence on foreign sources of defense critical items.

THE PROBLEM

Dependence presented American policymakers with an unprecedented dilemma. The United States traditionally enjoyed a nearly autarkic industrial base. The sheer size and technological sophistication of the American economy made it possible to produce domestically almost everything needed for U.S. national security. Unlike their counterparts in Western Europe and Asia, American military leaders had little experience with reliance on imported weapons systems.[5]

This period of military self-sufficiency ended in the 1980s, as rising dependence triggered a major outcry both within and outside the U.S. government.[6] Within the U.S. government, numerous studies highlighted the problem and advocated government intervention to preserve industries critical to national security. Outside of government, ailing industrial sectors, already buffeted by intense foreign economic competition, invoked national security claims as justification for protection and governmental support. At the same time, many industrialists and policymakers grew increasingly concerned about the competitiveness of many American industries (both defense and civilian), and advocated an activist industrial policy to bail out ailing sectors.[7]

Government officials clearly recognized the potential dangers of this growing dependence. A 1988 Pentagon report noted:

> From the national security perspective, foreign dependencies in technologies essential to defense production are inherently risky, and minimizing them should be a Department of Defense and national priority. . . . In a national emergency, the consequences of extensive dependence on foreign sources could be extreme.[8]

As we will see below, dependence created a number of specific problems related to mobilization for war and maintenance of future technological superiority. However, all these fears stemmed from a larger concern: how to control the nation's destiny in an unstable and unpredictable world.

Dependence on foreign defense products posed potential threats over the short, medium, and long term.[9] In the short term, foreign sourcing could lead to a lack of access to critical items and spare parts during a crisis. Over the medium term, foreign sourcing might impair the ability to obtain larger end-use items and manufacturing capabilities. The long-term risks of dependence proved most worrisome, because foreign sourcing could lead to a loss of domestic research and development capabilities in militarily important technologies. As a result, the United States might be placed in a position of permanent technological weakness over the course of several decades. For example, during the debates surrounding the creation of Sematech (see Chapter Five), the consortium's supporters argued that Japanese dominance of world semiconductor manufacturing threatened the United States' ability to develop the advanced semiconductors critical to military success on the battlefields of the twenty-first century.

These concerns were not restricted to low levels of the bureaucracy. In fact, the Reagan administration entered office based on a commitment to improve industry's ability to support national defense needs. However, while recognizing the problem, officials in the White House and many relevant executive agencies did not act to reduce foreign dependence, and opposed government programs designed to preserve or strengthen domestic production capabilities. A 1986 Pentagon study summarized the government's response:

> The real issue, beyond [dependence's] apparently growing pervasiveness, is that it is not being adequately dealt with. [Government] studies note that no positive action has been undertaken to correct or mitigate foreign dependency in any focused, comprehensive way.[10]

This inaction presents us with an empirical puzzle: Why did American leaders oppose protection of domestic defense-related industries in the face of these indications of growing dependence? This response is surprising when compared to the actions of foreign officials who did attempt to mitigate the effects of their own defense dependence. Only Great Britain pursued DIB policies similar to those of the United States. Among the states assuming more activist stances were France, Sweden, Japan, and Canada.[11]

Inaction also poses interesting questions from a theoretical standpoint. Realism, the dominant international relations theory since World War II, predicts that U.S. political leaders would actively intervene to support domestic industries in these cases. Realism views security as the state's highest goal in the anarchic international system.[12] It further posits that a state's leaders will seek to act decisively in response to situations that threaten this objective.

The United States has largely avoided intervention in response to defense dependence. In general, American policymakers did not use national security as a justification for protecting ailing defense industries. In only two industries, semiconductors and machine tools, did policymakers create activist rescue packages. And in both these cases resistance to intervention was great, stalling action for several years.

This research seeks to explain these policy responses. Two important questions form the focus of our analysis: (1) Why did American policymakers oppose intervention to support defense-related industries and minimize defense dependence in the bulk of cases? and (2) What explains the exceptions to these patterns?

As we move from systemic to domestic explantions for policy, several hypotheses warrant further examination. Interest-group pressures have traditionally served as the predominant explanation for trade protectionism. Thus, one could explain DIB policy based on the absence or prevalence of industry lobbying for protection.

A second potential hypotheses can be derived from recent theorizing on the role of the state and foreign policy. According to this views, DIB policy results from the ability of policymakers to act autonomously and insulate themselves from societal pressures. If these central decisionmakers prefer open markets, protectionism is highly unlikely.

A final domestic-level hypothesis examines the role of policymakers' ideas about the world. It explains policy continuity by the persistence of a given policy idea or perspective on the world. When these ideas change, policy change is likely to follow.

My main conclusion is that policy responses are best explained by the persistence of shared ideas and images among American policymakers. Specifically, decision-makers' strong beliefs in the efficacy of free and open trade acted to prevent them from considering activist policy responses—even when faced with clear indications of significant defense dependence.

This situation gradually began to change in the mid to late 1980s as a result of changes in policy ideas shared by U.S. decisionmakers. As new developments in economic theory began to filter into the policymaking process, U.S. officials had reason to believe that they had developed more effective means for determining which industries were truly critical for national security purposes. Activist government responses were created only in those cases, such as machine tools and semiconductors, where industries met these criteria.

RESEARCH DESIGN

I base my conclusions on an examination of four cases that present a variation in the government's response. Two of these cases—the debate over creating a government program to support high-definition television (HDTV) and the govern-ment response to support for the domestic ball bearing industries—resulted in rejection of government support or intervention. These cases, which will be discussed in Chapters Six and Seven, are explained most parsimoniously by reference to policymakers' shared policy ideas.

In the case of U.S. policy toward promoting high-definition television, domestic interest groups, led by the American Electronics Association (AEA) along with some Bush administration officials, advocated the creation of an extensive government support program. This program was designed to aid commercial industry, but would also create significant spin-offs for defense purposes. Initially, the program gained some support among government officials, especially Secretary of Commerce Robert Mosbacher. However, these initial indications of support for HDTV programs were eventually squashed by the president and top-level White House officials. In the end, the government response was limited to support for basic laboratory research and the creation of industry-wide HDTV standards.

The ball bearing case offers a typical example of the workings of Section 232 of the 1962 Trade Expansion Act.[13] Faced with significant foreign competition, domestic bearings producers requested protection on the basis of the industry's important role in defense production. A required Commerce Department investigation into the industry's health indicated that grounds for intervention did exist. However, President Reagan ultimately rejected the industry's claims.[14]

Our other two cases—the semiconductor and machine tool cases—present exceptions to the general policy line of the 1980s and offer a more interesting analysis of policy ideas and their impact. In these cases, which are discussed in Chapters Four and Five, the administration did protect domestic producers through Voluntary Restraint Agreements (VRAs). But, more importantly, they also agreed to provide financial support for public-private consortia: Sematech and the National Center for Manufacturing Sciences. Creation of these organizations entailed major policy innovations, indicating significant policy learning by policymakers. These consortia represent the first time the U.S. government directly funded joint private sector R&D on the basis of an industry's military and commercial importance.

Acceptance of intervention in these cases was related to the nature of each industry. Both are considered "critical industries"—technologies that supply essential components in a wide range of weapons systems and whose production has significant spillover effects on other sectors of the economy. Thus, there existed a strong case that support for semiconductors and machine tools did not involve targeted industrial policy or interference with market forces. The critical nature of these industries helped their supporters overcome policymakers' traditional opposition to targeted industrial support, that is, government picking of winners and losers.

My analysis is based on what Alexander George has called the method of structured, focused comparison.[15] The cases were chosen according to several criteria. First, they are arguably the most important and most heated defense industrial debates of the 1980s. In all of these cases, partisan conflict was extensive and policy debate moved out of specialized channels into the broader political arena.[16] Dependence was clearly identified and domestic groups invoked national security as a rationale for protection in every case. Each sector also faced severe competitive pressures from overseas, especially from Japan. Because the industrial sectors faced similar competitive pressures, they present us with a useful framework for comparison. Moreover, the differing results permit the comparison of cases where new ideas promoted change and where they failed to do so.

The industrial sectors examined in the case studies differ across a number of important variables, including maturity of the industry, the nature of the industry's relationship to direct military needs, and political clout. Although all of the industrial sectors involved manufacturing, they differed in their maturity and in the manner in which they were perceived by policymakers and the public. Both ball bearings and machine tools are mature, established industries. In contrast, semiconductor manufacturing and HDTV were considered emerging high-technology sectors.

In addition, each industry differed in terms of its relationship to direct defense needs. For instance, ball bearings and HDTV involved direct inputs into military systems, while semiconductor manufacturing and machine tools were not directly consumed by the military. Instead, they manufactured items for military use.

None of the sectors enjoyed substantial political clout similar to that of the textile, steel, automobile industries. While the National Machine Tool Builders Association enjoyed relatively close contacts within the administration and Capitol Hill, the ball bearing industry did not even employ a full-time Washington staff. Similarly, HDTV enjoyed support from the American Electronics Association, but did not have an established grassroots constituency. Finally, while the semiconductor manufacturing industry did not maintain an active Washington office, it did employ a high-powered lobbying team to influence Congress and the administration.

While the case study approach suffers from some shortcomings when compared to statistical approaches, it offers the advantage of facilitating intensive analysis of a few important cases.[17] The specific method used in this research is what Eckstein calls "disciplined-configurative," where analysis of the case studies is designed to test specific theoretically grounded hypotheses.[18]

The individual case studies will be guided by a series of general questions framing our analysis:[19]

1. What is at stake in the policy dispute? Specifically, where and how does the fear of foreign dependence manifest itself?
2. What are the positions of the actors in the dispute? How do they define the issue? What policy ideas are important?
3. What are the various policy options proposed for resolving the issue?
4. What is the result? Did government officials intervene to "rescue" the affected industry? Why or why not?

By using these questions to guide each case study, we can gain a better understanding of the links between shared ideas and policy making. Moreover, we can also develop insights into the future contours of American DIB policy.

Realism and the Concept of Relative Gains

The results of these cases present a puzzle for analysts, because the most widely accepted international relations theory-realism-predicts that defense dependence would trigger an active response from government leaders. Neorealists base this prediction on their recognition that states are constantly concerned with questions of relative position and power.[20] When faced with potential alterations in military and economic power, states will react to these shifts.[21]

Realists argue that a state's willingness to enter into cooperative arrangements depends on its assessment of the relative gains from such a move. Will state X gain more from cooperation than state Y? If so, state Y may be less willing to cooperate. This concern constrains cooperation, but does not preclude it.[22] However, a state is unlikely to cooperate if other states benefit to its own disadvantage. As Mastanduno has noted, "a nation-state in pursuit of relative gains will seek to avoid or restructure relationships or cooperative ventures in order to reduce or eliminate gaps in benefits that favor its partners."[23]

The extent of a state's emphasis on relative gains depends on the specifics of the situation and the nature of the issue area. Relative gains considerations are generally more important in military than economic relations. Furthermore, relations between allies will be freer from relative gains considerations than are relations between adversaries. When a common enemy poses a clear and present danger, states may actually welcome increases in an ally's relative capabilities.[24] Indeed, the presence of a pressing Soviet threat encouraged U.S. support for the development of indigenous defense industries in Western Europe and Japan. As we will see below, the diminution of the Soviet threat has increased allied tensions regarding defense industrial base policies. Despite these caveats, realists expect that such considerations are never completely absent.[25]

A state's power position in the international system also affects its policy options, choices, and relative gains calculations. A state's concern with relative gains varies inversely with the gap separating it from rivals or potential rivals. An internationally hegemonic state should be especially immune to relative gains concerns. This occurs because powerful states enjoy a number of advantages, including abundant resources, large populations, and international market power. Powerful states enjoy wider ranges of action and wider margins of safety.[26]

However, as the power of the hegemonic state declines and the importance of military threats recedes, realists expect the hegemonic state to become more attuned to relative gains considerations and begin to act more like a "normal" country. In other words, the hegemon becomes less committed to supporting international regimes that offer gains to all states and begins to pursue policies that aid itself at the expense of its competitors.

In the realm of American DIB policy, greater concern for relative gains would, according to realism, be expected to manifest itself in state intervention to protect or subsidize domestic industries. It would involve a policy shift away from liberal internationalism toward neomercantilism. Indeed, as policymakers have begun to recognize America's relative decline, many have pressed for a shift toward policies embodying relative gains considerations.[27]

Despite these expectations, one must recognize that concern with relative gains and concern with dependence are not necessarily synonymous. No state can remain autarkic in an increasingly interdependent world. However, states do remain concerned about maintaining future independence and autonomy, and strive to avoid situations that might threaten these goals. These concerns are particularly acute in national security related issue areas, prompting states to seek autarky in the production of critical military goods.[28]

While relative gains concerns prove most compelling on questions of national defense, direct security threats did not arise in the cases examined in this study. Instead, existing economic relationships between the United States and its allies (primarily Japan) potentially threatened America's future position in the development and application of advanced technology. The potential repercussions were not limited to the bilateral relationships between the United States and Japan (or other allies). Dependence also threatened the United States' ability to counter more direct and immediate military threats from the Soviet Union. Over the long term, defense industrial planners feared that foreign gains in nonmilitary domains could be exploited in both military and nonmilitary arrangements in the future.[29] The future importance of a given technology, such as semiconductors, proved more important than its existing military utility in spurring calls for action.

A systems level approach would predict that international changes, such as the decline of U.S. economic power, the diminution of the Soviet threat, and the rise of other powers such as the European Community and Japan, would make American policy more sensitive to relative gains considerations. However, recent events do not confirm this hypothesis. Until quite recently, relative gains considerations have not played a major role in U.S. policy. Despite indications of growing defense dependence, American policymakers did not act to protect threatened defense-related industries.

BACKGROUND TO THE ISSUE AREA

The concept of dependence has a long history in political thought.[30] It figures prominently in the works of political theorists such as Machiavelli, Montesquieu, and Rousseau as well as political economists such as Malthus and Adam Smith. For example, Adam Smith, best known for his development of laissez-faire economic theories, also argued that "It is of importance that the kingdom depend as little as possible upon its neighbors for the manufactures necessary for its defense; and if these cannot be maintained at home, it is reasonable that all other branches of industry be taxed in order to support them."[31]

In the postwar era, the concept of "dependence on trade" was first explored comprehensively in Hirschman's *National Power and the Structure of Foreign Trade*.[32] More recently, the 1970s saw a flurry of theorizing regarding the concept of interdependence with the works of Keohane and Nye and others introducing a number of new concepts into international relations theory.[33]

For my purposes, it is best to view dependence in terms of vulnerability. Dependence refers to a situation where the cost of disengagement from a given relationship is high. Herein, dependence (or defense dependence) refers to a situation where reliance on a foreign source raises the potential that one's ability to produce critical weapon systems and/or secure the most advanced technology for the development of a future weapons system could be compromised.[34] This might occur through a cut-off of supplies or through domestic industry's inability to maintain access to leading edge research and technology.

In discussing dependence, one must remember that dependence does not always produce extreme vulnerability. Dependence limits a government's options; it does not eliminate them. As Baldwin notes,

> Discussions of dependency often portray the dependent actor as "having no alternatives" or having "alternatives closed off." This kind of rhetoric never means what it appears to mean. The statesman always has alternatives. When someone says that the United States has no alternative to importing oil . . . they really mean that alternatives involve costs that the parties are unwilling or unable to bear. Clearer understanding of dependency relations would be achieved if alternative relations were described as more or less costly rather than as existent or non-existent.[35]

In this sense, dependence becomes vulnerability and affects a relationship when the opportunity costs of foregoing the relationship are high or intolerable.

An example might help clarify this point. National autarky is very difficult to achieve in the modern interdependent, global economy. For example, the United States is dependent on the supply of high technology consumer items and investment from Japan. Yet, at the same time, Japan is dependent on U.S. export markets along with American military support, creating a situation of mutual dependence comparable to a relationship of mutual nuclear deterrence.[36] Because of this mutual dependence, neither side can abandon the relationship without weakening itself.

Even with these caveats, dependence remains an undesirable situation for both states, as problems might arise when asymmetries in interdependence develop.[37] If Americans come to value Japanese goods and investment more than the Japanese value American export markets or military goods, dangers might emerge. For example, Japanese Defense Agency (JDA) officials recognize the potential threats caused by Japan's dependence on American military products and have made its elimination one of their top priorities.[38]

Because of such costs, nearly everyone agrees that dependence is undesirable. While many see dependence (or interdependence) as inevitable or unavoidable, most theorists and policymakers would agree that its effects should be mitigated. This is especially true in the military sphere, where nations have traditionally sought to preserve domestic capability to produce critical weapon systems. The puzzle facing us is to explain why American political leaders did not act more boldly to mitigate the effects of defense dependence during the 1980s.

The Emergence of Dependence

As we have seen, defense dependence first emerged as an issue for U.S. defense planners in the early 1980s. By the late 1980s, it was no longer a small blip on policymakers' radar screens; dependence had become an important public policy issue.[39]

This issue arose as part of a larger set of concerns over America's rising technological interdependence and a growing sense that America was in decline. In 1987, the publication of Paul Kennedy's *The Rise and Fall of Great Powers* sparked a heated public debate.[40] Kennedy argued that the United States suffered from "imperial overstretch," a tendency of great powers to maintain their military commitments at the expense of long-term investment in productive capabilities.[41] Kennedy and others, dubbed the "declinists" by Samuel Huntington, argued that the United States faced the possibility of losing its predominant international position as had previous hegemons such as Great Britain.[42]

The declinist argument was soundly criticized by Samuel Huntington, Joseph Nye, and others.[43] These authors argued that "decline" simply represented the growth of other economies and the restructuring of global economic shares from the anomalous position of uncontested U.S. hegemony in the 1950s. They noted that only the United States maintained the military, economic, and political capabilities needed to remain a global superpower.[44] No other state could match these resources.

Despite heated debate, most analysts agreed that the United States' global dominance had eroded. While their interpretations of these trends differed, they generally agreed that certain trends were disconcerting.[45] Between 1980 and 1986, U.S. imports of foreign high-technology products rose from 11.5 to 18.6 percent of total domestic consumption, with the United States posting its first-ever high-technology trade deficit in 1986. Between 1973 and 1987, the United States' world share of inward foreign direct investment[46] rose from 9.9 to 25.2 percent. As of 1989, foreign-owned firms in the United States were estimated to account for nearly one-quarter of U.S. exports and one-third of U.S. imports. In a report released in 1992, the industry-led Council on Competitiveness concluded that U.S. businesses were competitively weak in over one-third of the industries deemed critical to future economic growth.[47]

The weaknesses of America's commercial industries spilled over into the defense sector and contributed to defense dependence. These trends were reinforced by the growing commonality between commercial and military technologies. Of the twenty-two key technologies identified in the DoD's 1989 Critical Technologies Plan, sixteen overlapped with technologies identified in the Commerce Department's 1990 Emerging Technologies Report. In contrast to the past, modern weapons had become highly dependent on commercial high technology products. For example, one European industrialist suggested in 1991 that electronic equipment would account for over 40 percent of future combat aircraft costs.[48] A comparison between the navy's F-4 Fighter and its replacement, the F-18, further confirms these trends. Electronics components composed 2 percent of the F-4 and 43 percent of the F-18.[49]

As commercial and military technologies became more similar, policy makers also found that commercial technology advances had begun to outpace military advances. As Michael Sekora, former director of technology planning at the Pentagon noted, some composite materials used in weapons are "not nearly as sophisticated as what you could buy in your local sporting goods store."[50]

In the past, defense R&D advances had often been transferred to commercial sectors, a process described as spin-off.[51] For example, early advances in the American semiconductor and commercial aircraft industries grew out of military R&D programs. In the 1980s, roles were reversed as "spin-on" began to replace spin-off, and commercial advances outpaced the military's state-of-the-art technologies. For example, the Patriot missile still contains microprocessors that were first developed in the 1970s and were several generations behind commercial standards by the late 1980s.

These trends had two effects. First, they made military technology increasingly dependent on commercial R&D advances; second, they reduced the Pentagon's ability to drive technological change. In the 1960s, approximately 70 percent of U.S. produced computer chips went into military equipment; in 1991, 8 percent of chips were used for this purpose.[52] R&D expenditures indicate similar trends. In 1960, DoD accounted for one-half of all U.S. R&D expenditures and one-third of all R&D performed by the Western industrialized countries. In 1990, it accounted for one-third of total U.S. R&D spending and one-sixth of R&D in the industrialized world.[53]

As a result of these changes, many defense analysts became more and more concerned about the health of the national industrial base. However, they also noted that U.S. commercial business had lost its technological lead in several key high technology sectors. Thus, eroding commercial competitiveness also contributed to defense dependence. Although aggregate data on defense dependence does not exist for the United States, the industry-level information cumulatively indicates a deepening of dependence over the last ten to fifteen years. Table 1.1 identifies the major government-sponsored DIB studies that identified problems with defense dependence.

In a general sense, defense dependence was not a new phenomenon. The United States had been dependent for defense goods in the past, especially on foreign sources of raw materials such as oil, cobalt, titanium, and other strategic minerals. Indeed, the Strategic Stockpile and the Strategic Petroleum Reserves were established to counter the threats of these raw material dependencies.[54] But, by the 1980s, dependence had moved into the new area of manufactured goods. This type of dependence concerns us here.

Significant defense dependence did not develop in the area of major systems. For example, only a few complete systems, such as the Harrier AV-8B jet, the 120mm gun for the M1 tank, and the Beretta hand gun, were procured offshore. Dependence on foreign sources existed mainly in the area of subcomponents and parts, the crucial building blocks of modern weapons systems. A number of specific problem areas also received attention. For example, the market for surface acoustic wave technology, used in radar and communications circuits, was 80% controlled by Japanese and Korean firms.[55]

Weaknesses in these critical industries made many weapons systems almost completely dependent on foreign sources for critical components. As one analyst quipped, "many of today's systems are about as American as a Ford Escort."[56] In 1987, Admiral James Lyons, commander of U.S. forces in the Pacific, noted: "All of the critical components of our modern weapon systems, which involve our F-16s and F/A 18s, our M-1 tanks, our military computers, — and I could go on and on — come from East Asian industries. I don't see a change in that, during the foreseeable future. Some day, we might view that with concern, and rightly so."[57]

Dependence: Underlying Causes

Defense dependence developed as part of the larger phenomenon of globalization of America's defense industries.[58] Driven by a confluence of technological, economic, and political/military pressures, globalization manifested itself in a number of ways: increased foreign investment in U.S. industry, cross-border alliances between U.S. and foreign defense firms, and simple foreign dominance in U.S. markets.

From a technological perspective, globalization was driven by the rapidly rising costs of weapons systems. As weapons systems became more complex their costs rose exponentially, creating a situation known as structural disarmament. According to Thomas Callaghan, structural disarmament is "what happens when a nation's defense budget, plus exports, provides too small a market to bring armament development and production costs down to a politically affordable level."[59]

The roots of structural disarmament lie in the increased technological sophistication of weapons systems. Technological improvements cost money, making each new generation of weapons much more expensive.[60] By increasing the unit cost of weapons, fewer systems can be produced and purchased.

Defense industries responded to this dilemma by entering into joint ventures and

Table 1.1

Major U.S. Government Studies of Defense Dependence

DATE	STUDY	AGENCY	PROBLEM AREAS
1983	*Industrial Responsiveness Study*	Industry/DoD	Hawk, Phoenix, TOW missiles,and ten other systems
1983	*NRC Machine Tool Study*	Industry/DoD	machine tools
1984	*BluePrint for Tomorrow*	Air Force	engines, tactical missiles
1985	*Precision Guided Munitions (PGMs)*	JCS	twenty PGMs
1985	*Defense Industrial Base Study*	GAO	M1, Harpoon,and three others
1985	*Industrial Responsiveness Analysis*	Industry/DoD	27 systems and subsystems
1985	*Effects of Foreign Dependency*	JLC	M1, Sparrow, F-16 and ten others
1986	*Precision Bearings Study*	JLC	precision bearings
1987	*Optics Study*	JLC	precision optics

Year	Study	Agency	Focus
1987	*Dependency/Vulnerability Study*	NDU	seventeen PGMs
1987	*Semiconductor Study*	DSB	semiconductors
1990	*Foreign Vulnerability of Critical Industries*	DARPA/TASC	machine tools, semiconductor and automatic test equipment
1990	*Dependence of U.S. Systems on Foreign Technologies*	DoD/IDA	Micro-electronics, certain advanced materials, flat panel displays
1991	*Adequate Insurance for Critical Dependencies*	Rand/DARPA	Tritium, HDTV, acoustic technology, DRAMs
1992	*Study of Three Weapon Systems*	Commerce Department	Ceramic packages, wire rod, precision bearings

Source: Author; Friedberg (1989). p. 411. Note, this data omits studies completed as part of investigations under Section 232 of the Trade Expansion Act of 1962. For data on those studies, see U.S. Department of Commerce, *The Impact of Imports on National Security*, July 1989. Abbreviations: DSB-Defense Science Board; NDU-National Defense University; JLC-Joint Logistics Commanders; TASC-The Analytical Science Corporation; IDA-Institute for Defense Analyses.

strategic alliances with the purpose of entering new markets and increasing production runs for major systems. Longer production runs increase efficiency and significantly reduce production costs.[61] This drive for production efficiency was a major force pushing globalization. Given the small size of their domestic markets, European states were especially active in creating collaborative programs. The European Fighter Aircraft (EFA), developed jointly by Great Britain, Spain, Germany, and Italy, offers a well-known example.[62]

These pressures ultimately helped lead to a major shake-up in the international defense industry. This transformation took two forms: mergers and acquisitions (M&As) within borders, and cross-border linkages.

With their smaller domestic markets, European firms led the way in promoting consolidation. Between 1985 and 1990, European defense and aerospace firms were involved in roughly 220 mergers and acquisitions with other national firms. Roughly forty transnational mergers and acquisitions occurred during the same period.[63] Among the best known of these cross-border purchases were the French company Thomson-CSF's purchase of the Dutch firm Philips's defense divisions, the merger of the helicopter divisions of France's Aerospatiale and Germany's Messerschmitt-Bolkow-Blohm, and the joint purchase of the U.K.'s Plessy by Britain's GEC and Germany's Siemens.

While somewhat more cautious than their European counterparts, American firms were also involved in these transactions. In the 1970s, only a handful of cross-border M&As occurred. However, their frequency rapidly expanded until thirty-five M&As were completed in 1990 and 1991.[64] Between 1985 and 1990, U.S. firms merged with, or took over, eighty-four European aerospace companies.[65] Foreign purchase of U.S. dual-use firms was also extensive. According to one database, foreign firms made 608 total or partial acquisitions of U.S. high technology firms between October 1988 and April 1992.[66]

Economic and political/military factors reinforced these technological changes. Economically, extensive overcapacity burdened Western defense firms. Simply put, there were too many contractors chasing too few contracts. This produced a plethora of different weapons systems in the hands of NATO forces. For example, by the mid-1980s, NATO fielded over two dozen antitank weapons, a variety of tanks, over fifty kinds of ammunition, almost 100 different tactical missiles, and two dozen families of combat aircraft.[67]

It is somewhat ironic that U.S. policy helped create this overcapacity. After World War II, European and Japanese industry was shattered. As part of its overall containment policy, the United States government helped reestablish indigenous defense industries in allied states. In many cases, the United States simply transferred designs and technology for production in overseas plants. These items were then purchased for use by U.S. and NATO forces.[68] Since the 1950s, the U.S. has formally entered into eighty-seven government-to-government licensed production agreements with nineteen countries.[69] Among the systems built under this program were the Starfighter jet and European production of the Hawk, Bullpup, and Sidewinder missiles.[70]

These industries eventually developed indigenous design/production expertise and created systems that competed with American designs. As defense budgets rose in the early 1980s, such overcapacity was a manageable problem. However, spending peaked in 1985, and as spending declined both governments and private defense firms were forced to respond. Defense firms, encouraged by their home governments, responded with cross-border collaboration and mergers.

U.S. political leaders were among the most active in pushing for rationalization through globalization. The heart of their effort was NATO's Rationalization, Standardization, and Interoperability (RSI) policy, known colloquially as the "Two Way Street." First announced in 1975, RSI was designed to reduce overcapacity and promote NATO's use of common weapons systems. RSI was driven by military considerations, as NATO leaders feared that the variety of systems would prevent allied forces from fighting together effectively. Their solution was to have all forces fight with the same, or at a minimum, interoperable weapons. Although RSI's ambitious goals remain unfulfilled, the program played an important role in increasing interalliance defense trade.

Finally, as we have seen, dependence arose out of the growing weakness of many critical American industries. American industry grew less robustly in the 1980s. A variety of causes have been cited: sluggish domestic productivity growth, closed foreign markets, declining educational standards, poor management, and flawed government policies.[71] As defense technologies became more entwined with the commercial industrial base, these commercial weaknesses had a negative effect on defense independence. Chapter Three provides additional discussion of these broader economic trends.

The Policy Debate over Dependence

Parties on both sides of this debate recognized the potential threat of dependence on foreign goods for military purposes. Indeed, concern over dependence had a long history in American political thinking. Alexander Hamilton's 1791 *Report on Manufactures* advocated a system of industrial and commercial tariffs to render the United States independent of foreign nations for military and other essential supplies.[72] For the bulk of our history, American leaders heeded Hamilton's advice, creating a domestic arsenal system and erecting high tariff barriers for commercial and military industries alike.

This mercantilist legacy gradually weakened through the 1930s and 1940s as American policy shifted toward acceptance of open markets for defense goods.[73] Because of its large domestic market and World War II's economic destruction within Europe, American leaders enjoyed a period of uncontested military and economic hegemony that lasted until well into the 1960s. As a result of this market dominance, few U.S. government officials questioned the propriety of a policy promoting open defense trade.

Given this tradition, American military planners were ill-prepared to respond when the tables were turned and foreign defense products began entering U.S. markets. Most analysts raised similar points when discussing the dangers of dependence. The concerns fell into three interrelated categories: military, technological, and political. Those who emphasized military issues were largely concerned with security of supply and mobilization. Would foreign suppliers be able to provide the U.S. military with the goods it required in a crisis? Others argued that foreign control of U.S. markets would contribute to the long-term erosion of the American industrial base. Moreover, the U.S. military could lose its qualitative edge if world-class technological capabilities were based overseas. Finally, those concerned with political factors feared that foreign businesses might use their control over technology to affect American political decisions. Precious freedom of maneuver might be lost.

Military planners were especially concerned about foreign dependence's impact on crisis mobilization, that is, the ability to produce weapons systems in sufficient quantity and at sufficient speed to meet military demand in a national security emergency.[74] Would lost access to foreign supplies or production bottlenecks overseas hamper military production at home?

The Reagan administration entered office convinced that industrial weakness was an Achilles heel for American defense efforts. Its defense programs included a strong commitment to improve mobilization response in the face of the Soviet threat. Fred C. Ikle, undersecretary of defense for policy, took the lead on these issues. As part of his defense program, President Reagan created a special Emergency Mobilization Preparedness Board (EMPB) within the National Security Council (NSC) to address some of the problems related to dependence.[75]

Despite a rhetorical commitment to improved mobilization response, few concrete policy changes ensued. The mobilization weaknesses identified in the late 1970s remained unchanged in the 1990s. Even the forty-two day effort of the Persian Gulf War taxed American mobilization capabilities.[76]

Most discussions of mobilization raised questions about the reliability of nondomestic suppliers. Echoing frequently voiced concerns, Edward Olsen emphasized "the doubtful reliability of allies under duress. Their political reliability cannot be guaranteed during a crisis or war. Some are not even reliable supporters of U.S. positions in peacetime. . . . [P]ermitting the continuing decline of our smokestack and other industries essential to U.S. national defense will remain a dangerous strategic myopia."[77]

Overseas suppliers might be less reliable for a number of reasons. In some cases, foreign policy differences might lead home governments to prevent transfer of military goods. For example, Sony withheld transfer of TV cameras for missile guidance during the Vietnam War and, in 1983, under pressure from Socialist members, the Japanese Diet blocked an American subsidiary of Kyocera from supplying ceramic packaging for use in U.S. cruise missiles.[78] American efforts to block U.S. subsidiaries in Europe from supplying pipeline equipment to the Soviet Union also fall within this category. In fact, American policymakers are among the most frequent users of this policy tool—the entire U.S. export control system is based on this concept.[79]

Beyond political differences, foreign suppliers might be less reliable for a variety of reasons outside of the home government's control. These complicating factors include the supplier's distance from the United States, economic and political instability in the supplier's country, and its proximity to potential battle sites. In a time of war or major international crisis, these factors could coalesce to cut American industry off from key suppliers.

Concerns over reliability arose in the aftermath of the Gulf War, as the Bush administration was forced to intervene with foreign governments on over thirty occasions to guarantee delivery of crucial military parts. As one high-level administration official commented: "If the foreign governments were neutral or were not disposed to help us out, we could have run into some real problems. We were sweating bullets over it and the military was sweating bullets, too."[80]

If foreign suppliers were unable to meet U.S. military needs, the credibility of the American deterrent force might come into question. In the 1980s, defense analysts argued that NATO forces were insufficiently supplied for a protracted conflict. For example, in 1982, a House Appropriations subcommittee found that U.S. military forces could not sustain combat operations in a major contingency. In one case, it determined that the navy could not sustain full combat operations for more than a week.[81]

These problems posed a serious threat to the credibility of NATO's flexible response policy. If conventional forces could not be reinforced and sustained, the credibility of NATO's conventional deterrent would erode. In fact, Supreme Allied Commander-Europe John Galvin was forced to admit in 1988 that deficiencies in NATO's combat forces would require him to employ nuclear weapons within two weeks of an all-out Warsaw Pact attack in Europe.[82] For those concerned with industry's mobilization capabilities, the solution was a greater reliance on domestic sources.

These arguments regarding mobilization were not new. Many of the same points were raised in the aftermath of the Korean and Vietnam wars. What was different about the 1980s discussion was that traditional mobilization concerns combined with new fears of technological dependence. For the first time, fears about the defense sector were seen as part of a larger process of deterioration among all American industries.

These technological anxieties took several forms. First, many analysts feared that foreign firms might not supply the Pentagon with their most technologically advanced materials, reserving their best supplies for domestic needs. As foreign companies gained an increasingly larger market share, manufacturing could move offshore, with technology development soon to follow. In these cases, the Pentagon could lose access to new developments, and technological innovations would not be incorporated into future weapons systems.[83] As several analysts wrote in 1986,

> it is unlikely that the international exchange of scientific information can be a complete substitute for the erosion of a domestic research base. . . . Japanese scientific and business communities in [electronics] and other fields are quite closed. . . . As a result, technological information . . . is likely to move much more rapidly within Japan than between Japan and the rest of the world.[84]

Loss of access to cutting-edge technology was worrisome because the American military traditionally relied on technological superiority to overcome numerical inferiority. Losing this technological edge could have potentially disastrous repercussions. In a 1990 report, the Defense Science Board (DSB) highlighted these fears. It noted that Nikon often sold its semiconductor "stepper" manufacturing equipment in Japan up to 24 months before it was made available to nondomestic firms.[85] A 1991 General Accounting Office(GAO) investigation found this practice to be even more pervasive. Its review of fifty-nine U.S. firms involved in the computer industry determined that almost half had faced significant delays in receiving top-of-the-line equipment from Japanese suppliers.[86] Susan Tolchin succinctly summarized the fears of many analysts: "One need not be much of a visionary to see the effect of a loss of cutting edge technology. Semiconductor design changes on average every two and one-half years. It follows, then, that Japan's policy of saving the newest and best computer chips for itself means that American products that depend on computer chips will become less versatile."[87]

Second, analysts feared that non-domestic firms might not supply goods specifically tailored to unique U.S. military requirements. Bernard L. Schwartz, CEO of Loral Corporation, outlined these dangers in a 1989 speech:

> The foreign owner controls the enterprise in critical ways that may or may not support U.S. defense objectives. Overall, the real risk of foreign ownership stems from America's losing control of today's defense technology and its ability to influence investments in tomorrow's technology. . . . Once ownership control passes out of U.S. hands, there is no assurance that the company's priorities will continue to support the priorities of the U.S. defense establishment.[88]

Schwartz's reservations were based on trends in industries such as integrated circuits. In the mid-1980s, Japanese firms reportedly refused to develop bubble memories, an offline storage device, which met DoD specifications. Had the U.S. firm Intel refused to step in, the Pentagon would have lost access to this technology.[89] American officials were similarly critical of Japanese firms' reluctance to pursue and share advances in gallium arsenide—a new electronic material used in semiconductors.[90]

Third, many observers feared the more long-term effects of defense dependence on the American manufacturing base. As U.S. businesses lose contracts to non-domestic firms, they may also lose sufficient demand to keep production lines open and be forced to go out of business. This has three perverse effects: (1) U.S. ability to produce weapons at home further declines, (2) jobs and critical skills are lost, and (3) commercial competitiveness erodes. For many administration critics, government inaction was threatening to create a hollow industrial base.

Technological dependence fed political concerns: Would foreigners use their technological and financial power to coerce the United States or, at a minimum, make certain policy options more costly? Many feared that foreign interests might turn the tables on the United States. American leaders, long used to wielding their financial and technological power to coerce desired policy changes, might now see similar tools employed against them. Prominent American business leaders argued that the country would no longer be "fully in control of its economic fortunes [that]...now depend, as never before, on the whims of its foreign creditors."[91] Former Defense Secretary Harold Brown predicted significant changes in the U.S.-Japan relationship:

A new situation will emerge as Japan equals, and more so should it surpass the United States in technological capability. The economic growth rate of the U.S. would decline further, and there would be a further relative degradation of the economic base on which rests U.S. geopolitical and military strength. . . . Psychological as well as technological and economic effects would be expected.[92]

As Brown's comments suggest, much of the concern on this count focused on Japan, the major supplier of high-tech goods to the United States. These fears were fanned by the 1989 publication of *The Japan That Can Say No* by Diet Member Shintaro Ishihara and Akio Morita, Chairman of Sony.[93] Morita and Ishihara argued that Japan should use its technological dominance to influence political events, asserting that "It has come to the point that no matter how much [the U.S. and U.S.S.R.] continue military expansion, if Japan stopped selling them the [computer] chips, there would be nothing more they could do.[94]

Such political concerns remained relevant even after the end of the Cold War, leading some to express fears that the United States was becoming a "techno-colony."[95] Former chairman of the Joint Chiefs of Staff (JCS) Admiral William Crowe, summarized the concerns of many military officers when he argued: "The Gulf War was unique because America enjoyed the unanimous support of all its allies. Even so, cooperation was difficult....The U.S. defense industrial base is already in danger of becoming too dependent upon foreign sources for strategic supplies. What if the next time we are called upon to respond, our allies decide it is in their best interest to sit it out?"[96]

Policy Options

These concerns over the ability to mobilize, the loss of technological dominance, and the maintenance of political independence all coalesced to put defense dependence on the policy agenda. But how can American leaders respond? Faced with growing dependence and the threats this poses for national security, policymakers have a range of generic options from which to select. They are: (1) Trade Protection, (2) Industry Promotion, (3) Global Sourcing, and (4) Status Quo.[97] In practice, policy responses will entail a mix of these options. However, these four options define the range of possibilities.

Trade Protection

The protection option has traditionally appealed to members of Congress, labor leaders, and those involved with declining industrial sectors. In short, it entails the use of trade quotas or tariffs to shelter the defense industrial base, combined with an autarkic procurement policy. The tools used for this purpose include the Buy American Act of 1933 as well various trade policy instruments such as Section 232 of the Trade Expansion Act and antidumping remedies.

This approach is best viewed as a form of neomercantilism, or what David Haglund has termed "Techno-Nationalism."[98] Its advocates sometimes assert that foreign firms are inherently untrustworthy. More commonly, they argue that foreign businesses cannot provide secure supply sources because of proximity to potential crisis zones, domestic instability, or other reasons. They also charge that foreign governments have employed unfair trade practices to control U.S. defense markets and erode the U.S. defense industrial base. The comments of William Phillips, Chairman of the National Committee for Industrial Defense (NCID), a lobbying group for small business suppliers to the Pentagon, indicate some of the key themes. In 1987, he warned:

> We have been moving great chunks of our defense industrial base right under the noses of the Soviets. . . . These overseas defense industrial base plants [in Europe and the Far East] on which the U.S. is becoming so dependent—often sole sources for vital components as U.S. producers have been driven from the marketplace—could be eliminated by the enemy in surprise air strikes.[99]

A similar argument was expressed by Congresswoman Mary Rose Oakar (D-OH), chair of the House Banking Subcommittee overseeing DIB issues. In a 1987 hearing, she asserted that "I think our Department of Defense should not be buying offshore anything that is consumed domestically in this country, if it can be acquired from a domestic producer."[100]

A protectionist approach can succeed in achieving its foremost goal—ensuring domestic sources of supply and protecting domestic suppliers from unfair foreign competition. "Buy American" policies can also stimulate demand for U.S. products, thus increasing productivity through lengthened production runs. Moreover, as this option's proponents note, governments have always intervened to support domestic defense industries. Continued intervention not only preserves national security; it also maintains jobs and industries within the United States.

However, the protection option may also entail high costs. Trade protection has generally failed to help revitalize domestic industries.[101] Effectiveness aside, protection also invites the possibility of retaliation from trading partners directly or indirectly affected by it.

Finally, and most importantly, defense protectionism raises the possibility that U.S. military forces might be supplied with technologically inferior systems. These fears have led the DoD to generally oppose measures to restrict the military's access to foreign technologies.[102] For example, in 1989, Deputy Secretary of Defense Don Atwood argued that "[international] alliances enable us to share research and development costs with our allies, and in so doing, free up vital national resources for other pressing problems. We need to stimulate more cooperation, not less."[103] More recently, Atwood's successor, William J. Perry, argued that the United States would not "create protected portions of industry to keep supply lines open."[104]

Industry Promotion

Another option for policymakers involves domestic remedies for ailing industries—what many observers call industrial policy. The term industrial policy has come to assume a number of different meanings in the American political system, leading to a great deal of confusion. For many, industrial policy has come to assume a negative meaning associated with government planning and socialism.[105]

As used here, *industrial policy* refers to government policies that target assistance to specific industrial sectors. Industrial policy is a somewhat more comprehensive tool than the protectionist option. As used in this study, protection refers to trade measures that restrict foreign involvement in supplying DoD or defense-related firms in the United States. In contrast, industrial policy refers to domestic efforts to support American firms. Specific industrial policies can assume a number of forms, and could include revised government regulations, bailouts of ailing firms, sector-targeted subsidies, labor retraining, and product-specific R&D.[106] Some economy-wide policy tools, such as tax and budget policies, can also be targeted to aid specific industrial sectors.

Although nearly every country in the world has an explicit government-sponsored industrial policy, the United States has traditionally avoided an explicit industrial policy to support American companies. (This issue is further discussed in Chapters Two and Three.) Yet, as commercial and military technologies became more closely related, many analysts argued that industrial policy was necessary to maintain a strong defense industrial base. Through targeted support for critical technologies such as semiconductors, advanced machine tools, and fiber optics, government officials could ensure secure supplies for the military while also enhancing the international competitiveness of the American economy. As one advocate noted, "The government, as the only buyer of US military equipment, has the *responsibility* to take the necessary steps to bring about these industrial changes."[107]

The creation of an industrial policy based on domestic measures, such as R&D subsidies, offers a number of benefits when compared to the trade protection options outlined above. For example, subsidies do not shelter domestic firms from foreign competition or restrict DoD's ability to purchase products from nonsubsidized firms or industrial sectors.

Nonetheless, subsidies do suffer from several shortcomings.[108] As with trade protection, R&D subsidies may trigger a foreign response that creates a bidding war in support for certain industrial sectors. Moreover, government support for these targetted sectors may starve other industries of resources such as capital and scientific talent.[109] These concerns, along with the difficulties of effectively choosing targeted sectors (see Chapter Three), have made some observers skeptical of industrial promotion activities.

Global Sourcing

Opponents criticized these plans as flawed and dangerously outmoded, representing a naive yearning for a return to Fortress America. In their view, continued reliance on free trade would guarantee both military security and economic prosperity. U.S. Defense Secretary Dick Cheney reflected this attitude in a 1992 interview, noting that "Buy American" policies "raise questions about my spending money on things I could get cheaper elsewhere, and it raises the specter of having to rely upon less than first-rate technology in certain areas."[110]

Supporters of global sourcing often cited the higher costs of domestic procurement.[111] They also feared that protection at home would invite retaliation abroad and adversely affect markets for American arms exports.[112] Finally, as American industry lost its technological edge, many noted that providing U.S. forces with top of the line materials required foreign purchase. In some cases, U.S. businesses were simply unable to provide the Pentagon with the requisite levels of quality products.[113]

In essence, proponents argued that technological change presented policy makers with no choice but to go global. According to one recent study, "The increasing cost and sophistication of weapon systems and the fall in defense budgets could present U.S. and European governments pursuing the next generation of modernization with new hard choices: import, cooperate or do without."[114]

The solution to these stark choices involved reliance on imports and greater cooperation with the NATO allies and Japan. Ultimately, this process might involve a deepening of the RSI concept toward a "Defense GATT" to eliminate defense trade barriers between the United States and its allies.[115]

A Defense GATT would have a number of benefits according to its proponents.[116] It would help the United States and its allies avoid duplicative R&D efforts, make production more efficient through expanded production runs, and also improve military efficiency through enhanced interoperability. As an added benefit, more open defense trade might serve to cement closer political and military ties between the allies.

Status Quo

Maintenance of the status quo did not imply simply doing nothing. What it did entail was a continuation of an ad hoc mix of policies that pursued several contradictory objectives at the same time. Program managers within DoD were directed to preserve the industrial base, improve cooperation with Japan and NATO allies, and promote competition for defense contracts. An internal DoD study summarized the results of these confusing and conflicting directives:

> The practical effect of this trichotomy is that the program manager who is responsible for developing and executing the acquisition program has no clear guidance on how to resolve these different priorities. As a result, the real world procurement policies and practices do not adequately address the issue of foreign dependency. There is little specific guidance at the component level and foreign dependency is not an issue of high priority with program or project managers.[117]

Faced with this broad array of options, American officials generally pursued policies combining components of options 3 and 4—a combination of global sourcing and muddling through. Given what realism leads us to expect, this result is somewhat surprising. Faced with clear indications of declining power, American officials did not adopt policies embodying a greater concern for relative gains considerations.[118]

The machine tool and semiconductor industries represent exceptions to these generalizations. In these cases, the government responded with an integrated approach that combined industrial policy measures with some level of trade protection. These responses were based on the development of new policy ideas that offered more sophisticated reasons for supporting certain industries. Although the outlines of a new DIB policy based on these new ideas are beginning to emerge, the semiconductor and machine tool cases still remain exceptions to the general policy line dating back to the end of World War II.

This mix of policy results, along with a general delay in the U.S. response to defense dependence, raises questions about the utility of system-level approaches as sole explanations of American defense industrial base policy. A more complete understanding of these issues requires turning to the domestic level of analysis. In Chapter Two, we explore these alternative explanations.

NOTES

1. U.S. Congress, House Committee on Armed Services, *The Ailing Defense Industrial Base: Unready for Crisis*, Defense Industrial Base Panel Report, 96th Congress, 2d Session, (Washington, D.C.: GPO, 1980). Hereafter referred to as Ichord Panel Report

2. The defense industrial base refers to "those sectors of a country's economy that can be called upon to generate goods, services and technology for ultimate consumption by the state's armed forces." See David G. Haglund, ed., *The Defense Industrial Base and the West* (London: Routledge, 1989), p. 1.

Outside of government, several analysts also raised concerns about the defense industrial base and rising foreign dependence. See, for example, Loren Thompson, "The Defense Industrial Base: Going, Going...," *International Security Review*, vol. 6, no. 2 (Summer 1981), pp. 237-72; Paul Seabury, "Industrial Policy and National Defense," *Journal of Contemporary Issues*, vol. 6, no. 2 (Spring 1983), pp. 5-15.

3. For an extensive review of various studies of this topic, see Roderick L. Vawter, *U.S. Industrial Base Dependence/Vulnerability: Phase I-Survey of Literature* (Washington, D.C.: National Defense University Press, 1986); Kevin Tansey and Rosa Johnson, "The Pentagon's Dependence on Foreign Sources," *GAO Journal*, no. 14 (Winter 1991-92), pp. 28-33.

4. See Arthur J. Alexander, *Adaptation to Change in the U.S. Machine Tool Industry and the Effects of Government Policy* (Santa Monica, Calif.: RAND Corporation, 1990), p. v. The ball bearing industry figures come from U.S. Defense Science Board, *Foreign Ownership and Control of U.S. Industry*, Report to the Undersecretary of Defense for Acquisition (Washington, D.C.: Department of Defense, June 1990), p. 63. This report was never officially released by DoD, but was leaked to the press by Rep. Mel Levine (D-CA) in 1991.

5. For a review of European experience with this dilemma, see Andrew Moravcsik, "Arms and Autarky in Modern European History," *Daedalus*, vol. 120, no. 4 (Fall 1991), pp. 23-46.

6. See Aaron Friedberg, "The End of Autonomy," *Daedalus*, vol. 120, no. 4 (Fall 1991), pp. 69-90.

7. For a review of these debates, see Otis L. Graham, *Losing Time: The Industrial Policy Debate*, (Cambridge, Mass/ : Harvard University Press, 1992). For a discussion of the general rise in protectionist demands during the 1980s, see I. M. Destler, *American Trade Politics: System Under Stress*, (Washington, D.C.: Institute for International Economics, 1986).

8. U.S. Department of Defense, *Bolstering Defense Industrial Competitiveness*, Report to the Secretary of Defense by the Under Secretary of Defense (Acquisition) (Washington, D.C.: GPO, July 1988), p. 47. This report was written by Robert Costello, then Under Secretary of

Defense (Acquisition). Hereafter referred to as the Costello Report.

9. For a discussion of these issues, see U.S. General Accounting Office, *Industrial Base: Assessing the Risk of DoD's Foreign Dependence* (Washington, D.C.: GAO, April 1994).

10. Vawter (1986), p. 12. In fact, the Department of Defense (DoD) made few attempts to establish a comprehensive data base of its own dependence of foreign-sourced components and systems. See U.S. General Accounting Office, *Adequacy of Information on the U.S. Defense Industrial Base* (Washington, D.C.: GPO, November 15, 1989); GAO, *Industrial Base: Significance of DoD's Foreign Dependence* (Washington, D.C.: GPO, January 1991).

11. On Great Britain, see Martin Edmonds, "United Kingdom National Security and Defence Dependence: The Technological Dimension," *Government and Opposition*, vol. 26, no. 4 (Autumn 1991), pp. 427-48. On France, see Edward A. Kolodziej, *Making and Marketing Arms: The French Experience and its Implications for the International System*, (Princeton, N.J.: Princeton University Press, 1987). On Sweden, see Michael K. Hawes, "The Swedish Defense Industrial Base: Implications for the Economy," in Haglund (1989). On Japan, see U.S. Congress, Office of Technology Assessment, *Global Arms Trade* (Washington, D.C.: GPO, June 1991), pp. 107-20. On Canada, see Dan Middlemiss, "Canada and Defence Industrial Preparedness: A Return to Basics?" *International Journal*, vol. 42 (Autumn 1987), pp. 707-30.

12. See Kenneth N. Waltz, *Theory of International Politics* (New York: Random House, 1979), p. 126.

13. Section 232 authorizes the president to intervene in cases where import penetration in domestic industries threatens national security. For background on Section 232, see Craig Anderson Lewis, "Waiting for the Big One: Principle, Policy, and the Restriction of Imports Under Section 232," *Law and Policy in International Business*, vol. 22, no. 2 (1991), pp. 357-408.

14. Congress, acting in the aftermath of Reagan's decision, did impose "Buy American" restrictions on DoD purchases of bearings.

15. The method is described in Alexander L. George, "Case Studies and Theory Development: The Method of Structured, Focused Comparison," in Paul G. Lauren, ed., *Diplomacy: New Approaches in History, Theory and Policy* (New York: Free Press, 1979), pp. 43-68.

16. Using concepts from John Kingdon, we can note that, in these cases, policy debate moved from a specialized agenda, which refers to the agenda of one agency, to the general agenda, where the president, prime minister, or other top officials become involved in the policy debate. See John W. Kingdon, *Agendas, Alternatives and Public Policies* (Boston: Little, Brown, 1984), p. 4.

17. Arend Lijphart, "Comparative Politics and the Comparative Method," *American Political Science Review*, vol. 65, no. 3 (September 1971), p. 691.

18. Harry Eckstein, "Case Study and Theory in Political Science," in Fred Greenstein and Nelson W. Polsby, eds., *Handbook of Political Science*, vol. 3 (Reading, Mass.: Addison-Wesley, 1975), p. 100.

19. George (1979), p. 55-57, offers a number of useful observations on this approach.

20. A useful discussion of the importance of relative gains is Joseph Grieco, *Cooperation Among Nations: Europe, America and Non-Tariff Barriers to Trade* (Ithaca, N.Y.: Cornell University Press, 1990). Other excellent discussions include: Duncan Snidal, "Relative Gains and the Pattern of International Cooperation," *American Political Science Review*, vol. 85 (1991), pp. 701-26; Robert Powell, "Absolute and Relative Gains in International Relations Theory," *American Political Science Review*, vol. 85 (1991), pp. 1303-20. For an exchange between all three authors, see "The Relative Gains Problem for International Cooperation,"

American Political Science Review, Vol. 87 (1993), pp. 729-43.

21. Reactions to reductions in economic and/or military power can take several forms. In general, states will seek to mobilize additional resources internally or seek some other means to offset the impact of shifts in relative power positions. Various responses are discussed in Michael Mastanduno, David A. Lake, and G. John Ikenberry, "Toward a Realist Theory of State Action," *International Studies Quarterly*, vol. 33, no. 4 (December 1989), pp. 457-74.

22. Waltz (1979), pp. 105-6.

23. Michael Mastanduno, "Do Relative Gains Matter? America's Response to Japanese Industrial Policy," *International Security*, vol. 16, no. 1 (Summer 1991), p. 79.

24. Grieco (1990), pp. 45-46.

25. Mastanduno (1991), p. 80.

26. See discussions in Waltz (1979), pp. 194-95 and David A. Lake, *Power, Protection and Free Trade: International Sources of U.S. Commercial Strategy, 1887-1939* (Ithaca, N.Y.: Cornell University Press, 1988), pp. 29-49.

27. For example, see Clyde Prestowitz, *Trading Places* (Paperback Edition)(New York: Basic Books,1989), and William S. Dietrich, *In the Shadow of the Rising Sun: The Political Roots of American Economic Deline* (University Park, Pa.: Pennsylvania State University Press, 1991).

28. See Moravcsik (1991).

29. See commentary by Joseph Grieco in "The Relative Gains Problem for International Cooperation," *American Political Science Review*, vol. 87, no. 3 (September 1993), pp. 734-35.

30. By far the best discussion of dependence as a concept is David A. Baldwin, "Interdependence and Power: A Conceptual Analysis," *International Organization*, vol. 34, no. 4 (Autumn 1980), pp. 471-506.

31. Adam Smith, *The Wealth of Nations*, quoted in Edward Mead Earle, "Adam Smith, Alexander Hamilton, Friedrich List: The Economic Foundations of Military Power," in Peter Paret, ed., *Makers of Modern Strategy* (Princeton, N.J.: Princeton University Press, 1986), p. 224.

32. Hirschman's work later had a profound impact on the *dependencia* school of thought. Hirschman has even reluctantly identified himself as the "grandfather" of dependency theory. See Albert O. Hirschman, "Beyond Assymetry: Critical Notes on Myself as a Young Man and on Some Other Old Friends," *International Organization*, vol. 32, no. 1 (Winter 1978), p. 45.

33. For example, see Robert O. Keohane and Joseph S. Nye, Jr., *Power and Interdependence: World Politics in Transition* (Boston: Little, Brown, 1977); Richard N. Cooper, *The Economics of Interdependence*, (New York: McGraw-Hill, 1968).

34. This definition is based on one employed by the GAO. See U.S. General Accounting Office (January 1991).

35. David A. Baldwin (1980), p. 500.

36. C. Fred Bergsten, "Economic Imbalances and World Politics," *Foreign Affairs*, vol. 65 (Spring 1987), p. 784.

37. Keohane and Nye (1977), pp. 10-11. Caporaso has well summarized the situation: "The dependence of actor B upon actor A is (1) directly proportional to B's motivational investment in goals mediated by A, and (2) inversely proportional to the availability of those goals to B outside the A-B relation." Quoted in David A. Baldwin (1980), pp. 499-500.

38. See Stephen Vogel, "The Power Behind 'Spin-Ons': The Military Implications of Japan's Commercial Technology," in Wayne Sandholtz et al., *The Highest Stakes: The Economic Foundations of the Next Security System* (New York: Oxford University Press, 1992), pp. 66-67.

39. For example, both the *New York Times* and *Wall Street Journal* ran front page articles on this phenomenon. See Richard W. Stevenson, "Foreign Role Rises in Military Goods," *New York Times*, October 23, 1989, p. A1; Tim Carrington, "Military's Dependence on Foreign Suppliers Causes Rising Concern," *Wall Street Journal*, March 24, 1988, p. 1.

40. Paul Kennedy, *The Rise and Fall of Great Powers* (New York: Random House, 1987). A similar argument is presented in David P. Calleo, *Beyond American Hegemony: The Future of the Western Alliance* (New York: Basic Books, 1987).

41. Kennedy (1987), pp. 514-15.

42. For an analysis of the British case, see Kennedy (1987) and Aaron Friedberg, *The Weary Titan: Britain and the Experience of Relative Decline, 1895-1905* (Princeton, N.J.: Princeton University Press, 1988).

43. See Joseph S. Nye, Jr., *Bound to Lead: The Changing Nature of American Power* (New York: Basic Books, 1990), and Samuel P. Huntington, "The U.S.: Decline or Renewal?" *Foreign Affairs*, vol. 67 (Winter 1988-1989); Susan Strange, "The Persistent Myth of Lost Hegemony," *International Organization*, vol. 41, no. 4 (Autumn 1987), pp. 565-71.

44. See, for example, Nye (1990), pp. 259-61.

45. These figures are from National Academy of Engineering, *National Interests in an Age of Global Technology* (Washington, D.C.: National Academy Press, 1991), pp. 25-26.

46. Foreign direct investment refers to "ownership of assets by foreign residents for purposes of controlling the use of those assets." See Edward M. Graham and Paul R. Krugman, *Foreign Direct Investment in the United States*, 2d ed., (Washington, D.C.: Institute for International Economics, 1991), p. 7.

47. Council on Competitiveness, *Gaining New Ground: Technology Priorities for America's Future* (Washington, D.C.: Council on Competitiveness, 1992), pp. 7-11.

48. Cited in GAO, *European Initiatives* (April 1991), p. 11.

49. Martin C. Libicki, Jack Nunn, and Bill Taylor, *U.S. Industrial Base Dependence/Vulnerability: Phase II-Analysis*, Mobilization Concepts Development Center, (Washington, D.C. National Defense University, September, 1987), p. 75.

50. Quoted in Andrew Pollack, "In U.S. Technology, a Gap Between Arms and VCRs," *New York Times*, March 4, 1991, pp. A1, D8.

51. See John A. Alic, et al. *Beyond Spinoff: Military and Commercial Technologies in a Changing World* (Cambridge, Mass.: Harvard Business School Press, 1992).

52. Ibid, pp. 59-60.

53. Carnegie Commission on Science, Technology, and Government, *New Thinking and American Defense Technology* (New York: Carnegie Corporation, August 1990), p. 11.

54. Internal DoD studies indicate that raw materials dependence has been widely recognized, prompting an active government response. The same is not true of dependence in manufactured components and finished goods. Libicki, Nunn, and Taylor, (1987), p. 73.

55. Benjamin Zycher, Kenneth A. Solomon, and Loren Yager, *An "Adequate Insurance" Approach to Critical Dependencies of the Department of Defense* (Santa Monica, Calif.: RAND Corporation, 1991), p. 22.

56. Ethan B. Kapstein, "Losing Control: National Security and the Global Economy," *National Interest*, Winter 1989-1990, p. 85.

57. "Interview with James A. Lyons, Jr.," *U.S. Naval Institute Proceedings*, Vol. 113 (July 1987), p. 67.

58. Globalization refers to a process whereby "U.S. defense increasingly relies on foreign technologies, foreign-sourced products, or domestic-sourced products purchased from local subsidiaries of foreign corporations." See Theodore H. Moran, "The Globalization of America's Defense Industries: Managing the Threat of Foreign Dependence," *International Security*, vol.

15, no. 1 (Summer 1990), pp. 57-99. This process was not limited to defense industries. In fact, globalization of civilian industry began much earlier and proceeded much more rapidly than defense globalization.

59. See Thomas A. Callaghan, Jr., *Pooling Allied and American Resources to Produce a Credible, Collective Conventional Deterrent*, Report prepared for the U.S. Department of Defense, August 1988, p. 23.

60. Studies of rising costs for new generations of British weapons systems indicate these trends. Cost increases range from 3.75 times more for a new generation of combat aircraft to 1.5 times more for a new generation of explosive shells. See Keith Hartley, "Defense Procurement and Industrial Policy," in John Roper, ed., *The Future of British Defence Policy* (Aldershot: Gower Publishing, 1985), p. 165.

61. For each doubling of production rates, unit costs can be reduced by 20 percent in aerospace production, 30 percent in electric components and 24 percent in equipment maintenance. See Simon Webb, *NATO and 1992: Defense Acquisition and Free Markets*, R-3758-FF (Santa Monica, Calif.: RAND Corporation, July 1989), p. 61. Moravcsik (1991), p. 67, offers similar figures. He notes that "a common rule of thumb for aerospace is that the unit price declines by 15-20 percent for each doubling of production."

62. On EFA, see Andrew Latham, "Conflict and Competition over the NATO Defence Industrial Base: The Case of the European Fighter Aircraft," in Haglund (1989), pp. 86-117; Elizabeth J. Kirk and Robert Goldberg, "U.S. and European Defense Industries: Changing Forces for Cooperation and Competition," AAAS Issue Paper No. 91-13S (Washington, D.C.: American Association for the Advancement of Science, 1991).

63. Defense Forecasts, Inc., *Foreign Investment in the U.S. Defense Industrial Base: A Sound National Strategy for America's Future*, (Washington, D.C.: Defense Forecasts, Inc., May 1992), p. 7. These figures omit numerous cross-border alliances, such as the EFA consortium and the EUCLID research effort, which focus on a single project or production of a single system. For background on these European efforts, see GAO, *European Initiatives* (April 1991); Kirk and Goldberg (1991); and Patrick Oster, "Europeans Shelving Rivalries over Big Weapons Contracts," *Washington Post*, September 1, 1991, p. c1.

64. See Steven Pearlstein, "Thomson-LTV Case Gives Foreign Companies Pause," *Washington Post*, August 20, 1992, p. B14.

65. Defense Forecasts, Inc.(May 1992), p. 7.

66. Linda M. Spencer, *High Technology Acquisitions: Summary Charts* (Washington, D.C.: Economic Strategy Institute, May 1992).

67. Jan Feldman, "Collaborative Production of Defense Equipment within NATO," *Journal of Strategic Studies*, vol. 7, no. 3 (1984), p. 284.

68. There are many sources on various defense cooperation efforts between the United States and its allies. On U.S.-Canada cooperation, see North American Defense Industrial Base Organization (NADIBO), *The North American Defense Industrial Base: A Half-Century of Defense-Economic Cooperation* (Alexandria, Va.: NADIBO, 1988); and Robert Van Steenburg, "An Analysis of Canadian-American Defence Economic Cooperation: The History and Current Issues," in David G. Haglund, ed., Canada's Defence Industrial Base (Kingston, Ont.: Ronald Frye, 1988), pp. 189-219. On efforts in Europe and Japan, see Reinhard Drifte, *Arms Production in Japan* (Boulder, Colo.: Westview Press, 1986); and Trevor Taylor, *Defence, Technology, and International Integration* (New York: St. Martin's Press, 1982), Ch. 2; Robert Zweerts with Kelly Campbell, "The Search for Integrated European Programme Management," in Jane Davis Drown, Clifford Drown, and Kelly Campbell, eds., *A Single European Arms Industry?* (London: Brassey's, 1990), pp. 77-79.

69. U.S. General Accounting Office, *Military Coproduction: U.S. Management of Programs Worldwide* (Washington, D.C.: GPO, 1989), p. 12.

70. Taylor (1982), p. 23.

71. For background, see Dertouzos et al., Council on Competitiveness, *Gaining New Ground: Technology Priorities for America's Future* (Washington, D.C.: Council on Competitiveness, 1991); Jeffrey A. Hart, R*ival Capitalists: International Competitiveness in the United States, Japan, and Western Europe* (Ithaca, N.Y.: Cornell University Press, 1992).

72. On Hamilton's view, see Earle (1986).

73. The development of U.S. trade policy is described in Destler (1986), pp. 1-36.

74. For background on mobilization, see Hardy L. Merritt and Luther F. Carter, *Mobilization and the National Defense* (Washington, D.C.: National Defense University Press, 1985); John N. Ellison, Jeffrey W. Frumkin, and Timothy W. Stanley, M*obilizing U.S. Industry: A Vanishing Option for National Security?*, (Boulder, Colo.: Westview Press, 1988).

75. The EPMB was established on December 17, 1981 under the auspices of National Security Defense Directive 47 (NSDD-47). Designed to coordinate interdepartmental policy on industrial mobilization, the body never functioned effectively and its functions were transferred out of NSC in the aftermath of the Iran-contra affair. See Ellison, Frumkin, and Stanley (1988), p. 7.

76. See John T. Correll and Colleen A. Nash, "The Industrial Base at War," *Air Force*, December 1991, p. 52.

77. Edward A. Olsen, "A Case for Strategic Protectionism,"
Strategic Review, vol. 15, no. 4 (Fall 1987), p. 66.

78. Tansey and Johnson (1991-92), p. 30; Jacob M. Schlesinger, "Kyocera's Ambivalent Role in Weapons," *Wall Street Journal*, February 5, 1991, p. A19.

79. See Michael Mastanduno, "The United States Defiant: Export Controls in the Postwar Era," *Daedalus*, vol. 120, no. 4 (Fall 1991), pp. 91-112. For background on the use of this tool in wartime, see Alan S. Milward, "Restriction of Supply as a Strategic Choice," in Gordon H. McCormick and Richard E. Bissell, eds., *Strategic Dimensions of Economic Behavior* (New York: Praeger, 1984), pp. 44-58.

It is somewhat ironic that many discussions of dependence's dangers were often based on the experience of U.S. allies who suffered as a result of dependence on American suppliers. For example, in his review of the potential dangers of dependence, Moran cited American refusal in 1964-1966 to transfer high performance computer licenses for use in French nuclear programs as well as the 1982 Soviet gas pipeline case. See Moran (1990), pp. 60-65. Friedberg cites the case of U.S. financial pressures affecting British policy in the 1956 Suez crisis. See Aaron Friedberg, "The Strategic Implications of Relative Economic Decline," *Political Science Quarterly*, vol. 104, no. 1 (1989), p. 413.

80. Stuart Auerbach, "U.S. Relied on Foreign-Made Parts for Weapons," *Washington Post*, March 25, 1991, pp. A1, A17.

81. Fred Hiatt, "U.S. Found to Lack Supplies for War," *Washington Post*, August 3, 1984, pp. A1, A10.

82. Such mobilization difficulties had long concerned NATO leaders. See, "An Exclusive AFJ Interview with General John R. Galvin, USA," *Armed Forces Journal International*, vol. 125, no. 8 (March 1988), p. 50.

83. When firms are based at home, the president can compel on-time delivery through use of the Defense Production Act (DPA) of 1950. This tool cannot be applied to foreign firms overseas. See Leon N. Karadbil and Roderick L. Vawter, "The Defense Production Act: Crucial Component of Mobilization Preparedness," in Merritt and Carter (1985), pp. 37-60.

84. Michael Borrus, Laura D'Andrea Tyson, and John Zysman, "Creating Advantage: How Government Policies Shape International Trade in the Semiconductor Industry" in Paul Krugman, ed. *Strategic Trade Policy and the New International Economics* (Cambridge, Mass.:

MIT Press, 1986), p. 94.

85. DSB Report in Spencer (May 1992), p. 63.

86. U.S. General Accounting Office, *International Trade: U.S. Business Access to Certain Foreign State-of-the-Art Technology* (Washington, D.C.: GPO, September 1991), pp. 3-4. Libicki, Nunn, and Taylor (September 1987) report similar findings, pp. 93-94.

87. Susan J. Tolchin, "The Impact of the LTV-Thomson Sale on U.S. National Security and Competitiveness," Testimony before the Subcommittee on Defense Industry and Technology, Committee on Armed Services, U.S. Senate, April 30, 1992, p. 10.

88. Bernard L. Schwartz, *Foreign Ownership of U.S. Defense Companies: Where Do We Draw the Line?* (Washington, D.C.: Foreign Policy Institute, 1989), p. 13.

89. Libicki, Nunn, and Taylor (September 1987), p. 92.

90. Ibid, p. 95. See also National Research Council, Committee on Electronic Components, *Foreign Production of Electronic Components and Army System Vulnerabilities* (Washington, D.C.: National Academy Press, 1985), pp. 33-37.

91. Felix Rohatyn, "Restoring American Independence," *New York Review of Books*, February 18, 1988, pp. 8-10.

92. Harold Brown, *U.S.-Japan Relations: Technology, Economics and Security* (Washington, D.C.: US/Japan Economic Agenda, 1987), p. 5.

93. This document was first published in Japan and widely circulated throughout the U.S. government in a translated edition. See Akio Morita and Shintaro Ishihara, *The Japan That Can Say No*, (Washington, D.C.: U.S. government translation, 1989). It was widely cited in congressional discussions in 1989. For example, see U.S. Congress, House Committee on Science, Space and Technology, *Federal Research Policy and the American Semiconductor Industry*, 101st Congress, 1st Session, November 8, 1989.

94. Morita and Ishihara (1989), pp. 3-4.

95. See David Gergen, "American as Techno-Colony," *U.S. News and World Report*, April 1, 1991, p. 88.

96. William J. Crowe, "Strategic Supplies Depend on U.S. Industries," Letter to the Editor, *Washington Post*, December 19, 1991, p. A21.

97. For other reviews of generic policy options, see Friedberg (1989), pp. 428-31, and Office of Technology Assessment, *Redesiging Defense*, pp. 84-91.

98. David Haglund, with Marc Bloch, "'Techno-Nationalism' and the Contemporary Debate over the American Defense Industrial Base," in Haglund (1989), pp. 234-77.

99. See U.S. Congress, House Banking Subcommittee on Economic Stabilization, *New Industrial Base Initiative*, 100th Congress, 1st Session, July 8, 28, September 15, 16, 23, 29, 30, 1987, p. 165. The NCID's goal was to promote awareness of DIB issues and to support the creation of industrial strategies to strengthen American manufacturing.

100. Ibid, p. 106.

101. See Jagdish Bhagwati, *Protectionism* (Cambridge, Mass.: MIT Press, 1988).

102. For background, see U.S. Department of Defense, Report to the U.S. Congress by the Secretary of Defense, *The Impact of Buy-American Restrictions Affecting Defense Procurement* (Washington, D.C.: DoD, July 1989).

103. Donald Atwood, Deputy Secretary of Defense, "Speech to the National Security Industrial Association," mimeo, July 17, 1989.

104. "Perry to Ruffle Feathers to Preserve Defense Industrial Base," *Defense Daily*, October 8, 1993, p. 49.

105. Michael Kinsley, "Who's Afraid of Industrial Policy," *Washington Post*, July 19, 1992, p. C7.

106. This definition is based on distinctions made in Graham (1992), pp. 79-81. Trade protection and Buy Domestic policies also fall in the category of sector-specific interventions. However, because they directly imply closing markets to foreign intervention, they are included within the protectionist policy option.

107. Jacques S. Gansler, "Needed: A U.S. Defense Industrial Strategy," *International Security* vol. 12, no. 2 (Fall 1987), p. 45.

108. For background, see Tyson (1992), esp. p. 280-86.

109. Moran (1990), p. 92.

110. "Cheney: Don't Expect Pentagon to Bail Out Industrial Base," *Aerospace Daily*, January 23, 1992, p. 115.

111. DoD has argued that the five year cost of legislation mandating domestic purchase of anchor chains was almost $7 million. See U.S. Department of Defense, (July 1989), p. A-65.

112. See David Silverberg, "Luster Fades over Cooperative Programs," *Defense News*, January 27, 1992, p. 6.

113. For example, an in-depth government review of foreign components in three major navy systems found that much foreign sourcing occurred because U.S. production was uncompetitive. U.S. Department of Commerce, Bureau of Export Administration, *National Security Assessment of the Domestic and Foreign Contractor Base: A Study of Three U.S. Navy Systems*, (Washington, D.C.: Department of Commerce, March 1992), p. 84.

114. Center for Strategic and International Studies, *The Atlantic Partnership: An Industrial Perspective on Transatlantic Defense Cooperation*, (Washington, D.C.: CSIS, May 1991), p. 8.

115. See, for example, Richard Burt, "Drop Barriers to Defense Trade in the West," *Wall Street Journal*, May 22, 1991, p. A14.

116. "William Taft, IV: His Message to NATO is 'Let's Get It Together,'" Interview, *Defense Week*, March 16, 1987, pp. 8-9.

117. Vawter (1986), pp. 11-12.

118. In his study of American responses to Japanese industrial policy, Michael Mastanduno (1991, pp. 108-13) reached a similar conclusion, arguing that relative gains have become more important but are still not a powerful factor in American policy making. Mastanduno may actually overstate the importance of relative gains considerations for U.S. policymakers. His three case studies are the FSX, HDTV, and the application of Super 301 trade law provisions to satellites. He identifies relative gains as most salient in the latter case. However, in this decision, policy was driven by a desire for "fair trade," that is, the elimination of unfair trade practices in Japan. Thus, the result can also be explained through reference to decision makers' commitments to fair trade and the absolute gains from open markets.

Similarly, Mastanduno overstates the importance of relative gains in the FSX case. Although congressional pressure prompted reconsideration of the deal, the final result was largely unaffected. Aaron Friedberg and Clyde Prestowitz both reach similar conclusions. See Prestowitz (1989), p. 57 and Friedberg (Fall 1991), p. 84.

2

Explaining Responses to Dependence

As we saw in Chapter One, realist theory does not offer a complete explanation for American defense industrial base policy in the 1980s. Based on their understanding of states as "defensive positionalists" (i.e., concerned with their position vis-a-vis existing and potential competitors in an anarchic international system), realists view relative gains as a state's dominant foreign policy concern. Realists would thus expect states to avoid situations of severe dependence if possible. Realists would further predict that defense dependence should trigger an active government response, taking several possible forms: protection of domestic industries, insurance through stockpiling or other measures, or active intervention through subsidies, tax incentives, and so on.

This is not what happened. When faced with growing defense dependence, American political leaders did not react in a manner designed to support relative gains. Instead, they clung to traditional policy patterns in place since World War II and argued that the American defense industrial base was best preserved through open markets and free defense trade among the allies. Even in the exceptional cases of machine tools and semiconductors, opposition to government intervention was substantial.[1] To understand American policy, we must turn to other suggested explanations for the variation in the degree of government intervention. In this literature, three major categories of explanation have been proposed: interest group pressures, state autonomy, and shared images.

INTEREST GROUP EXPLANATIONS

Until quite recently, interest group explanations for protectionism dominated the literature on U.S. trade policy. These studies, which focused on the role of societal pressures on policy making, developed out of concepts of pluralism developed in the 1950s and 1960s.[2] The interest group approach explains foreign economic and DIB policy as the result of domestic bargaining and contention among politically organized groups.

Students of U.S. trade policies view the American government as relatively passive in most cases. The government's role is limited to ensuring access for the best-organized groups and ratifying and implementing agreements worked out among competing interest groups.[3] Policy outcomes are explained by examining the power of various interest groups with the most powerful groups prevailing in policy disputes.

E. E. Schattschneider's *Politics, Pressures and the Tariff* still remains the classic interest group analysis.[4] In this work, Schattschneider attributes the passage of the 1930 Smoot-Hawley Tariff Act to the role of interest group pressures. Indeed, interest group pressures in support of Smoot-Hawley were so strong that they overrode the nearly unanimous opposition of professional economists. Schattschneider argues that, in passing Smoot-Hawley, Congress was simply responding to the overwhelming weight of interest group pressures. More recent studies of U.S. trade politics continue to emphasize the role of interest groups and their protectionist demands. Stephen Cohen reaches the following conclusion: "If a special interest group is big enough, persistent enough, sufficiently well-organized, and sufficiently articulate and truthful, it eventually will secure some form of accommodation in the form of trade policy or legislation."[5]

A major reason for this pattern is that the benefits of protection (or subsidy) are distributed asymmetrically.[6] The benefits of a specific protectionist action are concentrated on a small group of firms or industrial sectors, while its costs are dispersed among consumers of the given product. This produces asymmetries in the intensity of interest among groups, with protection-seekers enjoying better organization and resources. Based on these advantages, these groups are more effective in gaining protection for themselves.

The interest group approach yields two hypotheses relevant to our cases: (1) it predicts an increase in protectionist demands in the face of declining market share and worsening economic competitiveness for American firms, and (2) it predicts that these societal pressures will result in a more protectionist/interventionist U.S. DIB policy.

These hypotheses appear to have some validity. As America's relative economic position eroded and new rivals such as Japan and the Newly Industrialized Countries (NICs) emerged, demands for protection rose across the board. For example, from 1979 to 1985, 693 countervailing and antidumping duty petitions were filed. These petitions were almost nonexistent during the 1970s.[7]

Demands for defense protectionism rose at a similar pace. Petitions filed under Section 232 averaged about one every two years from 1962 to 1979. Ten petitions were filed between 1981 and 1988.[8] Congressional activity in this area also rose. Hearings on the DIB indicate that a majority of affected interest groups supported greater DIB protection.[9] In addition, American labor unions are consistently supportive of neomercantilist measures. In contrast, only two interest groups have consistently advocated free trade measures: The American League of Exports and Security Assistance (ALESA), and the Aerospace Industries Association of America.

Yet even these two groups have supported industrial policy measures that offer expanded government support to American defense firms.

Protection-seeking industries were aided by changes in the structure of the U.S. government. In the aftermath of Watergate, congressional procedures and structures became substantially decentralized. These shifts were felt throughout the Congress but the changes were especially profound in both trade and defense policy. Policy entrepreneurs throughout Congress began to test the traditional dominance over trade policy held by the Senate Finance and House Ways and Means Committees. On DIB issues, the Armed Services Committees' dominance came under fire. The House and Senate Banking Committees became particularly active with Senator Alan Dixon (D-IL) and Representative Mary Rose Oakar (D-OH) using their subcommittees as "bully pulpits" in support of domestic producers.[10]

Given this constellation of forces, we would expect to see an increase in protectionism and concern for relative gains by American policy makers as the U.S. position in the world economy declined. However, as the case studies will indicate, this did not occur.

Faced with this unexpected outcome, other analysts have sought to explain the U.S. government's ability to block protectionist demands by reference to changes in the preferences of societal groups. As U.S. firms have become more global, protectionist sentiment has weakened and support for free trade has grown.[11] With a growing dependence on foreign trade, many American firms have become skeptical of domestic protection because it may invite retaliation in foreign markets. At the same time, firms have lost their national orientations, viewing themselves as global entities.[12] In 1989, National Cash Register (NCR) President Gilbert Williamson reflected this trend when he remarked, "I don't think about [U.S. competitiveness] at all. We at NCR think of ourselves as a globally competitive company that happens to be headquartered in the U.S."[13]

This antiprotectionist tide has been most strongly felt in sectors where the costs of protection have limited consumer impact but disproportionately affect industrial groups such as importers and exporters.[14] For example, auto manufacturers opposed voluntary restraint agreements for steel because they contributed to higher car production costs. Similarly, American computer manufacturers asserted that the 1986 Semiconductor Agreement had forced them to quadruple their memory upgrade prices.[15]

As globalization proceeds, this suggests that we may expect an increase in anti-protectionist pressures.[16] However, in the debates concerning the DIB in the late 1980s, these counterpressures from American business were limited. The bulk of affected actors supported DIB protection. Even today, these pressures are largely absent in the defense field. In the well-publicized 1992 effort by French firm Thomson-CSF to purchase the defense divisions of LTV, for example, no American defense firm publicly favored the sale.

Domestic protectionist or antiprotectionist pressures cannot explain the outcome of the DIB debate in the United States. The demand for defense free trade among societal actors was quite limited, but the expected outcome of growing protectionism did not appear. From the interest group perspective, we have a paradoxical result:

government rebuffing strong domestic pressures.

STATIST EXPLANATIONS

While useful in highlighting the constellation of societal forces producing various policies, the interest group approach neglects several important components of the policy process. Among its most striking limitations is its neglect of the impact of institutional structures and the role of the state. The state is not a passive apparatus; it is an important actor that helps shape the institutional framework in which societal actors and state actors operate. As many recent analyses have asserted, the state can indeed act autonomously.[17] By ignoring this fact, the society-centered approach "captures only the demand for policy, not its supply."[18]

The central core of the statist argument focuses on the autonomy of government institutions. Researchers have developed a variety of definitions for autonomy. However, for our purposes, the most useful definition views autonomy as a government structure that is centralized and differentiated from society.[19] Statists argue that, ceteris paribus, states with insulated and centralized government bureaucracies tend to be more successful in developing and implementing policies that run counter to the demands of outside pressure groups. These insulated state actors tend to prevail in conflicts between the state and civil society over the definition of national interests.

The United States, viewed as a "weak" state, and Japan, a "strong" state, are presented as a classic contrast in much of the literature. For example, Chalmers Johnson argues that Japan's centralized bureaucracy has permitted it to develop a highly effective national industrial policy.[20] In contrast, the decentralized and fragmented nature of the American state has eased the ability of private interests to influence policy and obtain special "pork barrel" benefits from the government.

At first glance, the statist argument appears to offer useful insights regarding U.S. DIB policy. Judith Goldstein has effectively utilized this approach in her studies of the state's role in trade policy. She notes that U.S. leaders have consistently supported free trade concepts since the mid-1930s. In keeping with this commitment, they created institutions embodying a free trade bias. Institutional continuity contributed to the persistence of free trade policies.[21]

In the 1930s, the failure of the Smoot-Hawley tariffs and their contribution to the Great Depression convinced American policymakers of the many benefits of a free trade policy, leading to the creation of institutions supportive of this policy line. Prominent among these was the Reciprocal Trade Agreements Act of 1934, which created a system of presidential dominance of trade policy, especially in the realm of international liberalization efforts like the GATT.

This shift in institutional responsibility resulted in part from congressional recognition that the president could best counter protectionist pressures and guarantee continued U.S. commitment to free trade.[22] With congressional acquiescence after Smoot-Hawley's failure, the executive branch established insulated trade institutions, such as the International Trade Commission (ITC).[23] The creation of these institutions does not imply that societal groups consistently failed to obtain preferential treatment;

in some cases, especially in agriculture,[24] the president or the ITC provided protection to domestic interests. However, these cases have been rare, and congressional input has been limited to a largely symbolic role.[25]

This emphasis on the insulation of political institutions may also offer useful explanations for the absence of DIB protection. The statist approach yields a hypothesis that explains policy inaction by reference to the autonomy of government institutions. Because these bodies are relatively immune to societal pressure, they are able to develop and implement their own policy preferences, even in the face of significant societal opposition. According to this perspective, insulation aided government leaders in rebuffing societal demands for defense protectionism.

Our case studies indicate that none of the relevant agencies was immune from congressional or interest group input. Like other components of the American state, they were relatively permeable to societal pressures. The Department of Commerce, a key player in all of these cases, is commonly categorized among the least insulated and weakest agencies in the U.S. government.[26]

The Commerce Department assumes a lead role in investigations under Section 232 of the 1962 Trade Expansion Act.[27] Since it is not an administrative agency, Commerce is often bombarded by political pressures as its studies proceed. For example, more than 200 members of Congress contacted the Commerce Department and the White House to support VRAs for the U.S. machine tool industry in 1985 and 1986.[28]

This lack of insulation contrasts significantly with the insulated status of the ITC, the administrative agency that oversees the bulk of U.S. trade investigations.[29] Goldstein and others who emphasize the insulation of the American trade apparatus have focused largely on the ITC.[30] Since the ITC's role in the DIB debate is limited, their arguments concerning insulation of the U.S. trade bureaucracy are less applicable.

Other agencies involved with the DIB, including the DoD, are also relatively open to public pressures.[31] Indeed, defense analysts often complain of congressional micromanagement of defense programs. Selected figures on the scope of congressional activity offer some confirmation for this argument. Over 107 committees and subcommittees play some role in defense policy debates. In the mid-1980s, Congress made an average of over 2,000 changes to the president's defense budget and required anywhere from 450 to 680 different reports on various Pentagon activities.[32] This range of activity indicates that the Pentagon cannot be considered insulated.

One of the more insulated sectors of the American state, the Defense Advanced Research Projects Agency (DARPA),[33] played an important role in many of 1980s debates. Many attribute DARPA's success to its insulation,[34] but even DARPA's operations are affected by outside pressures. In 1990, its director, Craig Fields, was removed because of his advocacy of a more proactive role for DARPA.[35] Similarly, in 1988, over DoD opposition, Congress reoriented DARPA's programs away from basic research toward greater involvement in the production of operational systems prototypes.[36] More recently, the Clinton administration has changed the agency's name to the Advanced Research Projects Agency (ARPA) to indicate yet another new mission and greater focus on "dual-use" research.

As these examples indicate, the insulation of government departments does not provide a fully adequate explanation for policy choices. But even if the relevant political institutions were highly insulated, this fact alone might not fully explain policy outcomes. The links between institutional structure and effective power are not always unidimensional. Strong, centralized states are not always more powerful and autonomous. As Ezra Suleiman has noted in his studies of the French state, centralization concentrates jurisdictions, but does not necessarily concentrate power.[37] In some cases, private interests may find it easier to capture power in a centralized state because they can avoid dispersion of resources. In contrast, a decentralized state may make the state more permeable but may also limit private actors' ability to concentrate resources and power.[38]

IDEAS AS CAUSES OF POLICY AND POLICY CHANGE

While serving as useful analytical tools, statist or institutional arguments alone cannot explain policy outcomes. The actual content of policy is not explained by an institutional approach;[39] we must turn to other models to understand how and why government officials come to choose their policy preferences. Similarly, this approach cannot adequately explain policy changes that occur independently of institutional change.[40]

To answer these questions, we must examine the impact of ideology and policy beliefs. Indeed, many institutional analyses recognize the importance of ideology. For example, Krasner's *Defending the National Interest* includes ideology as a central component of state power. Similarly, Goldstein's work closely links ideas and institutions. A better understanding of policy is derived by breaking this link between institutions and ideology and viewing ideology and policy beliefs as a separate explanatory variable.

Most studies of the American policy-making process have utilized the approaches discussed above. But more recently, some analysts have turned to an examination of the content of policymakers' ideas to help explain outcomes.[41] This approach does not discuss the ideas of individual leaders; it focuses on the shared collective beliefs of decisionmakers.[42]

Many foreign policy analysts are skeptical of analysis based on policy ideas. This skepticism results from difficulties in accurately determining an actor's beliefs and in separating out the independent impact of ideas. While these concerns are legitimate, they should not eliminate beliefs as a plausible explanatory variable for foreign policy behavior. This is especially true when, as in the DIB case, situational variables (both international and domestic) provide insufficient explanations for varying policy outcomes.

Policy ideas offer a useful addition to more traditional explanatory variables. This research defines policy ideas as "a set of concepts, axioms, and deductive inferences directed toward the analysis of a public problem. This set offers a causal explanation for a given social condition or problem 'state'; a forecast regarding future states, and a prescriptive inference for policy intervention on behalf of a desired outcome."[43] It is hypothesized that these policy ideas have an independent effect on behavior.

While this definition of policy ideas is generally accepted, some analysts downplay the independent effect of ideas. Many view policy beliefs as an intervening variable or "causal nexus"—a filter through which other factors must pass.[44] In this view, beliefs are positioned between the environment and behavior and mediate between interests and outcomes.

The "ideas as causal nexus" view captures a portion of reality, but it neglects the independent effects of policy ideas. Yet other explanations should not be discarded. Indeed, international factors and domestic politics place important constraints on policy and changes in these factors often do produce policy changes. However, as D. Michael Shafer has noted:

> Still, policymakers' ideas underpin the very definition of national security interests, threats to them and possible responses. Changes in these ideas may result in a redefinition of American interests and so in a change in policy without a change in circumstance. Conversely, their failure to change with events many lead policymakers to fail to adjust policy as needed.[45]

Material interests do not dictate policy ideas. In fact, the connection is often reversed. Ideas can profoundly affect one's perception of one's material interests. Ideas affect not only outcomes, but also the meaning and interpretation of available policy options.[46]

Ideas help filter policymakers' perceptions of the world. They affect policy outcomes because they lead decisionmakers to ignore or concentrate on certain sources of information or certain policy options. In many cases, existing policy ideas will make certain options off-limits. For example, Jacobs describes how American ambivalence toward the state prevented policymakers from seriously considering a centralized state apparatus to operate the Medicare program.[47] These effects are not limited to the U.S. experience. Checkel has similarly noted how dominant policy ideas prevented the Soviet Union from considering radical foreign policy changes until the mid-1980s.[48]

Ideas are so important because they are resistant to change.[49] When ideas do shift, change often results from a major disaster or crisis. But even a major crisis may not create a permanent shift in collective beliefs.[50] The persistence of collective ideas explains their important influence on decisionmakers.

As the foregoing suggests, obtaining a complete and rich understanding of policymaking requires that we examine the impact of policy maker's ideas. As Peter A. Hall notes, "It is ideas, in the form of economic theories and the policies developed from them, that enable national leaders to chart a course through turbulent economic times, and ideas about what is efficient, expedient, and just that motivate the movement from one line of policy to another."[51]

While true, we cannot simply assert that ideas matter. This approaches reductionism and tells us little about how important ideas are relative to other causal variables or how they intersect with other causes to produce outcomes. To do this, one must first explain why certain ideas were accepted by policymakers and also show that: (1) top policy makers held a consistent set of salient views, and (2) domestic interests supported positions opposed to the government's policy line. Policymakers' ideas cannot simply reflect group interests or material circumstances.

Unfortunately, assessing the independent impact of ideas is a difficult methodological task. In fact, strong evidence of independent causality may be impossible to find, especially when we cannot conclusively determine that statements from policymakers were not post hoc rationalizations. However, by employing what Alexander George has called the "congruence procedure," we can gain a much better understanding of the close links between beliefs and behavior.[52]

Under the congruence procedure, the analyst seeks to deduce policy options from the policy maker's beliefs. In addition to relevant secondary sources, data on these policy beliefs and ideas can be derived from three sources: (1) transcripts of private discussions,[53] (2) interviews, and (3) official public statements. Because private transcripts are not available, only the latter two sources will be employed in our case studies. Although they have some limitations, public statements do offer valid indicators of policy ideas. Official statements can act to constrain political leaders and also serve to reinforce existing beliefs. In an effort to reduce potential distortions and account for potentially deceptive statements, one should try to compare statements made before a variety of audiences and give greater credence to spontaneous or unrehearsed personally expressed views.[54]

Based on this analysis, the researcher then attempts to establish a congruence between beliefs and behavior, while also ruling out other causal factors. Finally, he or she must examine the process by which ideas are accepted and come to shape assessments of various situations and relevant policy options. Through this analysis, one seeks to show that other plausible options were not considered because they were inconsistent with existing policy beliefs.[55] The ultimate goal is to indicate correlation and to raise the possibility that correlation may be of causal significance.

Ideas clearly affect policy, but how do they work? According to Mark Moore, "Ideas simultaneously establish the assumptions, justifications, purposes and means of public action. In doing so, they simultaneously authorize and instruct different sectors of the society to take actions on behalf of public purposes."[56]

It is useful to consider policy ideas as similar to Thomas Kuhn's concept of scientific paradigms.[57] Much as paradigms guide scientific inquiry, policy ideas guide the policy process. Ideas have four different effects: (1) they define the conventional wisdom; (2) they suggest alternative policies that are plausibly effective; (3) they set out questions for which evidence is necessary; and (4) they keep alternative issue definitions off the policy agenda.[58] They serve as kind of prism that determines a policymaker's perception of a situation and determines the parameters for possible action.[59]

Ideas influence policy through their role in the creation and sustenance of policy monopolies. A policy monopoly is defined as a monopoly on political understandings concerning a given issue area and an institutional arrangement that bolsters that understanding.[60] Policy monopolies have two central characteristics: a definable structure responsible for policy making, and buttressing policy ideas that are connected to core values and can be communicated simply through images and rhetoric.[61]

Policy monopolies have been studied in the past using terms such as iron triangles and policy networks.[62] These concepts captured the closed nature of the policy process, but failed to highlight the critical importance of policy ideas in supporting this process. Ideas are the critical feature in the creation and maintenance of policy monopolies.

Policy monopolies are based on the creation of positive images associated with a given policy prescription. Governments are expected to fulfill certain widely accepted functions, such as providing for the national defense and promoting economic growth. When promoting new ideas, policymakers and outside interests strive to associate their preferred policies with these positive images.[63] When they succeed, the makings of a policy monopoly begin. When these new ideas are associated with the creation of new institutions, a policy monopoly has been created.

When effectively created, policy monopolies can be highly resistant to change. For example, Goldstein's discussion of U.S. trade policies indicates a fairly persistent trade policy monopoly in support of multilateralism and open markets.[64] But many policy monopolies, especially in the United States, are incomplete. Incomplete monopolies result in a loose confederation of interested parties who often share similar outlooks but disagree in policy preferences.

In the United States, policy monopolies are frequently created or destroyed, producing what have been called punctuated equilibria in politics.[65] When previously accepted ideas fail to generate effective solutions to long-standing problems, policy makers and outside actors search for new solutions. If new ideas become accepted in the political arena, they often provoke the destruction of existing policy monopolies. Baumgartner and Jones effectively describe the process:

> Destruction of policy monopolies is almost always associated with a change in intensities of interest. People, political leaders, government agencies, and private institutions which had once shown no interest in a given question become involved for some reason. That reason is typically a new understanding of the nature of the policies involved. . . . In the wake of crumbling images, policy monopolies that were constructed behind their shield have often weakened or even disintegrated.[66]

As new ideas become better understood and accepted, they often become embedded in new institutional arrangements that form the cornerstone of a new policy monopoly. If this institutionalization fails, creation of a policy monopoly is unlikely.[67] Far more likely is continued skirmishing over the definition of public problems and their solutions.

Baumgartner and Jones illustrate this process in their discussion of U.S. policies toward the nuclear power industry.[68] In the 1940s and 1950s, positive images of nuclear power dominated political debates; these images became embedded in an insulated decision-making structure—the Atomic Energy Commission. As negative images of nuclear power replaced the earlier sanguine view, the government regulatory structure also evolved. The Atomic Energy Commission's monopoly on decisionmaking was ended, and new groups, led by environmentalists, assumed a more prominent role in nuclear power debates. Today, opposition to nuclear power is so intense that no new reactors have been created since 1977.

Learning

As we saw above, policy ideas often promote stability in policy making because they are highly resistant to change. Nevertheless, policy ideas do change. What is more problematic is whether new policy ideas are digested by policy makers and serve to influence their decisionmaking in a positive manner. In other words, do policymakers learn?

As Etheridge, Nye, and others have shown, learning can and does occur.[69] Indeed, in many cases, the creation and destruction of policy monopolies is based on learning by policymakers.

Policy learning is defined as a "change of beliefs (or the degree of confidence in one's beliefs) or the development of new beliefs, skills, or procedures as a result of the observation and interpretation of experience."[70] When an actor has learned, he or she acts differently when confronted with the same (or similar) situation that prompted the actor's initial learning. Through learning, the actor develops new means for calculating risks and evaluating potential outcomes.[71]

Policy learning can take several forms and occurs on several levels.[72] This book is most concerned with government learning, which refers to the consensus of views among top level decision makers and the wider elite.[73] These views are embodied in formal statements and reflected in the behavior of key leaders. Because public statements often serve several purposes at the same time, one is often hard-pressed to distinguish between individual and governmental learning. Do changes in public statements signal individual learning or an appeal to elites who have already learned? In order to avoid this problem, we must seek changes in the public statements of numerous public officials.

It is important to recognize that organizations and governments do not learn in the literal sense. Instead, key individuals learn and these new perspectives are eventually translated into new organizational routines. When these new ideas and organizational routines persist, learning hypotheses may offer useful explanations for policy change.

Government learning is indicated by a number of changes in policymakers' ideas.[74] Specifically, government learning is indicated by three criteria:

1.   Growth of realism. Government leaders begin to better recognize different elements and processes operating in the domestic and international environment.
2.   Growth of intellectual integration. Decisionmakers are able to take different elements and fuse them together in their thought processes.
3.   Growth of reflective perspective. Decisionmakers reflect about the above two processes of problem conception and the results they seek to achieve.[75]

It is essential to distinguish between adaptation and learning.[76] Policymakers adapt to the new events on a daily basis; they rarely undertake the stressful task of systematically reformulating basic assumptions and goals.[77] Moreover, this definition of learning does not necessarily imply that new policies are normatively superior or more effective.[78] As Levy has stated: "Belief change is not always accurate, and knowledge does not always translate into skill."[79]   However, this view does assume that policymakers have made political accommodations to cope with the effects of experience.[80] These accommodations might include changes in doctrine, revised budgetary commitments, and the development of new institutional mechanisms. In the area of defense industrial base policy, learning may be indicated by changes in declaratory policy, expanded funding to support industry, and the creation of new bureaucratic organizations devoted to the issue.[81]

My conception of learning is thus similar to Mendelson's discussion of "evolutionary learning," an approach that links new ideas with political leaders' search for solutions to thorny political problems.[82]   Mendelson describes how Mikhail Gorbachev's frustration with the Soviet presence in Afghanistan increased the Soviet leadership's openness to new foreign policy ideas. The input of a wider circle of foreign policy advisors provided Gorbachev with a wider range of policy options regarding Afghanistan. This study charts a similar approach as it examines how American policymakers' inability to solve the problems of defense dependence and eroding competitiveness opened the U.S. public debate to new policy ideas.

Analysts of government learning have clearly indicated that policy ideas can change. But what causes this change? When policy ideas change, a number of factors are at work. Most political scientists have emphasized factors such as outside pressures and circumstances. Indeed, political leaders rarely accept policy ideas on their merits alone.[83] New ideas must come to the attention of political leaders, be understood by these leaders, and somehow accord with the state of political discourse at a given time. The external political situation is thus critical to the acceptance of new ideas. As Garrett and Weingast recently argued, "Only certain ideas have properties that lead to selection by political actors and to their institutionalization and perpetuation. It is not something intrinsic to ideas that gives them their power, but their utility in helping actors achieve their desired ends under prevailing constraints."[84]

Most theorists would accept these external factors as critical to policy evolution, but, unfortunately, most analyses stop at this point. The substance of ideas does matter—a point that many analysts are coming to respect.[85] Policies are unlikely to change unless new ideas emerge.

Policymakers will try new options only if someone creates an alternative plan to overcome existing problems.   These ideas can emerge from a wide range of sources—the material interests of outside interest groups, intellectual writings, or even internal governmental deliberations. They are often generated by individuals whom Kingdon has dubbed "policy entrepreneurs."[86]

The content of ideas profoundly affects the learning propensities of government officials, and, ultimately, the creation of new policy monopolies.[87] Beyond initial outside conditions, ideas are also judged on their economic, political, and administrative viability.[88] Economic viability relates to the ability of ideas to resolve ongoing economic problems. Policymakers will only accept new ideas if they view them as technically feasible; they must be convinced that a new idea can be implemented.

Political viability refers to the fit between new ideas and the existing goals and interests of dominant political actors. It also encompasses the symbolic associations linked to certain ideas.[89] If new ideas are automatically viewed as illegitimate, they are unlikely to influence policy makers. For example, Bradford Lee attributes American reluctance to accept Keynesian ideas in the 1930s to widespread beliefs that deficit spending presented a serious threat to the political system.[90]

In her study of the progress of developmentalism in Brazil and Argentina in the late 1950s, Sikkink similarly attributes societal receptivity to new ideas to the preexisting conceptual frameworks dominating each country.[91] In Brazil, the new ideas were accepted because they became linked with nationalist causes. In Argentina, by contrast, Peronist politicians succeeded in defining the new ideas as a "sell-out" to foreign interests. In the end, Argentineans rejected the developmentalist model as ill-suited to their unique needs.

Finally, administrative viability refers to "the degree to which new ideas fit the long-standing administrative biases of the relevant decision makers and the existing capacities of the state to implement them."[92] American policymakers must operate in a system that is decentralized and fragmented. Ikenberry's description is appropriate: "these structures are characterized by a fragmentation of political sovereignty across levels and branches of government and have left executive officials with a relatively modest bureaucratic planning capacity and few mechanisms for direct intervention in specific [economic] sectors."[93]

Because of this fragmentation, U.S. policymakers are attracted to administratively simple ideas. Creation of new government capacities is extremely difficult in the U.S. system. Thus, ideas calling for new capacities are suspect, and administrative simplicity is critical to the success of new ideas. For example, administrative simplicity helped ease passage of the 1986 Tax Reform Act.[94]

As we will see in our case studies, government DIB policy in the 1980s cannot be explained without reference to the power of policy ideas and learning. I hypothesize that U.S. government inaction in the face of growing defense dependence is best explained by the persistence of long-standing policy ideas concerning the efficacy of a limited government role in directly supporting defense-related industries. Because this model persisted after World War II and became institutionalized within the U.S. government, alternative policy options were not considered by top American officials. When domestic industries petitioned for protection, they faced substantial obstacles to overcoming the power of these shared political ideas.

These setbacks led outside groups, such as the Council on Competitiveness and various industry associations, as well as many bureaucrats inside government, to consider alternative arguments justifying DIB protection or support. These new models, often based on strategic trade theory, made a strong alternative case for government intervention, weakening the previous policy monopoly based on free trade and limited government intervention in markets at home.[95] Many of the strategic theorists argued that traditional theories did not capture the changing dynamics of international trade. As columnist Robert Kuttner put it, trade theory "doesn't fit a world of learning curves, economies of scale and floating rates."[96]

Because of the persistence of free trade conceptions within the U.S. government, strategic trade concepts were largely developed and refined in academia, think tanks, and other outside groups. Similarly, Margaret Weir has discussed how the private Committee for Economic Development (CED) served to make Keynesian ideas more intellectually palatable in the 1950s.[97]

As these concepts were refined and made more palatable, they were injected into the public policy debates regarding government intervention in support of the semiconductor manufacturing and machine tool industries. In both of these cases, new ideas became linked to specific policies that were administratively simple.[98] The creation of industry-led consortia was a relatively simple project. Because the consortia were industry-led, supporters of this concept did not contend with arguments that government was incapable of performing this task. In addition, support for consortia did not entail a new form of government activity. No new bureaucracies were created and no new functions were established. The government's role was restricted to funding support, a task of limited administrative complexity.

While the new ideas helped spur government support for the machine tool and semiconductor industries, policymakers did not alter their initial opposition to industrial policy and blanket trade protection. Instead, they developed new responses that permitted intervention without affecting their traditional opposition to market intervention. The new concepts were based on "an idea whose time has come."[99] We examine the origin and evolution of these policy ideas in the next chapter.

NOTES

1. Friedberg (1991) makes a similar point. See p. 73.

2. Among the best known pluralist works are: Robert Dahl, *Who Governs?* (New Haven, Conn.: Yale University Press, 1963); David Truman, *The Governmental Process: Political Interests and Public Opinion* (New York: Alfred A. Knopf, 1951); and Nelson W. Polsby, *Community Power and Political Theory* (New Haven, Conn.: Yale University Press, 1963).

3. Theodore J. Lowi, *The End of Liberalism* 2d. ed. (New York: W.W. Norton, 1979), p. 51.

4. E. E. Schattschneider, *Politics, Pressures and the Tariff* (New York: Prentice Hall, 1935).

5. Stephen D. Cohen, *The Making of U.S. International Economic Policy*, 2d ed., (New York: Praeger, 1988), p. 135. See also Robert Baldwin, *The Political Economy of U.S. Import Policy* (Cambridge, Mass: MIT Press, 1985).

6. See Mancur Olson, *The Logic of Collective Action* (Cambridge, Mass.: Harvard University Press, 1965).

7. For a listing of these cases, see Destler (1986), pp. 223-342. Most economic studies concur with these figures, but also note that the effects of protectionism have been overstated. The United States still remains more liberal than most of its major trading partners. See David B. Yoffie, "American Trade Policy: An Obsolete Bargain," in John Chubb and Paul Peterson, eds., *Can the Government Govern?* (Washington, D.C.: Brookings Institution, 1989), p. 117. John Ruggie makes a similar argument. See his "Embedded Liberalism Revisited: Institutions and Progress in International Economic Relations," in Emmanuel Adler and Beverly Crawford, eds., *Progress in Postwar International Relations* (New York: Columbia University Press, 1991), pp. 218-219.

8. U.S. Department of Commerce, Bureau of Export Administration, Office of Industrial Resources, *Section 232 Investigations: The Effects of Imports on National Security* (Washington, D.C.: Department of Commerce, July 1989).

9. Among the groups recently testifying in support of greater DIB protection are: NCID, the American Defense Preparedness Association, the American Gear Manufacturers Association, the American Electronics Association, the National Machine Tool Builders Association and the U.S. Business and Industry Council.

10. The banking committees became involved in DIB issues because of their jurisdiction over the Defense Production Act. Oakar chaired the House Banking Subcommittee on Economic Stabilization. This subcommittee, under both Oakar and her predecessor, John LaFalce (D-NY), was also especially active on issues related to industrial policy.

11. See Helen V. Milner, "Resisting the Protectionist Temptation: Industry and the Making of Trade Policy in France and the United States during the 1970s," *International Organization*, vol. 41, no. 4 (Autumn 1987), pp. 639-66; Helen V. Milner and David B. Yoffie, "Between Free Trade and Protectionism: Strategic Trade Policy and a Theory of Corporate Trade Demands," *International Organization* vol. 43, no. 2 (Spring 1989), pp. 239-72. A similar argument is made by I. M. Destler and John Odell; see their *Anti-Protection: Changing Forces in U.S. Trade Politics* (Washington, D.C.: Institute for International Economics, 1987).

12. These shifts have created a heated debate over the issue of whether governments should concern themselves with corporate nationality, that is, whether U.S.-owned firms should be treated differently from foreign firms based in the United States. For an introduction to this debate see Robert Reich, "Who is Us?" *Harvard Business Review*, (January-February 1990), pp. 53-64. For an alternative view, see Laura D. Tyson, "They Are Not Us: Why American Ownership Still Matters," *The American Prospect* (Winter 1991), pp. 37-49.

13. Quoted in George C. Lodge, *Perestroika for America*, (Boston: Harvard Business School Press, 1990), p. 67.

14. Destler and Odell (1987), pp. 2-3.

15. George Gilder, "How Computer Companies Lost their Memories," *Forbes*, June 13, 1988, pp. 79-84.

16. On the impact of globalization on corporate perspectives, see Robert B. Reich, "The Stateless Manager," *Best of Business Quarterly*, Fall 1991, pp. 85-91.

17. Among the most important statist works are: Theda Skocpol, *States and Social Revolutions* (Cambridge: Cambridge University Press, 1979); Stephen D. Krasner, *Defending the National Interest: Raw Materials Investments and U.S. Foreign Policy*. (Princeton, N.J.: Princeton University Press, 1978); Peter J. Katzenstein (ed.), *Between Power and Plenty* (Madison: University of Wisconsin Press, 1978); and Eric A. Nordlinger, *On the Autonomy of the Democratic State* (Cambridge, Mass.: Harvard University Press, 1981). For an excellent review of this research, see Peter Evans, Dieter Rueschemeyer, and Theda Skocpol, eds., *Bringing the State Back In* (New York: Cambridge University Press, 1985).

18. G. John Ikenberry, *Reasons of State: Oil Politics and the Capacities of American Government* (Ithaca, N.Y.: Cornell University Press, 1988), p. 26.

19. For other works that employ similar definitions, see Krasner (1978), pp. 55-61; Katzenstein (1978), pp. 306-323; and G. John Ikenberry, "Conclusion: An Institutional Approach to American Foreign Economic Policy," *International Organization* vol. 42, no. 1 (Winter 1988), pp. 219-43.

20. Chalmers Johnson, *MITI and the Japanese Miracle: The Growth of Industrial Policy* (Stanford, Calif.: Stanford University Press, 1982).

21. See Judith Goldstein, "Ideas, Institutions and American Trade Policy, *International Organization* vol. 42, no. 1 (Winter 1988), pp. 179-217; and "The Political Economy of Trade: Institutions of Protection," *American Political Science Review* vol. 80, no. 1 (March 1986), pp. 161-184. Similar arguments are presented by Stephen Haggard and Douglas Nelson. See Stephen Haggard, "The Institutional Foundations of Hegemony: Explaining the Reciprocal Trade Agreements Act of 1934," *International Organization* vol. 42, no. 1 (Winter 1988), pp.

91-119; and Douglas Nelson, "Domestic Political Preconditions of US Trade Policy: Liberal Structure and Protectionist Dynamics," *Journal of Public Policy* vol. 9, no. 1 (1989), p. 83-108.

22. Goldstein (1988), p. 187. Destler provides one of the best descriptions of the creation and subsequent operations of these institutions; see Destler (1986).

23. An insulated institution or decision arena is a policymaking site with a single or very few loci of decision making authority. In the U.S. system, these terms refer to decisionmaking arenas where congressional input is limited or nonexistent. Two of the best American examples are the Supreme Court and the Federal Reserve Board.

24. Goldstein has described how the impact of policy ideas produced different attitudes toward agriculture and manufacturing in the 1930s. Ever since, a strong free trade preference in manufacturing has been accompanied by an activist government role in support of agriculture. See Judith Goldstein, "The Impact of Ideas on Trade Policy: the Origins of U.S. Agricultural and Manufacturing Policies," *International Organization* vol. 43, no. 1 (Winter 1989), pp. 31-71.

25. Judith Goldstein and Stefanie Ann Lenway, "Interests or Institutions: An Inquiry into Congressional-ITC Relations," *International Studies Quarterly* vol. 33 (1989), p. 304, fn. 1.

26. Krasner (1978), p. 86.

27. For background on Section 232, see Lewis (1991).

28. For a discussion of this process, see Prestowitz (1989), pp. 407-10.

29. These distinctions have led some observers to recommend placing Section 232 investigations under ITC jurisdiction in an effort to blunt political pressures on investigators. See Lewis (1991), p. 377.

30. See, for example, Goldstein and Lenway (1989).

31. Some analysts argue that DoD is highly insulated from public pressures, arguing that DoD's budgetary resources and administrative authority permit it to pursue its goals in a relatively autonomous fashion. See, for example, Gregory Hooks, "The Rise of the Pentagon and U.S. State Building: The Defense Program as Industrial Policy," *American Journal of Sociology* vol. 96, no. 2 (September 1990), pp. 358-404.

32. Kenneth R. Mayer, "Problem? What Problem? Congressional Micromanagement of the Department of Defense," Paper prepared for delivery at the 1991 Annual Meeting of the American Political Science Association, Washington, D.C., August 29-September 1, 1991, p. 24.

33. Set up in 1958, in the wake of Sputnik, DARPA was designed as an independent agency within DoD that would take a long-range view of DoD's future technology needs. In effect, DARPA serves as DoD's "corporate" research organization, funding innovative "high-risk" research programs. It is independent of the individual military services and reports directly to the highest levels of DoD, now the Undersecretary of Defense for Acquisition. For a fuller discussion of DARPA, see Jacques S. Gansler, *Affording Defense* (Cambridge, Mass.: MIT Press, 1989), pp. 237-8; Michael E. Davey, "Managing Defense Department Technology Base Programs," Report No. 88-310, (Washington, D.C.: Congressional Research Service 1988); and Andrew Pollack, "America's Answer to MITI," *New York Times*, March 5, 1989, Section 3, pp. 1, 8. In 1993, the "Defense" was dropped and the agency in now known as ARPA.

34. See Burton I. Edelson and Robert L. Stern, "The Operations of DARPA and its Utility as a Model for a Civilian ARPA," (Washington, D.C.: Johns Hopkins Foreign Policy Institute, November 1989).

35. See John Burgess and Evelyn Richards, "Head of Pentagon High-Tech Agency is Reassigned," *Washington Post*, April 21, 1990, p. D10.

36. Edelson and Stern (November 1989).

37. Ezra N. Suleiman, "State Structure and Clientelism: The French State Versus the Notaires," *British Journal of Political Science* vol. 17, no. 4 (July 1987), p. 259.

38. Katzenstein (1978) echoes this point in his argument that analysts must consider the centralization of both the state and societal forces.

39. As Kathryn Sikkink notes, institutional approaches help explain the context of policy making, but they do not explain how certain groups and institutions develop historically specific ideologies. See Kathryn Sikkink, *Ideas and Institutions: Developmentalism in Brazil and Argentina* (Ithaca, N.Y.: Cornell University Press, 1991), pp. 9-11. A similar point is made in Peter F. Cowhey, "'States' and 'Politics' in American Foreign Economic Policy," in John S. Odell and Thomas D. Willett, *International Trade Policies: Gains from Exchange between Economics and Political Science* (Ann Arbor: University of Michigan Press, 1990), pp. 225-232.

40. For example, the 1986 Tax Reform Act established a dramatic shift in U.S. tax policy. This reform occurred without a change in the institutional structure of the policymaking process; the House Ways and Means and Senate Finance Committees continued to dominate the decisionmaking process. Beam, Conlan, and Wrightson attribute this result to changes in policy ideas. See David R. Beam, Timothy J. Conlan, and Margaret T. Wrightson, "Solving the Riddle of Tax Reform: Party Competition and the Politics of Ideas," *Political Science Quarterly* vol. 105, no. 2 (1990), pp. 193-217.

41. The literature in this field is wide ranging and extensive. Many studies focus on the role of individual decision makers' cognitive processes. For reviews of this literature, see Irving L. Janis and Leon Mann. *Decisionmaking: A Psychological Analysis of Conflict, Choice and Commitment*, (New York: Free Press, 1977); Robert Jervis, *Perception and Misperception in International Politics*, (Princeton, N.J.: Princeton University Press, 1976).

My research does not examine the psychological or cognitive components of decision-making. Instead, I am interested in the content of policy ideas and their impact on policy outcomes. For examples of similar approaches, see Goldstein (1988); John S. Odell, *U.S. International Monetary Policy: Markets, Power and Ideas as Sources of Change* (Princeton, N.J.: Princeton University Press, 1982); Peter A. Hall, ed., *The Political Power of Economic Ideas: Keynesianism Across Nations*, (Princeton, N.J.: Princeton University Press, 1989); Kathryn Sikkink (1991); D. Michael Shafer, *Deadly Paradigms: The Failure of U.S. Counterinsurgency Policy* (Princeton, N.J.: Princeton University Press, 1988).

42. Most analysts agree that a nation's policymakers often share similar beliefs and world views. Similarities in beliefs are most often attributed to similar personal backgrounds, education and training, and generational experiences. See Odell (1982), pp. 66-67. Numerous studies have highlighted the linkage between these shared images and subsequent foreign policies. For example, see Alexander L. George and Robert Keohane, "The Concept of National Interests: Uses and Limitations," in Alexander L. George, *Presidential Decisionmaking in Foreign Policy: The Effective Use of Information and Advice*, (Boulder, Colo.: Westview Press, 1980), pp. 232-233; Jerel A. Rosati, *The Carter Administration's Quest for Global Community: Beliefs and their Impact on Behavior*, (Columbia, SC: University of South Carolina Press, 1987; Deborah Welch Larson, *The Origins of Containment: A Psychological Explanation*, (Princeton, N.J.: Princeton University Press, 1985). For literature reviews, see Rosati (1987) and Stephen F. Walker, "The Evolution of Operational Code Analysis," *Political Psychology* vol. 11, no. 2 (1990), pp. 403-18.

43. See Paul R. Schulman, "The Politics of 'Ideational Policy,'" *Journal of Politics* vol. 50, no. 3 (1988), p. 265.

44. Rosati (1987), p. 168. Peter A. Hall and Aaron Friedberg reach similar conclusions. See Peter A. Hall, "Conclusion: The Politics of Keynesian Ideas," in Hall (1989), p. 390; Friedberg (1988).

45. Shafer (1988), p. 8.

46. Sikkink (1991), p. 244.

47. Lawrence R. Jacobs, "Institutions and Culture: Health Policy and Public Opinion in the U.S. and Britain," *World Politics* vol. 44 (January 1992), pp. 179-209.

48. Jeff Checkel, "Ideas, Institutions, and the Gorbachev Foreign Policy Revolution," *World Politics* vol. 45, no. 1 (January 1993), pp. 271-300.

49. For discussions of the immutability decisionmakers' ideas, see Jervis (1976) and Alexander L. George, "The 'Operational Code:' A Neglected Approach to the Study of Political Leaders and Decision Making" in Erik P.Hoffmann and Frederic J. Fleron, Jr., *The Conduct of Soviet Foreign Policy* (New York: Aldine Publishing, 1980), esp. 25-80.

50. Friedberg (1988), pp. 16-17.

51. Hall, "Conclusion: The Politics of Keynesian Ideas," in Hall (1989), p. 361.

52. See George (1979).

53. These sources might include decision memos, summaries of meetings, or transcripts of meetings. Such sources remain largely unavailable for the debates cited in this study.

54. See Rosati (1987), pp. 190-92.

55. Alexander L. George, "The Causal Nexus Between Cognitive Beliefs and Decision-Making Behavior: The Operational Code Belief System," in Lawrence Falkowski, ed., *Psychological Models in International Politics*, (Boulder, Colo.: Westview Press, 1979b), p. 103.

56. Mark H. Moore, "What Makes Public Ideas Powerful?" in Robert B. Reich, ed., *The Power of Public Ideas*, (Cambridge: Ballinger, 1987), p. 75.

57. Thomas L. Kuhn, *The Structure of Scientific Revolutions*, (Chicago: University of Chicago Press, 1962).

58. Moore (1987), p. 72.

59. George (1980), p. 45.

60.This definition is taken from Frank R. Baumgartner and Bryan D. Jones, *Agendas and Instability in American Politics* (Chicago: University of Chicago Press, 1993), p. 6. Much of the following section is based concepts developed by Baumgartner and Jones.

61. Ibid, p. 7.

62. See Gordon Adams, *The Politics of Defense Contracting: The Iron Triangle* (New Brunswick, N.J.: Transaction Books, 1982); and Hugh Heclo, "Issue Networks in the Executive Establishment," in Anthony King, ed., *The New American Political System* Washington, D.C.: American Enterprise Institute, 1978).

63. Kingdon (1984), pp. 16-19.

64. See Goldstein (1988).

65. Baumgartner and Jones (1993), pp. 3-24.

66. Baumgartner and Jones (1993), p. 8.

67. In his discussions of foreign policy learning, Jack Levy makes a similar point, arguing that the institutionalization of new knowledge is a critical factor in learning. See Jack S. Levy, "Learning and Foreign Policy: Sweeping a Conceptual Minefield," *International Organization* vol. 48, no. 2 (Spring 1994), pp. 287-89.

68. Baumgartner and Jones (1993), pp. 59-82.

69. See, for example, Lloyd S. Etheredge, *Can Governments Learn?* (New York: Pergamon Press, 1985); George W. Breslauer and Philip E. Tetlock, eds., *Learning in U.S. and Soviet Foreign Policy* (Boulder, Colo.: Westview Press, 1991); Joseph Nye, "Nuclear Learning and U.S.-Soviet Security Regimes," *International Organization* vol. 41, no. 1 (1988).

70. This definition is taken from Levy, (Spring 1994), p. 283.

48 Responding to Defense Dependence

71. Andrew Owen Bennett, *Theories of Individual, Organizational, and Governmental Learning and the Rise and Fall of Soviet Military Intervention, 1973-1983*, Ph.D. dissertation, Harvard University, February 1990, pp. 14-15.

72. For example, Tetlock discusses learning at the levels of the individual, the institution, the government, and the political culture. Philip E. Tetlock, "Learning in U.S. and Soviet Foreign Policy: In Search of an Elusive Concept," in Breslauer and Tetlock (1991). See, especially, pp. 40-42.

73. See Lloyd S. Etheredge and James Short, "Thinking about Government Learning," *Journal of Management Studies* vol. 20, no. 1 (1983), pp. 41-58; Bennett (1990).

74. Developing effective measures of learning has proved extremely difficult. For background, see Bennett (1990); Levy (Spring 1994), pp. 279-312.

75. Etheredge (1985), p. 66.

76. Philip E. Tetlock (1991), pp. 45-47.

77. Tetlock notes that certain types of levels of belief are more amenable to change. Changes in tactical beliefs are most common, while changes in fundamental assumptions are relatively rare. The frequency of changes in strategic policy beliefs and preferences falls between these two extremes. See Tetlock (1991), pp. 27-31.

78. For a discussion of the problems surrounding measurement of "efficiency learning" see Matthew Evangelista, "Sources of Moderation in Soviet Security Policy," in Philip Tetlock et al., eds., *Behavior, Society, and Nuclear War*, Vol. 2, (New York: Oxford University Press, 1991), pp. 270-271.

79. Levy (Spring 1994), p. 292.

80. Ibid, p. 270.

81. Alone, these indices are not sufficient to indicate that learning has occurred. As Levy (Spring 1994, p. 290) notes, not all policy change results from learning. Policymakers may learn new ideas but be prevented from putting these ideas into practice. For example, as we will see in Chapter Three, many American policy makers, especially members of Congress, adopted new ideas about the government's role in supporting industry during the early 1980s. Nonetheless, domestic political constraints blocked the adoption of an activist U.S. industrial policy in this period.

82. See Sarah E. Mendelson, "Internal Battles and External Wars: Politics, Learning, and the Soviet Withdrawal from Afghanistan," *World Politics* vol. 45 (April 1993), pp. 327-60.

83. This section is based on Hall, "Conclusion: The Politics of Keynesian Ideas," in Hall (1989), pp. 369-75.

84. Geoffrey Garrett and Barry R. Weingast, "Ideas, Interests, and Institutions: Constructing the European Community's Internal Market," in Judith Goldstein and Robert O. Keohane, eds., *Ideas and Foreign Policy: Beliefs, Institutions, and Political Change*, (Ithaca, N.Y.: Cornell University Press, 1993), p. 172.

85. See Goldstein (Winter 1989).

86. Kingdon (1984, pp. 129-30) offers a simple definition of policy entrepreneur. They are "advocates for proposals or the prominence of an idea."

87. See Kingdon (1984), pp. 131-51.

88. Kingdon offers a similar list of criteria affecting the acceptance of new policy ideas: technical feasibility, value acceptability within the policy community, tolerable cost, anticipated public acquiescence, and a reasonable chance for receptivity among elected decision makers. See Ibid., p. 138. See also Odell (1982), pp. 67-68.

89. On the use of symbols, see Charles Elder and Roger Cobb, *The Political Use of Symbols* (New York: Longman, 1983), and Murray Edelman, *The Symbolic Uses of Politics* (Urbana: University of Illinois Press, 1964).

90. Bradford A. Lee, "The Miscarriage of Necessity and Invention: Proto-Keynesianism and Democratic States in the 1930s," in Hall (1989), pp. 129-70.

91. Sikkink (1991), pp. 252-4.

92. Hall (1989), p. 371.

93. Ikenberry (1988), p. 41.

94. Beam et al. (1990).

95. For introductions to the strategic trade policy debate, see Paul R. Krugman, ed., *Strategic Trade Policy and the New International Economics*, (Cambridge, Mass.: MIT Press, 1986); J. David Richardson, "The Political Economy of Strategic Trade Policy," *International Organization* vol. 44, no. 1 (Winter 1990), pp. 107-35.

96. Robert Kuttner, "The Free Trade Fallacy," *New Republic*, Vol. 28, 1983, p. 16. For a rebuttal of these claims, see Patricia Dillon, James Lehman, and Thomas D. Willett, "Assessing the Usefulness of International Trade Theory for Policy Analysis," in John S. Odell and Thomas D. Willett, eds., *International Trade Policies: Gains from Exchange Between Economics and Political Science* (Ann Arbor: University of Michigan Press, 1990), pp. 21-54.

97. These ideas were eventually accepted by John Kennedy's Council of Economic Advisors and led indirectly to Kennedy's 1962 tax cuts. Margaret Weir, "Innovation and Boundaries in American Employment Policy," *Political Science Quarterly* vol. 107, no. 2 (1992), pp. 256-57.

98. See Ibid., p. 266-267.

99. One of the best discussions of the development of new policy ideas is Kingdon (1984), especially pp. 131-151.

3

Ideas and the American Defense Industrial Base

The previous chapter presented a summary of approaches to understanding government responses to defense dependence. We concluded that U.S. DIB policies could not be explained adequately without reference to the impact of policy ideas and their evolution over time. In this chapter, we review the initial acceptance and subsequent consolidation of these ideas. We also examine their enduring influence in restricting government efforts to act more resolutely to consider relative gains in its DIB policies.

We then turn to an examination of how these ideas became transformed during the 1980s, leading to policy shifts that have gradually transformed U.S. DIB policies. As concerns over defense dependence grew, traditional policy ideas came under attack. The development of new economic models for understanding the industrial base contributed to a search for new policies toward the DIB. These new models helped expand the range of "legitimate" policy alternatives available to U.S. leaders and helped directly contribute to the creation of Sematech and the National Center for Manufacturing Sciences.

But intellectual change did not transform policy toward all threatened industries. In a number of cases, policymakers rejected the lessons of the new models and instead continued their support for a more traditional policy line. This continuity resulted from analyses that questioned the true "criticality" of industries deemed as essential for national security by their supporters.

IDEAS AND THE DEFENSE INDUSTRIAL BASE

Ideas about the DIB are tightly linked with a larger set of ideas about the appropriate role for government in managing the economy at home and abroad. In the aftermath of World War II, American economic and defense policymakers shared two assumptions about the U.S. defense industrial base. First, in the international sphere, American leaders committed themselves to free trade as the best means to guarantee economic prosperity and preserve national security.[1] Through the GATT and other international institutions, the United States pursued overall free trade policies as part of an effort to bind a global anti-Soviet alliance.[2]

Although the GATT and other components of the postwar free trade regimes included exceptions permitting protection of industries critical to national security, the United States rarely employed them—especially in comparison to the Western European states and Japan—and willingly transferred technologies and production capabilities to its allies. Open defense trade was viewed as the most cost-effective means to preserve America's national security. Through standardization of weapons, costly duplication would be avoided and interoperability would be guaranteed. This would eventually contribute to cost savings for the alliance.[3] Efficiency was supported even if it ultimately had negative economic effects at home over the long term.

The second component of American defense industrial base policies concerned the relationship between government and industry within the United States. As they moved to open markets overseas, American leaders also carved out a limited government role in support of domestic industries.

For example, after World War II, the United States dismantled a whole range of institutions created to support industrial mobilization. Rejecting creation of a large-scale planning apparatus, administration officials instead turned to the market as the most efficient means for ensuring defense preparedness.[4] Indirect support, through government purchases, represented the Pentagon's primary tool for influencing the decisions of private businesses. Any commercial spillovers from this effort were, by design, indirect and unintended. One observer recently summarized this perspective:

> The problem is less a large military establishment per se than the near-religious insistence that commercial benefits are verboten, that civilian counterparts of defense-funded research and technology assistance are not permitted, and that we must be generous with technology transfers to allies but rigidly control them when there is even the slightest risk that they might fall into the wrong hands. These dynamics. . . are the result. . . . of a fundamentalist devotion to laissez-faire interacting with military goals.[5]

In contrast to other states, such as France and Sweden, where governments actively supported domestic defense industries, the Pentagon's relationship with industry often assumed adversarial tones.[6] Not until the early 1980s did defense planners begin to see defense industrial base problems as part of a more general pattern of U.S. industrial deterioration. It was in this context that calls for DIB intervention arose.

Throughout much of the postwar period, these two concepts of free trade and nonintervention dominated defense industrial policy and planning and bolstered a strong policy monopoly. Table 3.1 highlights the dominant ideas.

These ideas helped contribute to American DIB policies designed to support allied arms industries even if this had negative ramifications for American economic interests. They also helped restrict the Pentagon's ability to directly support industries deemed critical to defense.

Table 3.1
Dominant Ideas about the American Industrial Base

General Beliefs:	In an unstable, polarized world characterized by zero-sum competition,[7] a strong commitment to an effective military defense is necessary.
Specific Beliefs:	American defense is best preserved when market forces are allowed to prevail. Thus, military forces will be supplied by the "winners" of market competition at both home and abroad. Government intervention will only conflict with the free operation of market forces.
Common Policy Project:	Maintenance of open markets along with a limited role for government offer the most effective means to fulfill these objectives.

Before examining the impact of these policies over time, we must first explain their initial attractiveness. To understand this question, we must examine the factors that prompt political leaders to accept new ideas. What features led American leaders to first accept these policy ideas?

As we saw in Chapter Two, new policy ideas are accepted by policymakers if they are viewed as economically, politically, and administratively viable. In the early 1950s, the two-track DIB strategy met all these criteria. These policies were assumed to offer the best possibility of meeting an ever-expanding Soviet threat at a reasonable cost. Reliance on market forces also enjoyed strong resonance both economically and politically. More importantly, these administratively simple strategies required few government capacities beyond spending.

The Cold War presented the United States with a dramatically changed strategic environment and the possibility of a future war even more devastating than World War II. Preparedness for this type of conflict would be expensive, if not prohibitive. At the time, many analysts argued that the Soviet threat required a complete transformation of American political institutions, advocating the creation of what Aaron Friedberg has called a "garrison state."[8] But American political leaders faced two significant constraints to expanding their defense program: a limited ability to extract taxes and resources from the population, and a limited ability to direct and steer overall economic development.[9] While typical of "weak" states, these constraints are also partially attributable to the United States' unique "liberal" and individualistic ideology.[10]

American "hands-off" DIB policies emerged within these preexisting constraints of limited extractive scope and directive capability. Ideological and political factors helped contribute to a policy combining basic R&D support with a reliance on the private sector to supply weapons for U.S. military forces. The system was unique when compared to the arsenal systems of European states and 19th-century America, but it proved attractive to American leaders because of its economic, political, and administrative viability. It was relatively low cost[11], required limited administrative capabilities, and was associated with politically attractive images.

More direct government support for industry was deemed unnecessary because many leaders assumed commercial products would develop almost automatically from government research efforts. This spin-off paradigm proved attractive to policy makers because: (1) it appeared to cost nothing as the original investment was justified on national security grounds, and (2) it appeared to support technological development without involving the government in an active "steering" capacity.[12]

As Sikkink has noted, policy ideas develop through three different stages: adoption, implementation, and consolidation.[13] Adoption depends on the above-cited factors relating to the viability of new ideas. Successful implementation requires that ideas become embedded in state institutions. Finally, to be consolidated, an idea must be supported by a strong elite and societal consensus. When both implementation and consolidation succeed, a robust policy monopoly usually results.

Throughout most of the postwar period, a strong and consistent elite consensus supporting market forces helped ease the implementation and consolidation of these ideas.[14] The outlines for postwar DIB policy were established in the immediate aftermath of World War II and became consolidated over the period from the 1950s to the late 1970s.[15]

In terms of defense free trade, these policies did not originally involve extensive U.S. imports of foreign military systems or their components. America's economic predominance, combined with European and Japanese weaknesses, made the Allies highly dependent on U.S. weaponry. The possibility of American defense dependence was never considered. In many cases, technology was not simply transferred to allies. Instead, American officials supported the development of indigenous production facilities to coproduce American systems. In Japan, these American initiatives laid the groundwork for the contemporary defense industry, as Japanese firms consciously utilized this assistance to develop world-class capabilities in both civilian and defense industries.[16]

Programs in Europe were even more comprehensive. Among the most important programs were the provision of machine tools under the Mutual Defense Assistance program and a concerted policy of offshore procurement by the American military.[17] Under an agreement first made in 1958, the United States has since formally entered into eighty-seven government-to-government licensed production agreements with nineteen countries.[18]

As European and Japanese industries recovered, these states began their own indigenous production of new weapons systems. As more states entered the arms market, the sheer variety of systems skyrocketed to a point where NATO troops could not fight together effectively.[19]

In 1975, the United States responded to this dilemma by reinforcing its free trade commitments in the Rationalization, Standardization, and Interoperability initiative, known colloquially as the "Two Way Street." RSI was designed to enhance NATO standardization, encourage alliance technological and industrial strength, encourage competitive national weapons programs, increase U.S. purchase of European military hardware, and increase European purchases of U.S. hardware.[20] Every administration from Ford to Bush expressed strong commitments to RSI, promoting some expansion in inter-Alliance defense trade. For example, within ten years, the U.S. balance in defense trade with Europe declined from an 8-to-1 to a 2-to-1 surplus.[21]

While they were working to maintain open defense markets, American policymakers also sought to limit government intervention in the defense business at home. These policies first emerged out of a heated national debate over the future of U.S. science policy as Senator Harley Kilgour (D-WV) led a failed effort in 1942 and 1943 to create a national Office of Technology Mobilization to offer centralized guidance and steer U.S. science policy toward commercial needs.[22] As late as 1953, the Truman administration appeared willing to consider a more activist government role supporting the DIB. However, the Eisenhower Administration was much less supportive of this activist line and realigned policy directions to return to a greater emphasis on private sector initiatives, an approach that persists today.[23]

Despite limits on direct intervention, Pentagon policies did affect American businesses. For example, as we will see in Chapters Four and Five, government procurement was a crucial factor in the early development of the semiconductor and machine tool industries.[24]

Although some have asserted that the United States has an industrial policy based in the Pentagon,[25] this argument overstates the impact of DoD policies. The Pentagon's efforts cannot be considered as industrial policy because they did not involve the development of a coherent set of institutional arrangements or creation of a coherent industrial strategy.[26] Even when Pentagon officials implicitly recognized the importance of key industries, they failed to even consider activist policies designed to preserve these capabilities.[27]

The policy line developed in the 1950s persisted and was not actively contested until the late 1970s. Extensive spending on defense R&D and production was encouraged but was highly constrained. Since World War II, defense R&D spending has served two main purposes: (1) to develop existing weapons systems, and (2) to examine innovative concepts for future weapons. Even today, support for basic technology activities is almost non-existent as over 90 percent of military R&D is devoted to the production of specific weapons systems.[28] Pentagon planners have pursued these objectives at the expense of the long-term development of a strong technology base at the level of components, materials, and processes.[29]

Although technological advancement was the key to both economic growth and national security, commercial and military activities were kept completely separate.[30] Yet, even in cases where the Pentagon sought to strengthen domestic industry, its focus was quite narrow. The Very High Speed Integrated Circuit program, established in 1980, is a case in point.[31] VHSIC, which spent over $900 million in ten years, was designed to improve transfer of civilian semiconductor technologies to military systems through the use of Pentagon R&D contracts. However, most analysts viewed the program as an ineffective response to the problems of defense dependence.[32] Instead of supporting a healthy technology base for semiconductors, VHSIC was designed for one narrow objective—the development of components for specialized military systems.

When policy did move in a different direction, it normally took the form of simple protection. These rare exceptions were defensive measures, driven almost exclusively by domestic pressure groups, not by a desire to strengthen domestic capabilities critical to national defense.[33] For example, political pressures prompted the creation of special DoD programs to support the U.S. mohair and anthracite coal industries.[34]

These reactive measures did little to strengthen American industry or provide "breathing space" so that industry could take steps to become more competitive. In some cases, trade protection had the perverse effect of harming domestic industries. For example, the 1986 Semiconductor Agreement with Japan created a severe shortage of memory chips and damaged a number of U.S. computer firms.[35] Borrus also charges that the VHSIC program hurt U.S. firms by encouraging them to specialize in esoteric defense technologies with limited commercial potential.[36]

These defensive, ad hoc policies have been criticized on both theoretical and policy grounds.[37] But they still persist—largely as the result of the dominance of policy ideas dating back to the late 1940s. Such problems were recognized at DoD and other government agencies. In a 1988 report, DoD noted that:

> The policies of other governments to subsidize and protect their industries are not matched by the United States Government. U.S. Government policies and actions to level the playing field in international trade have been inadequate. . . . Rare instances of U.S. Government efforts to foster domestic manufacturing are best characterized as efforts to correct the results of prior neglect, and usually focus on lagging rather than leading industries.[38]

Rumblings of Change

These DIB policies persisted for two related reasons. First, American firms were prospering and dominated world markets in both military and civilian industries. Such success was largely attributed to government policies that allowed free market forces to flourish. As long as American hegemony remained unthreatened, few saw a need to reexamine these assumptions. As one group of researchers noted, "The important point about the spin-off paradigm is not that it was a half-truth at best, but that the unusual circumstances of the postwar world did not force Americans to question it."[39]

Second, these policies persisted because few alternative ideas existed. The doctrines of free trade and nonintervention at home had become so entrenched in elite thinking and government institutions that no coherent alternative existed. Alternative approaches based on more active government intervention to support the DIB were almost automatically discounted.[40] When politicians called for protectionist measures, they did so cautiously, asserting that they were not protectionists and were only seeking a temporary exception to prevailing free market policies.

This consensus began to shift in the late 1970s as America's impressive economic growth sputtered and Japan and Western Europe developed into formidable economic rivals. In trying to cope with these economic changes, politicians and analysts searched for new policy ideas both overseas and at home. The concept of industrial policy (IP) soon emerged.

In general terms, industrial policy was not a new idea, as it embodied a concept of national economic-social planning with deep roots in American history. Past American policies, such as support for agriculture, entail aspects of IP. Programs in Japan and Western Europe also offered models to emulate.

Past efforts to expand government support for industry had consistently failed. The defeat of Harley Kilgour's proposed Office of Technology Mobilization is a case in point. But the 1970s and 1980s were different. Declining U.S. economic power led to a more serious reexamination of the concepts surrounding the industrial policy idea. For the first time, researchers and policymakers began to seriously question the efficacy of traditional approaches based on market forces alone.

Emergence of New Ideas—Industrial Policy

The concept of industrial policy first emerged in American political debates in the late 1970s and early 1980s.[41] The case for industrial policy rested on four premises: (1) the United States was deindustrializing and suffering losses (both absolute and relative) in its manufacturing capabilities; (2) without assistance, U.S. firms and workers might not make the transition from old heavy industries to new high-technology industries; (3) the U.S. was losing its edge in export markets, thus threatening its global leadership position; and (4) other nations, especially Japan, had successfully pursued industrial policies.[42] Based on these premises, advocates concluded that "U.S. companies and the government should develop a coherent and coordinated industrial policy whose aim is to raise the real income of our citizens by improving the patterns of our investments rather than by focusing only on aggregate investment levels."[43]

As Charles Schulze has noted, the industrial policy plans of the early 1980s had two aspects: "picking the winners" and "protecting the losers."[44] In other words, policymakers would strive to identify cutting-edge industries with high growth potential. Government would then strive to foster both public and private investment in these sectors. At the same time, it would seek to support and help rehabilite declining industries through measures such as trade protection, subsidies, and tax incentives.

During the early stages of the IP debate, members of Congress and outside experts proposed a whole range of plans for a radical reworking of U.S. government institutions and policies. One of the more widely debated proposals, developed by Rep. John LaFalce (D-NY) and the congressional leadership, involved creating an Industrial Development Bank to aid ailing firms with restructuring and a new Economic Cooperation Council to coordinate trade and technology policies.[45] Strong opposition by the Reagan administration, combined with a return to economic prosperity around 1983, ultimately defeated these far-reaching plans.

The IP concept was subjected to a harsh critique on economic, political, and theoretical grounds. Economists contended that industrial policy could actually weaken the American industrial base.[46] According to critics, support for a strategic industry would certainly benefit that sector and related industries. However, the effects on other industries might be negative.[47]   At a minimum, intervention in support of one industry would divert resources from other industries or from other productive investments, such as education and physical infrastructure. Intervention would also tend to raise costs for consumers and downstream industries that purchase the protected industry's products.

Industrial policy critics further argued that government support for critical sectors could dampen domestic competition. Without domestic competition, U.S. firms would be protected from the market pressures so vital to continued innovation and technological development. Finally, critics contended that an American industrial policy would trigger a foreign response, creating a tit-for-tat economic battle that would damage U.S. firms.

Politically, IP was criticized as a surefire means to create unnecessary subsidies and protectionist barriers to aid sunset, not newly emerging industries. The proposals were viewed by critics such as Charles Schultze as another effort to create a centralized planning mechanism that would interfere with market forces. The IP debate became partisan in the 1984 presidential election as President Reagan painted Democratic candidate and IP supporter Walter Mondale as the champion of big government and high spending.

While these charges were politically potent, the critique of IP on administrative grounds was most persuasive. Any new government IP agency, according to its opponents, simply would not work. Herbert Stein argued, for example, that "experience with government economic development programs. . . demonstrates what should be obvious a priori, the dominant influence of personal or regional political considerations."[48]   Commerce Secretary Malcolm Baldridge echoed Stein's points: "Interventionist government policies have really not worked in the past, and there is no reason to believe that we can make them work now. . . . No government agency is astute enough to target the right industries.[49]

Critics effectively argued that government was incapable of picking the critical industries of the future. As a result, special interests, primarily declining industries, would capture any U.S. IP. As Brookings's Schultze noted, "the surest way to multiply unwarranted subsidies and protectionist measures is to legitimate their existence under the rubric of industrial policy."[50]

Economic recovery slowed the groundswell of support for a government-led policy, but the defeat of the early 1980s proposals is also attributable to the nature of the proposals themselves. Simply put, industrial policy advocates failed to prove the viability of their remedies in either economic, political, or administrative terms. This experience led IP advocates to scrap the term industrial policy as too controversial.[51] It also had an important "chilling effect" on debates regarding DIB policy. Proactive sectoral interventions were almost automatically rejected. What emerged in its place was an almost exclusive reliance on tax and trade policy as the means to support domestic industries.[52]   These policies were purely reactive, driven by political pressures from declining industries. Even worse, protection was not coupled with requirements that the sheltered U.S. industry support its own revitalization.

New Ideas Redux—Strategic Industries

The economic growth of the mid-1980s did little solve the structural problems weakening the competitive edge of U.S. industries. This situation was dramtically worsened by the Reagan administration's macroeconomic policies, which combined expansive fiscal policy with tight monetary policy.[53] This combination resulted in a highly overvalued dollar in overseas markets. An overvalued dollar had the effect of increasing imports and decreasing U.S. exports, creating the largest trade deficits in U.S. history.

As a result of this situation, foreign investors flocked to the United States and foreign products streamed into the country. These pressures rocked U.S. companies, especially those in traditional manufacturing industries such as steel and automobiles.[54]

All these factors created significant pressures for government officials to "do something."

Because of these pressures to act, government inaction sparked significant controversy. In the mid-1980s, a number of new pressure groups began pushing an industrial policy agenda with a new name: competitiveness. These groups, such as the American Business Conference, the National Association of Manufacturers, and the private sector Council on Competitiveness, also became involved indirectly in DIB issues. This interest linked them with traditional defense industry representatives such as the American Defense Preparedness Association and the National Security Industrial Association.

These groups represented a significant lobbying force, but originally achieved very little in terms of comprehensive legislative accomplishments. However, Congress did pass several bills strengthening government R&D activities.[55] The Stevenson-Wydler Act of 1983 enhanced technology transfer from the government-run research laboratories. Similarly, the National Cooperative Research Act of 1984 reformed antitrust laws to encourage joint R&D by private firms.

Despite the political defeat of IP proposals, they found a fertile intellectual climate as new concepts, such as strategic trade theory, began emerging in academic circles by 1984 and 1985. These concepts represented a major sea change--one of the first intellectually coherent challenges to the existing policy monopoly based on the policy ideas noted in Table 3.1. As David Yoffie noted, "For the first time since David Ricardo published Principles of Comparative Advantage in 1817, the classical theory of international trade has been challenged by well-respected academic economists."[56]

Analyzing the success of the export-oriented economic strategies of Japan and other Asian states, some economists began questioning traditional theories of international trade, which failed to explain how resource-poor states like Japan and Singapore could became economic powerhouses. Faced with these anomalies, economists created new models that sought to account for dramatic changes in the world economy. The result was strategic trade theory.

Strategic trade theory differed from industrial policy in a number of respects. First, strategic trade theory rejected IP's emphasis on "protecting the losers." It instead focused on "supporting the winners," that is, assisting industries of the future.

Second, strategic trade ideas were based on the concept that governments could help create comparative advantage. By intervening to support certain critical sectors through subsidies, tax benefits, or closer cooperation with business, governments could reap the large external economies that result from these sectors and utilize them to enhance future growth prospects.

Third, strategic trade theorists developed much more sophisticated measures for determining "worthy" industries. IP advocates focused their efforts on industries with high growth potential and high value-added per worker. The ultimate effect of this definition was to include nearly all U.S. manufacturing industries. As we will see below, strategic trade theory developed much more refined measures for strategic industries.

A final related point concerns each school's suggested policy prescriptions. Strategic trade theorists were generally quite circumspect in their policy prescriptions, pursuing what Laura Tyson termed "cautious activism." In their view, very few industries met the "strategic" criteria. Even more importantly, government had very few feasible options for assisting these industries. In contrast, some of the IP advocates of the 1980s envisioned a centralized planning apparatus, such as Rep. LaFalce's industrial development bank, that would help steer spending and investment throughout U.S. industry.

Strategic trade theory entails a number of complex arguments based on recognition of a number of important changes in the world economy.[57] Supporters of these new approaches argued that certain industries were strategic. Analysts differed over what was considered strategic, but all identified strategic industries as those of high value to a nation's overall economy.[58] In general, these benefits entailed supernormal profits or significant external economies or spillovers to other parts of the economy.[59]

Borrus, Tyson and Zysman's discussion of the semiconductor industry illustrates what was meant by spillover effects: "If the United States loses its ability to compete effectively in semiconductors, it may lose its ability to innovate in both the semiconductor industry and in related electronics industries and its ability to diffuse electronics-based product and process innovations in a whole variety of actual and potential user industries."[60] Because spillovers were so important, dependence on foreign sources in strategic industries could become quite dangerous, affecting not only the target industry but also upstream suppliers and downstream customers.

Strategic industries were also identified by the importance of what analysts called "learning by doing."[61] Certain industries, such as commercial aerospace, may require such large commitments of resources that world markets might permit entry by only a small number of firms. In these cases, governments could assist firms in establishing credible national positions. These firms would then enjoy "first mover advantages," whereby the first firm to enter an industry is also the first to enjoy rapid declines in costs and increasing market share. According to strategic trade theorists, these industries often provided higher-paying and higher-skilled jobs as well as substantial spillover benefits.

This analysis drove a number of policy recommendations. Because these industries were so important to both economic prosperity and national security, government intervention was required to preserve a U.S. stake in world markets.

Because innovation in military technologies was becoming increasingly dependent on commercial industrial advances, such intervention was also critical to strengthening of the DIB.

According to strategic trade proponents, comparative advantage no longer depended on natural resources and endowments. Governments could act to create comparative advantage by implementing policies such as R&D subsidies, expanded pressures to open foreign markets, domestic protection, and so on. Japan and other Asian nations had pursued such policies quite effectively. U.S. businesses could not compete successfully against subsidized foreign competition without policies designed to support these industries and place them on a level playing field.

The intellectual reception for these ideas was not been unanimously positive, with many economists deriding the new concepts as "industrial boosterism."[62] In the views of critics, strategic trade theory suffered from many of the same pitfalls highlighted in the industrial policy debates of the early 1980s. They contended that the dynamics of the American political system would lead to support for politically powerful industries as opposed to strategic sectors. However, their most potent criticisms concerned the difficulties of actually measuring the characteristics of a strategic industry.[63] Without clear guidelines for selecting strategic industries, government intervention was unlikely to succeed.

Strategic trade advocates acknowledged the difficulties in rigorously measuring concepts such as externalities and first mover advantages. However, they ultimately concluded that these practical difficulties did not justify continued commitment to the free trade ideal.[64] They instead advocated a less far-reaching approach, ultimately dubbed "cautious activism" by Tyson and "sophisticated neomercantilism" by Moran.

While academia failed to unanimously embrace strategic trade theory, policy makers gave the ideas a somewhat warmer reception. Indeed, these models provided policymakers with new tools for making judgments regarding the industrial base and the types of industries requiring government support.[65] Most importantly, they offered a rationale permitting government to support market winners, not subsidize the losers among declining industries.[66] Since many strategic industries were important to defense, these new concepts also came to play an important role in DIB debates.

The Diffusion of New Ideas

These ideas came to be accepted through a process described by John Kingdon as "softening up."[67] Due to the presence of preexisting policy monopolies, new policy ideas are rarely accepted immediately. They must first circulate widely and endure, as IP ideas did throughout the 1980s. Eventually, a bandwagon type of effect occurs. Kingdon describes this process well: "Gradually, the idea catches on. People in and out of government speak of a 'growing realization,' an 'increasing feeling,' a 'lot of talk in the air,' and 'coming to a conclusion.' After some degree of diffusion, there seems to be a take-off point."[68]

New ideas become serious policy alternatives as a result of this bandwagon effect. Given the appropriate outside conditions, a window of opportunity develops and new policy ideas become accepted. Windows of opportunity develop when an existing consensus becomes unstable as older understandings and policy prescriptions fail to offer solutions for pressing problems.[69]

This bandwagon effect emerged gradually in the DIB debates of the mid-to-late 1980s. As policymakers grew increasingly frustrated with their inability to stem the tide of eroding competitiveness for many American industries, they gradually became more open to new approaches and new ideas. Since these new ideas offered a potential solution to the problems plaguing the DIB, both Congress and some in the administration seized upon them.

The decisions to support the machine tool and semiconductor industries represent the first manifestations of a broader intellectual change. The old ideas were not scrapped completely, but they were weakened considerably. While not completely broken, the preexisting policy monopoly was seriously weakened. This weakening helped expand public support for intervention in the semiconductor and machine tool cases.

This trickling of support for new ideas became a flood by 1988. At that time, the Pentagon published a report entitled Bolstering Industrial Competitiveness, better known as the "Costello Report" after its principal author, Undersecretary of Defense for Acquisition Robert Costello. The Costello Report was the first official government document that explicitly linked the strength of the DIB to broader economic competitiveness and advocated an activist response to support both military and commercial firms. The report specifically discussed the importance of strategic industries and argued that DoD must develop "a synchronized capability to analyze the structure and performance of critical industries; the impacts on these industries of changes in economic policy...and the development and evaluation of policy instruments aimed at fostering a healthy defense industrial base and contributing to sustainment of a healthy national industrial base."[70] Further reports, from both government and think tanks, seconded the conclusions of the Costello Report.[71]

These efforts culminated in a rush to create critical technology lists, an exercise that grows directly out of the strategic trade theory debate.[72] Within government, DoD, the Department of Commerce, and the White House Office of Science and Technology Policy all created critical technology lists. Outside of government, the Council on Competitiveness, the Air Force Association, the National Center for Manufacturing Sciences, and a number of other groups created similar lists of their own. Congressional advocates even forced a reluctant Bush administration to create a quasi-public Critical Technologies Institute to support these efforts. This intellectual transition has reached its apogee in the Clinton administration's efforts to establish a comprehensive technology policy to support American industry.[73]

Such list making was not designed as a sterile intellectual exercise. Policymakers sought to identify critical industries with the explicit purpose of creating policies to support those industries.[74] The process of list making highlights an issue raised above: the difficulty of developing rigorous measurements for strategic industries.

Because of these problems, government definitions of key industries did not seek to measure externalities or other components of strategic industries. Instead, they sought other means to capture an industrial sector's importance. For example, the

Department of Commerce defined commercial critical (or emerging) technologies as those that offer substantial economic benefits for U.S. industry by the year 2000. Technologies were included if they had the potential to: (1) create new products and industries of substantial size, (2) provide large advances in productivity or in the quality of products produced by existing industries which supply large, important markets, or (3) drive the next generation of R&D and spinoff applications.[75]

Because of these distinctions between theoretical and practical definitions, this study will use the term strategic industry to refer to industries meeting the criteria of externalities, learning by doing, and first mover advantages. In contrast, critical industry will refer to industries meeting the criteria outlined in the 1990 Commerce Department report.

THE ARGUMENT IN BRIEF

What do these changes indicate for American DIB policies and responses to defense dependence? The development of a coherent case for supporting strategic industries is essential to understanding the U.S. government's policies in the 1980s. As we saw earlier, up until the mid-1980s, government policies affecting DIB were based on openness to foreign trade and a presumption against government intervention at home. When policy deviated from these dual goals—as in the case of U.S. textile producers and other industries—intervention was reactive and based on domestic political pressures.

The problem facing policymakers was that they lacked methods to determine which industries were worthy of government support, that is, they lacked the capability to pick winners and losers. Domestic politics drove decisions as policymakers could not effectively analyze the criticality of industries and the necessity for government support. Moreover, protectionism was not viewed as a viable solution to the problems of defense dependence.[76] Thus, for much of the 1980s, DIB policy can best be characterized as "business as usual" and "muddling through." Policymakers, such as Robert Costello and Malcolm Baldridge, expressed concerns about defense dependence, but felt hamstrung in their efforts to address these problems.

Strategic trade theory and its related concepts offered a tool for breaking this impasse. These concepts did two things: (1) they offered a means to select industries that would effectively contribute to broader economic growth, and (2) they offered an intellectual rationale for the use of new policy instruments other than outright protectionism. In effect, these ideas enhanced the flexibility of the state—"the ability of executive officials to provide themselves with the broadest array of options."[77] The new ideas expanded policymakers' flexibility in responding to the relative gains problems resulting from defense dependence. These intellectual changes were an essential precursor to changes in U.S. DIB policy that continue today.

As we will see in subsequent chapters, policymakers applied these new ideas in a fairly sophisticated manner, an indication that significant learning had occurred. Indeed, all of the indicators of learning discussed in Chapter Two appeared in these episodes. First, policymakers became more realistic, recognizing that other states, especially Japan, did not view international trade in the same manner as the United States.

Second, policymakers improved their abilities to integrate various concepts and policies into a unified public program. For the first time, policymakers used domestic policy tools, such as support for R&D consortia, to attack U.S. industrial problems. In the past, only protectionism had been employed to address industrial weakness. In the cases of the machine tool and semiconductor industries, policymakers tackled a national security problem—growing defense dependence—with a variety of both domestic and international economic tools.

Finally, the cases also indicate growing reflective perspective among policy-makers. Instead of simply protecting all defense-related industries, government officials sought tools that would help them determine worthy candidates for intervention. By the late 1980s, strategic trade ideas were widely understood in Washington, but concepts were not used as a means to simply support any industry with military significance. Instead, they were applied to support industries with importance on both commercial and military grounds. Figure 3.1, published in a 1991 Office of Technology Assessment report, presents a widely held perspective on the nature of critical industries and the linkages between military and civilian technolo-gies. The industries designated as "technological roots" were most frequently cited on various critical technology lists.

Based on these criteria, our cases highlight a mix of policy responses.[78] In the cases of machine tools and semiconductors, the critical industry argument was largely uncontested and government intervention was approved.[79]

In the case of the ball and roller bearings industry, the sector's military importance was recognized. However, at the same time, most analysts downplayed the industry's commercial significance. As a result, the bearing industry's pleas for intervention were rejected.

Our last case, the controversial debate over government support for the high-definition television industry, provides further evidence that policy learning may have occurred. In this instance, a vocal and powerful private lobby pressed for government subsidization of what they viewed as a strategic industry. HDTV advocates even used the semiconductor and machine tool cases as examples they sought to emulate. Employing a sophisticated analysis based partly on strategic trade concepts, policymakers successfully countered the claims of HDTV supporters, arguing that HDTV had limited commercial or military significance.[80]

In the next four chapters, we examine each of these industries, with the goal of explaining the government's response (or nonresponse) to defense dependence in each case. In the majority of cases during the 1980s, such as those discussed in Chapters Five and Six, past policy ideas persisted, preventing the creation of active responses to defense dependence. The Reagan and Bush administrations rejected similar calls for intervention by producers of, among other items, precision optics, gears, industrial fasteners, plastic injection molding machinery, and nuts and bolts.

In our exceptional cases, machine tools and semiconductors, the industry's supporters created effective intellectual cases in support of government action. These

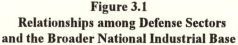

Figure 3.1
Relationships among Defense Sectors
and the Broader National Industrial Base

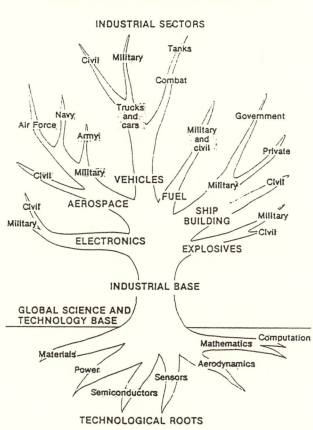

Source: U.S. Congress, Office of Technology Assessment (July 1991), p. 40.

arguments were ultimately adopted by policymakers. These new ideas not only prompted policy innovations to support these two critical industries, but have also become widely accepted among policymakers. This intellectual transition forms the foundation for the Clinton Administration's industrial policy proposals under consideration today.

NOTES

1. This development is well covered in the literature. For example, see Goldstein (1988), Destler (1986) and Douglas Nelson (1989).

2. See Robert A. Pollard, *Economic Security and the Origins of the Cold War, 1945-1950* (New York: Columbia University Press, 1985). For a discussion of early U.S. efforts to build up Japanese industry, see Stuart Auerbach, "The Ironies That Built Japan, Inc.," *Washington Post*, July 18, 1993, pp. H1, H12.

3. This commitment is largely theoretical/ideological, as hard data on the economic costs and benefits of free defense trade is limited. See Feldman (1984), p. 299, fn. 4.

4. See Richard R. Nelson, "Government Stimulus of Technological Progress: Lessons from American History," in Richard R. Nelson, ed., *Government and Technical Progress: A Cross-Industry Analysis* (New York: Pergamon Press, 1982), pp. 451-482.

5. Robert Kuttner, *The End of Laissez-Faire* (New York: Alfred A. Knopf, 1991), p. 196.

6. Industry representatives and members of Congress strongly criticize the Pentagon's heavy regulation of defense firm operations. See Senator John McCain (R-AZ), "The Self-Destruction of America's Defense Industrial Base," *Armed Forces Journal International*, June 1990, pp. 40-46; Center for Strategic and International Studies, *Deterrence in Decay: The Future of the U.S. Defense Industrial Base* (Washington, D.C.:, CSIS, March 1987); Gansler (1989).

7. These points are raised in George and Keohane (1980), pp. 232-233.

8. For an excellent discussion of this issue, see Aaron L. Friedberg, "Why Didn't the United States Become a Garrison State?" *International Security*, vol. 16, no. 4 (Spring 1992), pp. 111-113.

9. Ibid, p. 114.

10. See Louis Hartz, *The Liberal Tradition in America* (New York: Harcourt, 1955); and George C. Lodge and Ezra F. Vogel, eds., *Ideology and National Competitiveness*, (Boston: Harvard Business School Press, 1987).

11. Given extensive U.S. defense spending, it might seem odd to view the American defense program as low cost, but as Friedberg (Spring 1992) notes, this two-pronged DIB policy cost much less than the alternatives (nationalization, garrison state) under consideration at the time. In addition, it also cost significantly less than the DIB policies pursued by the Soviet Union.

12. John A. Alic et al. *Beyond Spinoff: Military and Commercial Technologies in a Changing World* (Cambridge, Mass.: Harvard Business School Press, 1992), p. 60. Ironically, neither of these assumptions is true, as spin-offs from defense research are rare. Successful spin-offs have generally required significant investments from private industry.

13. Sikkink (1991), p. 2.

14. However, the general public's support for free trade was always less extensive and has weakened considerably over the past decade. Indeed, our cases highlight this trend, as government officials have faced considerable societal opposition to open markets for defense goods. For a review of elite and general public opinion, see, William Schneider, "The Old Politics and the New World Order," in Kenneth Oye, Robert Lieber, and Donald Rothchild, *Eagle in a New World: American Grand Strategy in the Post-Cold War Era* (New York: Harper Collins, 1992), pp. 41-44, 55-61.

15. Few sources cover the history of the American DIB. For useful introductions, see Jacques S. Gansler, *The Diminishing Economic and Strategic Viability of the U.S. Defense Industrial Base*, Ph.D. dissertation, American University, (Ann Arbor: University Microfilms, 1978), pp. 45-65, Bruce L. R. Smith, *American Science Policy Since WWII* (Washington, D.C.: Brookings Institution, 1990).

16. See Vogel (1992). See also U.S. General Accounting Office, *Technology Transfer: Japanese Firms Involved in F-15 Coproduction and Civil Aircraft Programs* (Washington, D.C.: GAO, June 1992).

17. This latter program was quite extensive. Examples of these programs include support for European ammunition production, the adoption of a NATO common infantry round and a 1954 order for 450 Hawker Hunters to be built in Great Britain. Trevor Taylor (1982), p. 20.

18. U.S. General Accounting Office (1989), p. 12.

19. These problems first received extensive attention within NATO in a highly critical 1974 report by consultant Thomas Callaghan. Callaghan argued that duplication was crippling the alliance, leading to a 30-40 percent loss of combat effectiveness and waste in the range of $10 to $15 billion per year. Callaghan offered no documentation to support these figures. Indeed, as Trevor Taylor (1982, p. 29) notes, Callaghan probably exaggerated the disadvantages of duplication. Nonetheless, Callaghan's figures were widely accepted by policymakers.

The Callaghan report was originally prepared under contract for the State and Defense Departments. It was widely circulated within the U.S. government and NATO and was later published by the Washington-based Center for Strategic and International Studies. See Thomas A. Callaghan, Jr., *U.S. Economic Cooperation in Military and Civil Technology* (Washington, D.C.: CSIS, 1975).

20. For background on RSI, see Feldman (1984); Taylor (1982); and Ethan B. Kapstein, "International Collaboration in Armaments Production: A Second Best Solution," *Political Science Quarterly*, vol. 106, no. 4 (Winter 1991-92), pp. 657-673.

21. RSI and related initiatives are based on a series of bilateral agreements, known as Memoranda of Understanding (MOU), which authorize the U.S. Secretary of Defense to waive the 1933 Buy American act in order to improve weapons standardization and interoperability. Congress has strongly opposed MOUs because the opening of American markets has not been accompanied by similar openness in European markets. See U.S. Congress, House Committee on Government Operations, *International Procurement and Waivers of the Buy American Act: U.S. Business at a Disadvantage*, 101st Congress, 2d Session, (Washington, D.C.: GPO, November 29, 1990), p. 7.

Recent GAO studies have raised questions whether the 8:1 figure was overstated. In addition, they also argue that the existing imbalance in favor of American exports is overstated. U.S.-European defense trade now approaches a rough balance. See GAO, (April 1991).

Despite (or perhaps because of) these dramatic changes, cooperative programs continue to receive mixed reviews on both sides of the Atlantic. See, for example, Phillip Taylor, "Weapons Standardization in NATO: Collaborative Security or Economic Competition?" *International Organization*, vol. 36, no. 1 (1982), pp. 95-112; James A. Russell, "Collision on the Two-Way Street," *Defense Week*, March 3, 1986, p. 4.

22. Smith (1990), pp. 40-43.

23. Ibid, p. 131.

24. These developments are discussed in Jay Stowsky, "From Spin-Off to Spin-On: Redefining the Military's Role in American Technology Development," in Waybe Sandholtz et al., *The Highest Stakes: The Economic Foundations of the Next Security System* (New York: Oxford University Press, 1992), pp. 114-40.

25. See, for example, Hooks (1990); Stowsky (1992).

26. See Krasner (1984), p. 238. This contrasts with the efforts of "strong" states such as France and Japan, that developed coherent industrial strategies for supporting their domestic defense firms. On France, see Kolodziej (1987). On Japan, see Vogel (1992).

27. Hooks (1990), pp. 382-3.

28. Alic et al.(1992), p. 105.

29. Gansler (1989), p. 220. For example, the Pentagon's Manufacturing Technology (MANTECH) program, which supports innovations in manufacturing processes, constitutes only 0.1 percent of DoD's procurement budget. On MANTECH, see U.S. Congress, Senate Commitee on Armed Services, *Manufacturing Programs Undertaken by the Department of Defense and the Department of Commerce*, 102nd Congress, 1st Session (Washington, D.C.: GPO, 1991); Manufacturing Studies Board, National Research Council, *Industrial Prepared-ness: National Resource and Deterrent to War* (Washington, D.C.: National Academy Press, 1990). MANTECH was created in 1947 by the Air Force; it is now a DoD-wide program. During the 1980s, its annual funding averaged $160 million. (See testimony on p. 18. in same hearing.)

30. This separation reached its zenith in 1970 when Congress, concerned over DoD funding of university research, passed the Mansfield Amendment which stated that DoD funds could be used only to support projects with *direct* relation to military functions or operations.

31. For background on VHSIC, see Alic et al. (1992), pp. 268-272; Glenn R. Fong, "State Strength, Industry Structure and Industrial Policy: American and Japanese Experiences n Microelectronics" *Comparative Politics*, vol. 22, no. 3 (April 1990), pp. 273-99. Fong; and Anna Slomovic, *An Analysis of Military and Commercial Microelectronics: Has DoD's R&D Funding Had the Desired Effect?*, RAND Graduate School Dissertation (Santa Monica, Calif.: RAND Corporation, 1991).

32. Alic et al. (1992), p. 272; Michael Borrus, *Competing for Control: America's Stake in Microelectronics* (Cambridge, Mass: Ballinger, 1988), pp. 250-1.

33. See Destler (1986), pp. 158-63.

34. See Robert Higgs, "Beware the Pork Hawk," *Reason*, vol. 21 (June 1989), pp. 28-34.

35. See Gilder (1988).

36. Borrus (1988), p. 250.

37. See Yoffie (1989), pp. 120-22.

38. Costello Report (DoD, July 1988), p. 15. Emphasis in original.

39. Alic et al.(1992), p. 10.

40. As Kingdon (1984, pp. 141-2) notes, the distinctive American distrust of government solutions varies according to issue area. However, it is particularly strong in issue areas like the DIB, which are related to trade and technology. For discussion of how this bias affected policy debates and rhetoric in the 1980s, see William Schneider, "Talking Free Trade but Acting Protectionist," *National Journal*, May 2, 1987, p. 1082.

41. This period saw an explosion in books touting industrial policy. See, for example, Ira Magaziner and Robert Reich, *Minding America's Business* (New York: Vintage, 1982); Lester C. Thurow, *The Case For Industrial Policies* (Washington, D.C.: Center for National Policy, 1984); Barry Bluestone and Bennett Harrison, *The Deindustrialization of America* (New York: Basic Books, 1982).

42. Charles L. Schultze, "Industrial Policy: A Solution in Search of a Problem," *California Management Review*, vol. 24 (Summer 1983), pp. 5-6.

43. Magaziner and Reich (1982), p. 4.

44. Charles L. Schultze, "Industrial Policy: A Dissent," *Brookings Review*, vol. 12, no. 1 (Fall 1983), p. 4.

45. See Graham (1992), pp. 159-61.

46. For a discussion of theoretical objections to industrial policy, see Paul R. Krugman, "Targeted Industrial Policies: Theory and Evidence," in *Industrial Change and Public Policy* (Kansas City, Mo.: Federal Reserve Bank of Kansas City, August 1983), pp. 123-134; Gene M. Grossman, "Strategic Export Promotion: A Critque," in Paul R. Krugman, ed., *Strategic Trade Policy and the New International Economics* (Cambridge, Mass.: MIT Press, 1986), pp. 48-68; Geoffrey Carliner, "Industrial Policies for Emerging Industries," in Krugman (1986),

pp. 164-166.

47. Critics also contended that support for high value-added (i.e., capital-intensive) activities, without a similar increase in aggregate investment, might actually generate unemployment, as these activities tend to employ fewer workers. For a discussion, see Krugman (August 1983).

48. Quoted in Graham (1992), p. 142.

49. Ibid.

50. Schulze (1983), p. 12.

51. However, similar ideas reemerged under new terms such as competitiveness, industrial base, and technology policy.

52. Graham (1992), pp. 216-19; David C. Mowery and Nathan Rosenberg, "New Developments in U.S. Technology Policy: Implications for Competitiveness and International Trade Policy," *California Management Review*, vol. 32, no. 1 (Fall 1989), pp. 107-24.

53. For background, see Destler (1986), pp. 177-96; Robert Z. Lawrence and Charles L. Schultze, eds., *An American Trade Strategy: Options for the 1990s* (Washington, D.C.: Brookings Institution, 1990), esp. pp. 2-10.

54. For a discussion of these industries, see Hart (1993), pp. 237-64.

55. For background on these efforts, see Wendy H. Schacht, *Technological Advancement and U.S. Industrial Competitiveness*, CRS Report No. 88-689 SPR (Washington, D.C.: U.S. Library of Congress, 1988).

56. Yoffie (1989), p. 131.

57. For introductions to strategic trade theory, see Paul R. Krugman, "Introduction: New Thinking About Trade Policy," in Krugman (1986b, pp. 5-10; Richardson (Winter 1990); Klaus Stegemann, "Policy Rivalry Among Industrial States: What Can We Learn from Models of Strategic Trade Policy?" *International Organization* vol. 43, no. 1 (Winter 1989), pp. 73-100.

The complexity of these ideas has led many of the theory's proponents to question whether policymakers are capable of effectively implementing such a policy. See, for example, Paul Krugman, "Is Free Trade Passe?," *Economic Perspectives*, vol. 1, no. 2 (Fall 1987), p. 142.

58. See Beltz (1991, pp.9-10) for a good review of various definitions. It is important to note that strategic industries and high-technology industries are not necessarily synonymous. Similarly, the strategic trade theorists did not equate "strategic" with an industry's importance to national defense.

59. Krugman (1986b), pp. 15-17. He notes (at p. 17) that external economies cannot be directly measured: "the only way to make such assessments is to combine detailed knowledge of the industries with heavy reliance on guesswork."

There is a technical distinction between spillovers and externalities. *Spillovers* refer to specific appropriable downstream or upstream effects. For example, efficient semiconductor manufacturing has a spillover effect on computer manufacturing by making computer components cheaper and more effective. *Externalities* are "spillovers and linkages that cannot be appropriated, priced and marketed." See Richardson (1990), pp. 119-20. These distinctions are theoretically important, but had limited effect on policy debates, as analysts frequently conflated the two concepts.

60. Michael Borrus, Laura D'Andrea Tyson, and John Zysman, "Creating Advantage: How Government Policies Shape International Trade in the Semiconductor Industry," in Krugman (1986b), p. 93.

61. See Giovanni Dosi, Laura D'Andrea Tyson, and John Zysman, "Trade, Technologies and Development: A Framework for Discussing Japan," in Chalmers Johnson, Laura D'Andrea Tyson, and John Zysman, eds., *Politics and Productivity: The Real Story of Why Japan Works* (New York: Harper Business, 1989), pp. 9-10.

62. The opposition's case against strategic trade concepts differed little from the anti-IP case. Opponents argued that market forces would work best, and, even more importantly, that the U.S. government was incapable of providing the type of guidance required by industry. See, for example, Pietro S. Nivola, "More Like Them? The Political Feasibility of Strategic Trade Policy," *Brookings Review*, (Spring 1991), pp. 14-21.

63. See, for example, Anne O. Krueger, "Free Trade is the Best Policy," in Lawrence and Schultze (1990), pp. 82-86; Krugman (1987); Richardson.

64. For a useful discussion of these points, see Tyson (1992), pp. 10-14; Moran (1993), pp. 30-40.

65. Rigorous measurement of externalities and other factors contributing to strategic industries has been extremely difficult. These problems led many strategic trade theorists to question whether these concepts could be effectively translated into practical policies. See, for example, Krugman (Fall 1987).

66. Paul Peterson has similarly noted how changes in professional economists' views on deficits helped provide President Reagan with the intellectual ammunition required to introduce major tax cuts in 1981. See Paul Peterson, "The New Politics of Deficits," in John E. Chubb and Paul E. Peterson, eds., *The New Direction in American Politics* (Washington, D.C.: Brookings Institution, 1985), pp. 389-96.

67. Kingdon (1984), pp. 134-137.

68. Ibid., p. 147.

69. See the discussion in Judith Goldstein and Robert O. Keohane, "Ideas and Foreign Policy: An Analytical Framework," in Judith Goldstein and Robert O. Keohane, eds., *Ideas and Foreign Policy: Beliefs, Institutions, and Political Change* (Ithaca, N.Y.: Cornell University Press, 1993), pp. 25-26.

70. Costello Report (DoD, July 1988), p. 11. Emphasis in original.

71. For a listing and discussion of various reports, see James A. Blackwell, Jr., "The Defense Industrial Base," *Washington Quarterly*, vol. 15, no. 4 (Autumn 1992), pp. 189-206.

72. For a review and analysis of the various lists, see Mary Ellen Mogee, *Technology Policy and Critical Technologies: A Summary of Recent Reports*. Discussion Paper No. 3 of the Manufacturing Forum (Washington, D.C.: National Academy Press, December 1991). See also, U.S. General Accounting Office, *High Technology Competitiveness: Trends in U.S. and Foreign Performance* (Washington, D.C.: GAO, September 1992).

73. For discussions, see James Fallows, "Farewell to Laissez Faire," *Washington Post*, February 28, 1993, pp. C1, C3; Sylvia Nasar, "The Risky Allure of 'Strategic Trade,'" *New York Times*, February 28, 1993, p. D1.

74. Many of the cases studied here predate the more recent clamoring for critical technology lists of various sorts. Yet lists were not necessary to justify support for the semiconductor and machine tool industries as few observers questioned their critical nature. Both industries have appeared on every government or private sector list. Mogee (December 1991), pp. 16-19.

75. See U.S. Department of Commerce, Technology Administration, *Emerging Technologies: A Survey of Technical and Engineering Opportunities* (Washington, D.C.: GPO, Spring 1990).

In contrast, DoD defined militarily "critical" technologies as those that meet several criteria: (1) they enhance performance of conventional weapons systems or provide new military capabilities; (2) they improve weapon systems availability, dependability, or affordability; (3) they are pervasive in weapons systems; and (4) they help strengthen the industrial base. See U.S. Department of Defense, *Report to Congress on the Defense Industrial Base: Critical Industries Planning* (Washington, D.C.: DoD, October 1990), p. 19 This set of criteria has been widely criticized as too broad to offer useful policy guidance. See, for example, Lewis M.

Branscomb,ed., *Empowering Technology* (Cambridge, Mass: MIT Press, 1993), pp. 50-54.

76. See Costello Report (DoD, July 1988), p. 27.

77. Ikenberry (1988), p. 206.

78. This study assumes that congressional pressures supporting intervention will exist in every case. Krauss and Reich make a similar assumption in their analysis of U.S. trade and technology policies. See Ellis S. Krauss and Simon Reich, "U.S. Policy and International Competition," *International Organization*, vol. 46, no. 4 (Autumn 1992), p. 869.

79. *Intervention* refers to the creation of national sector specific policies to address the actual or potential presence of defense dependence. A *national response* refers to government action that requires coordination and approval by several agencies as well as White House-level authorization.

80. However, as we will see in Chapter Seven, DARPA did fund R&D for advanced displays, a central component in HDTV.

4

Relief for the Machine Tool Industry?

American DIB policy, as we have seen, has relied almost exclusively on market forces as the best means to provide U.S. troops with effective weapons. This hands-off policy persists, even though many economic indicators highlight growing foreign dependence and erosion of the industrial base. Policy ideas dating back to the early 1950s continued to influence policymakers throughout the 1980s, preventing them from contemplating more active support for the DIB. The lingering power of these policy ideas makes the decision to actively support the U.S. machine tool industry especially remarkable.

The machine tool sector was the one of the first industries whose decline was widely cited for its dangerous impact on U.S. national security. Indeed, the 1980 Ichord Panel report paid special attention to the machine tool industry's plight, noting that "import penetration into certain industrial sectors, such as machine tools. . . suggests an unacceptable dependency on foreign sources for key elements of defense production."[1]

As the U.S. machine tool sector continued to deteriorate, demands for action grew. During the early and mid-1980s, reversing the industry's slide became a cause celebre for many advocates of a government industrial policy.

In the end, the machine tool industry's supporters succeeded in convincing the Reagan administration to negotiate trade protection for U.S. firms and to create a package of domestic initiatives to revitalize the industry. Yet success was slow in coming as the Reagan administration delayed action for more than three years. This success is largely attributable to the industry's ability to educate key policymakers about the importance of machine tools, and policymakers' own search for new solutions to the unfamiliar problem of defense dependence.

BACKGROUND: THE AMERICAN MACHINE TOOL INDUSTRY

The machine tool industry is quite small and accounts for only 0.10 percent of

U.S. gross national product and 0.06 percent of total U.S. employment.[2] U.S. firms are also quite small. The largest firm, Cincinnati Milacron, ranked 357th on the Fortune 500 list in 1987. Indeed, if the whole U.S. machine tool industry were merged into one firm, the new entity would rank only 139th in size on the Fortune 500.[3]

Until the 1960s, machine tools was a craft industry with limited economies of scale. These characteristics changed in the 1970s with the advent of numerical control (NC) and computer numerical control (CNC) machine tools which depend on sophisticated computer technology. These new technologies required larger capital investments to automate factories and also created learning curve effects similar to those found in other high technology industries.[4] This transformation triggered some mergers and consolidation, but U.S. machine tool firms still remained relatively small in comparison to their foreign counterparts.

Despite its small size, the machine tool industry plays an important role in supporting overall U.S. manufacturing. Machine tools, which cut and shape metal, are essential components for advanced manufacturing. In a nutshell, they are the machines that make machines. As a British study noted,

> Machine tools is a nodal industry. It is the transmission point of new technology to the rest of manufacturing industry. An innovative and competitive machine tool industry contributes significantly to the rapid diffusion of new technology and to the realization of the competitive benefits that this makes possible for the rest of manufacturing industry.[5]

Without a strong machine tool industry, overall manufacturing competitiveness and productivity suffer.

Machine tools are equally important to U.S. national security, as DoD and private U.S. defense firms purchase approximately 20 percent of the industry's output.[6] Machine tools have received priority treatment by defense mobilization planners as far back as World War I. In 1948, Congress passed the National Industrial Reserve Act declaring, in a national policy that persists today, that "the defense of the U.S. [requires] a national reserve of machine tools. . . for the production of critical items of defense material."[7]

Although planners recognized the importance of machine tools, past mobilizations, especially those of World War II and Korea, were hampered by inadequate tool supplies. In response, military leaders created a series of programs to ensure adequate supplies in future conflicts. Among the machine tool-specific defense programs were the General Reserve of stockpiled machine tools and the Machine Tool Trigger Order Program.[8] The Trigger Order Program, created during the Korean War, authorizes the government to enter into standby contracts with manufacturers to be implemented in emergencies. Although the program languished for decades, it was reinstated in the 1980s—further recognition of the defense importance of machine tools. DoD's MANTECH and Industrial Modernization Incentives Program (IMIP) also provided support for machine tool firms.

Decline of the Industry

Despite paying lip service to the importance of the machine tool industry, policymakers did little to enhance the competitiveness of machine tool manufacturers during the postwar period. The Trigger Order and General Reserve Programs existed in statute but were moribund for all practical purposes. Neither program could evolve to keep pace with rapid changes in machine tool technology. For example, DoD estimated in the 1980s that approximately 80 percent of tools in the General Reserve were obsolete.[9]

Like many other U.S. industries, machine tool manufacturers saw their competitive edge erode in the 1970s. The industry's decline was based on a number of factors, including mismanagement, reduced demand for metal products, an overvalued dollar, and targeting by foreign competition.[10] Indeed, one could argue that the industry's decline was an overdetermined outcome. However, many observers agreed on one point: government policies were often more harmful than supportive of the industry's interests.

While American industry declined, its competitors, especially those in Japan and Germany, prospered.[11] In the late 1960s and early 1970s, Japanese firms, working with support from MITI, capitalized on low labor costs and an overvalued dollar to enter U.S. markets with low cost tools. By the 1980s, the Japanese also began dominating the high end of the machine tool market. For example, by 1987, Japan's Fanuc produced over 70 percent of the world's machine tool controllers—a sector created and traditionally dominated by U.S. firms.[12]

World market shares shifted dramatically as the Japanese machine tool industry prospered. Until 1969, the United States was the world's leading machine tool producer; by 1986, U.S. output was less than 40% of Japanese totals. Until 1977, the United States was a net exporter of machine tools. The United States has been a net importer ever since, with domestic producers accounting for only half of U.S. consumption.[13] Table 4.1 indicates the broad trends affecting U.S. firms.

These commercial impacts also affected defense markets. For example, according to the National Machine Tool Builders Association (NMTBA), DoD procurement of foreign machine tools doubled between 1982 and 1985, with navy procurements quadrupling over this period.[14]

Government subsidies and industrial policy were widely cited as the central factor in the rapid rise of Japan's machine tool industry.[15] In the 1960s and 1970s, MITI initiated a comprehensive effort to strengthen domestic machine tool manufacturers. It encouraged firms to merge into larger units and also supported industry efforts to develop standard modular products that could be manufactured more cost-efficiently. The most important support came from a broad 10-15 percent R&D subsidy through tax credits, loans, and the proceeds arising from a government monopoly on bicycle, motorbike, and powerboat racing.[16]

In the eyes of the U.S. industry and its supporters, MITI's support program provided Japanese firms with an unfair trading advantage that allowed them to capture market share from American firms. Yet, despite clear evidence of the Japanese challenge, the American business response was anemic. As one expert put it, by the

Table 4.1
Machine Tool Orders, Shipments, and Foreign Trade, 1970-1985
(Millions of U.S. Dollars, except as noted)

	1970	1975	1978	1979	1980	1981	1982	1983	1984	1985
New Orders	912	1277	4346	5621	4755	2945	1457	1697	2916	2528
Shipments	1433	2452	3014	3877	4692	5096	3605	1846	2285	2545
Shipments (1967 prices)	1265	1429	1384	1607	1710	1691	1123	565	684	744
Backlog (end period)	761	1281	2399	5165	5135	3300	1194	1045	1674	1657
Exports	396	922	1188	1391	1756	2158	1611	1121	1175	1249
Imports	164	361	947	1123	1425	1613	1468	1480	2025	2759
Net Exports	232	561	241	268	331	545	143	-359	-850	-1510
Imports-as % of domestic consumption*	13.7	19.1	34.2	31.1	32.7	35.4	42.4	67.1	64.5	68.3

*Domestic Consumption is defined as shipments minus net exports.

Source: U.S. Department of Commerce, *Statistical Abstract of the U.S.*, various years. Compiled in Hooley, p. 3.

mid-1980s the industry was in "almost total disarray."[17]

THE SEARCH FOR SOLUTIONS

The industry's rapid decline, and the absence of an effective private sector response, led to calls for government intervention. These efforts dated back to the late 1970s when individual Congressmen and Senators pleaded to expand public support for the machine tool sector. Similarly, the industry considered filing an antidumping suit in the 1970s, but ultimately refrained from acting.[18]

As the industry's decline continued, concern about defense dependence grew. Congressional concern was often couched in clear relative gains terms combined with a call for a comprehensive government response. For example, on March 22, 1982, Sen. John Danforth (R-MO), Chairman of a key Senate Finance Subcommittee, wrote to Defense Secretary Weinberger that, "in view of this industry's key role as manufacturer of the basic tools that are used in America's defense industries, our growing dependence on imports must also be considered in a broader context than that of U.S. trade policy."[19] Later that year, Sen. Howard Metzenbaum (D-OH) noted in a letter to President Reagan that government inaction was "particularly unconscionable when we consider how Japan has unfairly nurtured its own machine tool industry at America's expense."[20]

These pressures arose during a period of intense congressional debate over various industrial policy proposals (see Chapter Three). This was a time when the government was divided over a petition for trade relief from Houdaille Industries, a major U.S. machine tool manufacturer.[21]

In a petition filed in early 1982, Houdaille charged that Japanese firms, working with MITI, had created an illegal export cartel to control U.S. markets. Employing a little-known section of the tax code, Houdaille asked the president to deny the investment tax credit to American purchasers of certain machine tools produced in Japan. The Houdaille petition provoked debate at the highest levels of government.[22] All of the foreign policy departments, including State and DoD, opposed the petition. They were joined by the Treasury Department and the Office of Management and Budget (OMB). These officials argued that action would damage U.S-Japan ties and adversely affect American machine tool users by raising the cost of imported tools. Only the Commerce Department and the U.S. Trade Representative's Office (USTR), along with some support from the departments of Labor and Agriculture, favored a firm approach. But even the petition's supporters felt uncomfortable. As Prestowitz has noted, "[Commerce and USTR] believed that Japanese actions, coupled with lack of action on the American side, created a particularly disadvantageous environment for U.S. industry, and wanted to alter it. The difficulty was that American law provided no way for them to do so, except by finding Japan to be acting unfairly."[23]

Because the Cabinet could not agree on an appropriate response, the status of Houdaille's petition was not resolved until President Reagan and Japanese Prime Minister Nakasone exchanged handwritten notes on the subject.[24] Ultimately, in September 1983,[25] the free trade position won out and President Reagan rejected the

Houdaille petition.

Filing for Trade Protection

As the Houdaille case was winding down, the National Machine Tool Builders Association[26] initiated another effort to spur action by filing a petition with the Commerce Department under Section 232 of the Trade Expansion Act of 1962.[27] Section 232, also known as the national security clause, authorizes the president to take action to adjust imports to protect national security.[28] These remedies can take several forms, ranging from tariffs and quotas to economic sanctions to domestic responses such as subsidies and tax credits. Section 232 was rarely employed; since its inception, the clause had only been used to restrict oil imports.

In opting to file for protection under Section 232, the NMTBA assumed a calculated risk. Trade remedies based on Section 232 were rare. Yet, NMTBA representatives felt that an emphasis on machine tools' defense criticality offered the best chances for success. As one industry representative argued, "We felt that if 232 didn't apply to machine tools, it didn't apply to anybody."[29]

Although Section 232 remedies do not require a finding of unfair foreign practices, NMTBA still charged the Japanese with industrial targeting. Its petition restated many of the arguments raised in the Houdaille case and emphasized MITI's "unfair" subsidies to Japanese firms. In response to this challenge, NMTBA sought outright protection and asked that imports be limited to 17.5 percent of domestic consumption.[30] These quotas would remain in place for five years.

The NMTBA petition was not welcomed inside government circles. Even Commerce Department officials, who were sympathetic to the industry's plight, tried to dissuade NMTBA from filing.[31] Still, as directed by law, Commerce began its investigation of the industry's claims. The Commerce Department study pushed the question of the NMTBA petition into the technical realm. For the remainder of 1983, concerns about the U.S. machine tool sector centered on the Houdaille petition. Yet, as the one-year statutory deadline for completing the investigation approached in March 1984, a heated public debate about the machine tool industry was restarted.

THE POLICY DEBATE: WERE MACHINE TOOLS CRITICAL?

The first salvo in this effort came with the November 1983 publication of the National Research Council's report, The Machine Tool Industry and the Defense Industrial Base.[32] The report's basic theme was that the U.S. government had to do more to support U.S. firms, but it also cautioned that instruments other than trade policy were needed to truly strengthen the machine tool industrial base. The committee concluded that "the government will have to look into means to overcome the comparative advantages of foreign producers where attributable to hidden subsidies. . . . the U.S. government cannot wash its hands of the industry's concerns."[33] Among the report's many policy proposals was the innovative suggestion that government and industry cooperate to establish joint industry-wide research centers.

The U.S. government had never assumed an active role in supporting joint industry research programs.

In addition, the National Research Council's report also noted that previously suggested remedies did not offer effective solutions to growing defense dependence. Stockpiling, promoted through the Pentagon's General Reserve program, was found to be especially ineffective. According to the Council, stockpiling "does little more than perpetuate obsolescent methods."[34]

Meanwhile, the Commerce Department investigation was formally completed in February 1984. Based on this analysis, Secretary Baldridge recommended to the White House that the industry be granted import relief for a period of five years.

The White House did not react enthusiastically to Baldridge's pleas. He was originally opposed by the president and every economic agency in the government, who consistently opposed all protectionism on theoretical grounds.[35] Although lower-level Pentagon officials supported the industry, top DoD policymakers also opposed Commerce's position.[36]

The National Security Council opposed the petition on technical grounds, raising serious questions about the criteria used in Commerce's investigation. The NSC's concerns focused on the criteria for determining industry's ability to begin surge production during a protracted conflict.[37] These technical criticisms offered the president a tool for depoliticizing the conflict. In April 1984, he delayed a decision until the NSC had developed new guidelines for analyzing mobilization capabilities and demands.[38] In effect, he decided to do nothing.

The Intellectual Case for Activism

This delay placed the industry in a frustrating position. Commerce had recognized the need for action, as had many outside groups such as the National Research Council. Yet, the White House's decision placed NMTBA in a form of legal limbo. The White House had no deadline for action on 232 petitions,[39] raising the possibility that the decision process could go on indefinitely. Meanwhile, foreign penetration of the industry would continue.

Faced with this situation, the industry intensified its efforts to sell its case to policymakers. But, unfortunately, the machine tool industry was not a powerful force in Washington political circles. As noted above, the industry was quite small and did not employ large numbers of workers. The industry's small size was reflected in its trade association, the NMTBA. Moreover, the industry was concentrated in a few eastern and central states. This concentration severely restricted the industry's ability to gain wide support in Congress.

Even worse, the industry was not completely united behind the NMTBA petition. Several U.S. tool builders opposed the petition and resigned from NMTBA in protest. Similarly, NMTBA was opposed by other domestic associations such as the Machine Tool Importers Association of America.[40]

Faced with these constraints, the industry relied less on brute political pressure and more on arguments stressing the broader economic importance of machine tools. The NMTBA and its supporters soon began an intensive public relations campaign that faced two challenges. They had to first convince the Reagan administration that the machine tools sector was truly critical to national security and economic strength. Next, they had to convince them that government support would have a positive impact on the industry.

The easiest part of the industry's case concerned the economic importance of the machine tool sector. As noted earlier, the defense importance of machine tools was rarely questioned, a conclusion confirmed by the creation of the Trigger Order and Machine Tool Reserve Programs. Indeed, the NMTBA's decision to file for trade relief under Section 232 was driven in part by its recognition that few doubted the defense importance of machine tools. As one industry supporter noted, "Critics. . . will say that the industry is partly to blame for its precarious position. . . . Even if industry were 100% responsible for its present plight, any official believing machine tools essential to national defense would have no choice but to take whatever steps are necessary to preserve the industry that produces them."[41]

NMTBA also worked to convince officials of the importance of the machine tool sector for commercial manufacturing. This task proved somewhat more complicated, but, even here, few questioned the critical nature of this sector. The National Research Council's 1983 report directly addresses this point: "the most relevant reason for action is simply one of our own national defense. But such an effort will also help improve our whole national productivity and cannot be neglected either. The Committee believes that that argument will come to be of far greater importance to this country than any defense argument."[42]

Thus, despite its institutional weaknesses, NMTBA enjoyed one inherent advantage: Few questioned the importance of the industry. However, advocates faced significant opposition to their calls for intervention to preserve the machine tool industrial base. Opponents raised two points: (1) the industry was simply too weak and uncompetitive to ever restore itself, and (2) government action would not reverse this situation.[43]

Faced with these arguments, the industry presented a nuanced argument in support of government intervention. First, NMTBA painted a grim picture of the industry's plight. The association's original petition presented this case effectively. In 1985 and 1986, the industry's position grew even worse.[44]

Second, NMTBA continued to emphasize the contribution of unfair foreign competition to the industry's weakened state. Faced with a concerted onslaught from Japanese companies, U.S. firms simply could not survive. As James A. Gray, NMTBA's president put it, "Our members haven't been competing against companies, they have been competing against an entire nation."[45]

Finally, NMTBA had to prove that U.S. machine tool firms had the potential to become globally competitive in the future. Proving this point proved to be the most difficult, and most important component, of the NMTBA's case. For example, Krauss and Reich argue that President Reagan approved the Machine Tool Action Plan only after being convinced that the industry could again become competitive in the near future.[46]

In 1985 and 1986, the industry undertook a widely publicized series of self-help initiatives.[47] These efforts included expanded investment in plant and equipment, cooperative efforts to improve export performance, and the establishment of closer ties between customers and manufacturers.

These efforts were important, but the creation of the National Center for Manufacturing Sciences (NCMS) proved to be the most critical self-help initiative. NCMS was originally designed as a private R&D consortium of key U.S. machine tool manufacturers. A consortium is a collaborative R&D arrangement designed to leverage both financial resources and scientific and engineering expertise. These types of arrangements are quite common overseas; Japan's keiretsu system is a case in point.[48] However, R&D consortia are a relatively new phenomena in the U.S. Consortia were first legalized in 1984 with passage of the National Cooperative Research Act. Since that time, more than 250 consortia, involving over 1,000 U.S. businesses, have been formed.[49]

A machine tool consortium was not a new idea. The concept was originally proposed by the National Research Council in its 1983 report. Its authors based their proposal on several existing private consortia such as the Semiconductor Research Corporation (SRC) and Microelectronics and Computer Technology Corporation (MCC).[50] Others in the industry had also pressed for greater R&D cooperation.[51]

NCMS developed out of a series of 1985 and 1986 meetings sponsored by DoD and the National Research Council's Manufacturing Studies Board. NCMS originally operated on a $1 million start-up grant from NMTBA.[52] However, within months, fifteen members joined, and membership rose to seventy within one year.[53] Today, NCMS has 160 members and an annual budget of approximately $150 million.

NCMS was designed with broad purposes in mind. Its ultimate objective was to use joint R&D to revitalize the entire U.S. machine tool sector. Thus, it addressed the problem of defense dependence as well as the broader set of problems affecting American manufacturers. Unlike many other consortia, NCMS does not operate its own facilities or perform its own R&D; it funds joints research at universities, businesses, and laboratories, with a focus on projects with direct commercial benefits.

NCMS was touted by its supporters as the key tool in American efforts to create manufacturing excellence for both the defense and civilian sectors of the industrial base. It was designed specifically to reverse the limited government support given to industry in the past. As an NCMS board member argued, "For 40 years, the U.S. has put from $50 billion to $300 billion into defense of the world, while pretty much forgetting about any support of industry. Meanwhile, the vanquished—primarily Germany and Japan—have quietly been putting all their money into their industrial base."[54]

The Road to Success

The NMTBA's campaign proved quite effective, especially in swaying Congress, as a number of key leaders came around to support the industry's point of view. This support was quite broad, and included representatives without parochial interest in the issue. For example, Senator Robert Dole (R-KS), chairman of the Senate Finance Committee, became one of the industry's key supporters. Dole recognized the uniqueness of his position, noting that he supported the NMTBA petition despite "a huge agricultural constituency which is deeply opposed to protectionism."[55]

President Reagan learned directly of Congress's concerns in the fall of 1985. At that time, Reagan initiated a series of one-on-one and group meetings to garner bipartisan support for his tax reform plan. Many legislators also used this opportunity to press Reagan to take action on the NMTBA petition, still languishing after more than a year. The breadth of support convinced Reagan to hold a Cabinet-level meeting on the topic.[56]

Presidential interest spurred the lower levels of the bureaucracy into action. A revised Commerce Department report, incorporating new mobilization criteria, was forwarded to the White House in January 1986. This version differed slightly from the report filed almost two years earlier, but still recommended trade relief for seven classes of machine tools.[57]

This revised report did little to end interagency disputes over the NMTBA petition; a February 1986 Cabinet-level briefing (without the president) did little to reconcile the views of DoD, Commerce, and their more free trade-oriented brethren in the various economic agencies. The NSC remained opposed to the petition, arguing that current machine tool capacity was capable of supplying DoD in any relevant wartime scenario.[58]

In March 1986, the Cabinet met with the president to determine the available range of options.[59] According to reports, the meeting was very heated.[60] However, it appeared that the momentum was shifting in favor of the petition. Baldridge had succeeded in convincing Treasury Secretary James Baker to support the petition. Moreover, National Security Advisor Robert McFarlane, the petition's strongest opponent, was no longer in office. His successor, John Poindexter, was less strident in his opposition to the petition. The Pentagon remained divided,[61] but Defense Secretary Weinberger also joined in supporting action. Ultimately, a final decision was delayed again, as the president directed Richard Levine of the NSC staff and Assistant Secretary of Commerce Paul Freedenberg to prepare a final option memo for the president.

This memo, reviewed by President Reagan on May 20, 1986 (three years and two months after the original NMTBA filing), contained four options:[62] (1) place quantitative controls, as requested by NMTBA, on imports of selected machine tool types, (2) refuse to take action and permit market forces to operate, (3) initiate discussions with Japan and other major foreign suppliers to conclude a series of Voluntary Restraint Agreements (VRAs) on their exports, and (4) create a domestic policy package that would strengthen the competitiveness of machine tool firms.

The president ultimately did not decide on the correctness of the NMTBA petition, arguing that he would "defer a formal decision in the Section 232 case."[63] Yet, in explaining why he supported VRAs, Reagan cited the claims made in the petition, acknowledging that "the machine tool industry is a small yet vital component of the U.S. defense base," and "that high levels of imports can potentially erode U.S. capabilities to manufacture critical machine tool product lines."[64]

Reagan agreed to a combination of options 3 and 4 from the May 20 decision memorandum, supporting trade protection and a Domestic Action Plan. The president's plan had several parts.[65] First, he directed the Commerce Department to negotiate VRAs with Taiwan, West Germany, Japan, and Switzerland.[66] Second, DoD would improve communications with U.S. firms to provide them with earlier notification of future manufacturing requirements. Commerce would also offer assistance and data to U.S. firms. Third, funding for MANTECH and IMIP would be increased. Finally, the president authorized a $5 million annual appropriation (over three years) for NCMS. Later in 1986, Congress also passed "Buy American" legislation, which restricted DoD procurements of foreign-made machine tools.[67]

Based on this directive, the Commerce Department, led by Paul Freedenberg, entered into negotiations with the four targeted countries.[68] West Germany and Switzerland refused to enter into VRAs. However, on December 16, 1986, Reagan announced that Japan and Taiwan had agreed to limit their machine tool exports for five years beginning in January 1987.

The VRAs expired in December 1991, but were extended temporarily for an additional two years by President Bush.[69] The impact of the VRAs is the subject of some dispute.[70] However, the industry's ability to reinvest and revitalize itself during the "breathing period" provided by the VRAs reportedly played a major role in the Bush administration's decision to extend the import curbs.[71]

A POLICY SHIFT

Because of their dramatic nature, the machine tool VRAs received the bulk of attention in both the press and the analytic community.[72] This has shifted attention from the more far reaching changes embodied in the president's Domestic Action Plan. Particularly important was the decision to provide public funds for the NCMS consortium. Although limited funds were expended, this decision represents the first time that the federal government had provided direct support for an industry-led consortium.

In this case, the machine tool industry was deemed to have critical military and commercial significance. In response, policymakers agreed to create a targeted industrial policy to support American machine tool makers. While these efforts certainly did not rival those of Japan, they represented a significant shift in American DIB policies.

These new policies did not simply arise out of thin air. They gradually developed as a result of policymakers' efforts to try to respond to a changed world environment. As they searched for new means to bolster the DIB and deal with defense dependence, policymakers sought both new types of solutions and new means to identify critical industries.

The road to success was a long one. In addition to the public pressures exerted to support the machine tool sector, success also required an intellectual change among policymakers. This proceeded typically through a multistep process. First, government officials had to recognize that a problem existed. While this sounds simple, it took many years for this to occur. For example, in 1978, the Carter administration, led by DoD, opposed NMTBA initiatives that would have blocked the use of public funds to purchase foreign products "at less than fair value prices."[73]

Moreover, industry leaders also failed to rapidly recognize the extent of their weaknesses. The NMTBA itself opposed a predecessor to NCMS proposed in 1984.[74]

Second, policymakers gradually realized that old approaches would no longer succeed. As a result, they began searching for new approaches. Strategic trade concepts were not fully developed, but the basic ideas existed and were known to policymakers. The administration and Congress were certainly familiar with the Japanese and European industrial policy models actively debated in Washington during 1982 and 1983.

But these concepts could not simply be grafted onto the American political system. Because of the decentralized nature of the U.S. political system and a historical commitment to free market policies among the American elite, advocates have faced difficulties in creating a centralized, government-directed industrial policy similar to those in Japan, Sweden, and other states.[75] Indeed, as we saw in Chapter Three, these obstacles have been nearly insurmountable, forcing the U.S. government to employ restrictive trade and investment policies as proxies for the industrial policy tools employed in other nations.[76]

To some extent, the VRA decision represents a continuation of this use of trade policy as a proxy for industrial policy. However, the machine tool case also represents the first indication of change in the United States' defense industrial base policies. For the first time, an industry rescue package was developed on the basis of an industry's intrinsic national security performance instead of its political clout. As one industry representative put it, "Policy makers perceived—even among the free traders—that without a viable machine tool industry, manufacturing in the U.S. simply cannot succeed. Machine tools are a basic building block industry."[77]

Moreover, the government supported a new mechanism—the NCMS consortium—as a means to strengthen the DIB. Although NCMS started as a small program, it represented an important step beyond previous practices of supporting the DIB through procurement contracts alone.[78] Both industry and government recognized that protection alone could not succeed unless it was combined with efforts to revitalize the American machine tool industry at home. They also recognized that joint R&D, as promoted in the consortium model, was necessary to permit American firms to compete with their European and Japanese counterparts. In fact, consortia were designed to specifically emulate the close industry cooperation that was so common overseas.[79]

CONCLUSION

Compared to later responses, especially that of Sematech, the machine tool case represents a "mini" industrial policy. Limited dollars were spent, but the case for targeting critical industries had finally succeeded. Moreover, this decision occurred because of top officials' concerns over relative gains. In creating the government's comprehensive response, the White House specifically referred to the dangers of dependence. Fearing that continued open trade with foreign machine tool producers might provide other states with political leverage and insurmountable economic advantages, the White House overcame its traditional concerns about industrial policy and intervened to support U.S. machine tool firms.

An activist response would have been next to impossible even several years prior to the 1986 VRA decision. However, as policymakers became increasingly concerned about America's relative position vis-a-vis such key allies as Japan, they also sought out new means to provide support for defense critical industries. Concerns over relative gains overcame concerns regarding government intervention in the market. The result was a crack in a previously united front against an activist DIB policy. This crack would be further widened in 1987 when a similar crisis struck the U.S. semiconductor industry.

NOTES

1. Emphasis added. Ichord Panel Report (U.S. House Committee on Armed Services, 1980), p. 16.

2. Figures are for 1986. See William J. Corcoran, "The Machine Tool Industry Under Fire," in Donald L. Losman and Shu-Jan Liang, *The Promise of American Industry* (New York: Quorum Books, 1990), p. 232. For background of the machine tool industry, see also Anderson Ashburn, "The Machine Tool Industry: The Crumbling Foundation," in Donald A. Hicks, ed., *Is New Technology Enough?* (Washington, D.C.: American Enterprise Institute, 1989), pp. 19-84; Michael L. Dertouzos, et al. *Made in America* (Cambridge, Mass.: MIT Press, 1989), pp. 222-47; and Alexander (September 1990).

3. Corcoran (1990), p. 232.

4. Milner and Yoffie (Spring 1989), p. 266.

5. E. Scriberras and B. Payne, *The UK Machine Tool Industry* (London: Technical Change Centre, 1987), p. 64.

6. Corcoran (1990), p. 227.

7. Cited in U.S. Department of Commerce, *Petition Under the National Security Clause, Section 232 of the Trade Expansion Act of 1962 for Adjustment of Imports of Machine Tools*, Submitted by National Machine Tool Builders Association, March 10, 1983, pp. 64-65. Hereafter referred to as NMTBA 232 petition.

8. For background on these programs, see Corcoran (1990), pp. 242-44; Gary L. Guertner, "Machine Tools: Imports and the U.S. Industry, Economy, and Defense Industrial Base," Report No. 86-762E (Washington, D.C.: Congressional Research Service, July 17, 1986), pp. 26-32.

9. Corcoran (1990), p. 243.

10. For a general discussion of the causes for the machine tool industry's decline, see Dertouzos et al.(1989), pp. 236-41; Corcoran (1990), pp. 235-37. Some observers argue that defense needs helped lead the industry down a technological blind alley and contributed to its decline. See, for example, Anthony Di Filippo, *Military Spending and Industrial Decline: A Study of the American Machine Tool Industry* (New York: Greenwood Press, 1986). For an alternative view that attributes the decline to poor management by industry leaders, see Alic et al (1992), pp. 350-54.

11. On the German and Japanese experience, see Dertouzos et al.(1989), pp. 241-246.

12. Manufacturing Studies Board (1990), p. 38.

13. Figures are from Ashburn (1989), p. 77.

14. Testimony of Charles E. Gilbert, Jr. in U.S. Congress, House Banking Subcommittee on Economic Stablization (1987), *New Industrial Base Initiative*, p. 575.

15. For example, see David J. Collis, "The Machine Tool Industry and Industrial Policy, 1955-1982," in A. Michael Spence and Heather A. Hazard, *International Competitiveness* (Cambridge, Mass.: Ballinger, 1988), pp. 75-114; Prestowitz, pp. 376-381. For an alternative view, see Alexander, pp. 44-49.

16. Collis (1986), pp. 85-89.

17. Ashburn (1989), p. 77.

18. See DiFilippo (1986), pp. 127-129.

19. Quoted in NMTBA 232 petition, p. 70.

20. Letter dated August 3, 1982. Quoted in NMTBA 232 petition, p. 71.

21. The best sources on this episode are Prestowitz, pp. 381-390; and Max Holland, *When the Machine Stopped: A Cautionary Tale from Industrial America*, (Boston: Harvard Business School Press, 1989).

22. Clyde Prestowitz, a Commerce Department official at the time, provides an insider's perspective on this debate; Prestowitz (1989), pp. 382-90.

23. Ibid.., pp. 387-88.

24. Richard Hooley, *Protection for the Machine Tool Industry: Domestic and International Negotiations for Voluntary Restraint Agreements*, Pew Case Study in International Affairs, Case 120 (Pittsburgh, Pa.: University of Pittsburgh Graduate School of Public and International Affairs, 1989), p. 5.

25. September 1983 also saw the publication of an in-depth International Trade Commission report on the problems facing domestic machine tool manufacturers. The report was highly critical of U.S. firms, but did help maintain a public spotlight on the industry's plight. U.S. International Trade Commission, *Competitive Assessment of the U.S. Metalworking Machine Tool Industry*, USITC Publication 1428, September 1983.

26. Founded in 1902, the NMTBA, now known as the Association for Manufacturing Technology (AMT), represents over 287 U.S. machine tool firms, accounting for over 85 percent of the domestic industry.

27. According to industry representatives, the Houdaille petition and the 232 petition were not linked. Indeed, Houdaille's attorneys tried unsuccessfully to persuade the NMTBA to postpone its petition until the Houdaille case had been resolved. Author interview with industry representatives, 1991.

28. For background on Section 232, see Lewis (1991); and David D. Knoll, "Section 232 of the Trade Expansion Act of 1962: Industrial Fasteners, Machine Tools and Beyond," *Maryland Journal of International Law and Trade*, vol. 10 (1986), pp. 55-88.

29. Author interview.

30. In 1981, the most recent figures available in 1983, imports accounted for approximately 27 percent of domestic consumption. See Anderson Ashburn, "Machine Tools and National Security II," *American Machinist* vol. 127, no. 5 (May 1983), p. 5.

31. See Anderson Ashburn, "Machine Tools and National Security I," *American Machinist* vol. 127, no. 4 (April 1983), p. 5.

32. National Research Council, Committee on the Machine Tool Industry, *The Machine Tool Industry and the Defense Industrial Base* (Washington, D.C.: National Academy Press, November 21, 1983).

33. Quoted in U.S. Congress, Senate Committee on Foreign Relations, *U.S. Machine Tool Industry: Its Relation to National Security*, 98th Congress, 1st Session, November 28, 1983, p. 231.

34. Quoted in "Machine Tools: Defense Production Can't Be Stockpiled," *American Machinist* vol. 128, no. 1 (January 1984), p. 33.

35. "Baldridge Backs NMTBA on Import Relief," *American Machinist*, May 1984, p. 23.

36. Author interviews with DoD officials, 1991.

37. Hooley (1989), p. 6.

38. The new guidelines were not approved by the White House until mid-1985.

39. In 1988, in response to the NMTBA case, Congress amended Section 232 and imposed a ninety-day limit on presidential action.

40. See "Machine Tools: Will the Cornerstone Erode?" *Industry Week*, vol. 224, no. 8 (April 30, 1984), p. 78. For a broader discussion of antiprotectionism, see Destler and Odell (1987).

41. Ashburn (April 1983), p. 5.

42. Quoted in U.S. Congress, Senate Committee on Foreign Relations (November 28, 1983), p. 231.

43. See Krauss and Reich (Autumn 1992), pp. 880-82.

44. Corcoran (1990), pp. 230-37.

45. "Toolbuilders Seek Uncle Sam's Aid," *Industry Week*, November 29, 1982, p. 22.

46. Krauss and Reich (Autumn 1992), p. 882.

47. For a review, see U.S. Congress, Joint Economic Committee, *The Machine Tool Industry and the Defense Industrial Base*, 98th Congress, 1st Session, June 7, 1983, pp. 153-155.

48. For background on the *keiretsu* system, see Hart (1993), pp. 41-45.

49. For background on consortia, see John S. Wilson, "Collaboration in Research and Development: Selected Examples," in National Academy of Sciences, *The Government Role in Civilian Technology: Building a New Alliance* (Washington, D.C.: National Academy Press, 1992), pp. 131-51; U.S. Congress, Joint Economic Committee, *High Technology Consortia: The Federal Role*, 101st Congress, 1st Session, June 8, 1989; and U.S. Congressional Budget Office, *Using R&D Consortia for Commercial Innovation* (Washington, D.C.: CBO, July 1990).

50. Author interviews with Industry Representatives, 1991.

51. Anderson Ashburn, "Is There a Place for Joint Research?" *American Machinist*, vol. 128, no. 1 (January 1984), p. 5.

52. Although NCMS was incorporated in November 1986, plans for the consortium had long been on the drawing board and were widely discussed in both industry and policy circles. A formal organizational plan was completed in December 1985 and a chairman was appointed in January 1986. A prospectus for the organization was forwarded to the White House prior to the May 1986 decision to support VRAs. See "National Center for Manufacturing Sciences Gains Corporate Sponsors, Looks for Site," *American Machinist*, November 1986, p. 47.

53. Ibid.; "Research Center Opens in Michigan," *American Machinist*, September 1987, pp. 138-39.

54. Ernest Valhala, Chairman of NCMS Technical Review Board, quoted in Cheryl Eberwein, "Taking on Japan," *Corporate Detroit Magazine*, March 1992.

55. Quoted in Hongsuk Park, *American Politics and Foreign Economic Challenges* (New York: Garland, 1990), p. 183.

56. Hooley (1989), p. 8. Author interview.

57. The original Commerce Department report recommended relief for nine classes of machine tools. The change in the two reports was due to the NSC's alteration of the methodology for measuring mobilization requirements. See Hooley (1989), pp. 7-8.

58. Hooley (1989), p. 8.

59. The following details come from Ibid.., pp. 8-10.

60. Author interviews with Commerce Department and DoD officials, 1992.

61. Staff in the Office of the Secretary of Defense (OSD) opposed the petition, but Admiral William Crowe, chairman of the Joint Chiefs of Staff, and Richard Godwin, Under Secretary of Defense for Acquisition, strongly supported action. Author Interviews with Commerce and DoD officials, 1992.

62. Hooley (1989), p. 9.

63. Statement by the president, May 20, 1986.

64. Ibid..

65. Ibid..

66. According to several sources, the major import problem came from Japan. However, West Germany, Switzerland, and Taiwan were added to the list to prevent the appearance of "Japan-bashing." Author interviews with Commerce Department and DoD officials, 1992.

67. Implementation of these provisions has been spotty, as DoD has waived the restrictions on numerous occasions. See U.S. General Accounting Office, *Defense Procurement: DoD Purchases of Foreign-Made Machine Tools* (Washington, D.C.: GAO, February 1991).

68. Hooley (1989, pp. 9-11) provides background on these negotiations.

69. Stuart Auerbach, "President Extends Ban on Tool Imports from Japan and Taiwan," *Washington Post*, December 27, 1991, pp. D1, D11.

70. For background on this debate, see Bruce Stokes, "Tooling Up," *National Journal*, October 19, 1991, pp. 2544-48.

71. Stuart Auerbach, "Agencies Split on Imports of Machine Tools," *Washington Post*, December 6, 1991, pp. B1, B12.

72. For example, Hooley's (1989) case study—the only detailed public examination of this episode—does not discuss the domestic components of the machine tool action plan.

73. NMTBA's initiative was sparked by its anger over Chrysler's selection of foreign machine tool makers to supply tools for the turret of the XM-1 tank. DiFilippo (1986), p. 147-9.

74. "Limited Partnership for R&D is Proposed," *American Machinist*, vol. 128, no. 12 (December 1984), p. 23.

75. These comparisons are explicitly developed in Ellis S. Krauss and Jon Pierre, "Targeting Resources for Industrial Change," in R. Kent Weaver and Bert A. Rockman, eds., *Do Institutions Matter?: Government Capabilities in the United States and Abroad* (Washington, D.C.: Brookings Institution, 1993), pp. 151-87.

76. See Tyson (1992), pp. 286-89; and Hart (1993), pp. 263-64.

77. Author interview with industry representatives, 1991.

78. For background on the use of the procurement mechanism, see Donald F. Kettl *Government By Proxy*, (Washington, D.C.: Congressional Quarterly Press, 1988).

79. See Statement of Charles E. Gilbert, representing NMTBA, in U.S. Congress, Senate Committee on Armed Services, *Manufacturing Capabilities of Key Second-Tier Defense Industries*, 100th Congress, 1st Session, July 23, 1987, pp. 36-42.

5

The Semiconductor and Semiconductor Manufacturing Industries and the Creation of Sematech

As the Reagan administration was debating the machine tool VRA issue, the U.S. semiconductor industry lurched into a crisis of its own. After inventing the semiconductor device and dominating world markets for years, American firms faced a concerted onslaught from rapidly expanding Japanese competitors. Fearing the potential extinction of domestic production capacity, U.S. semiconductor firms turned to Washington for help.

As in the machine tool case, advocates for the U.S. semiconductor industry encountered significant obstacles in their efforts to initiate action. But, in the end, they succeeded even more remarkably than the NMTBA, prompting a dramatic change in policy that remains a model today. Policymakers noted at the time, and still recognize today, that the creation of the Sematech consortium was a seminal event.[1]

A significant evolution in policy ideas made this change possible. As strategic trade concepts filtered through the academic and policy communities, the case against market intervention was fatally weakened. As we saw in Chapter Four, the decision to support the U.S. machine tool industry resulted from a questioning of the traditional laissez-faire doctrine. As resistance faded, proponents also created a viable intellectual case for supporting the semiconductor industry through Sematech. By late 1987, these factors made Sematech's creation a relatively noncontroversial decision.

THE RISE AND FALL OF THE AMERICAN SEMICONDUCTOR INDUSTRY

A vast literature on the history of the American semiconductor industry exists.[2] The industry dates back to 1947, when Bell Laboratories invented the transistor.

Researchers jumped off from this breakthrough, racing to create the integrated circuit (IC)—the precursor to today's semiconductors. Intensely interested in miniaturizing electronic devices, the Pentagon funded a number of research programs supporting IC development. However, Texas Instruments, working without government support, invented the first working IC in 1958.

Invention of the IC prompted an explosion of research, eventually leading to the creation of the modern microelectronics industry. American firms capitalized on a strong R&D base and soon established a commanding lead in world markets. At the same time, the market for this technology grew rapidly. Between 1963 and 1973, the American IC market grew from $16 million to almost $2 billion.[3]

Government R&D funding and procurement of microelectronics played an indirect, yet important, role in these developments. In the most extensive case study of public policy toward the semiconductor industry, Richard C. Levin concluded that "the contribution of public policy in microelectronics has been modest, but nevertheless of considerable significance."[4] However, a 1977 MIT study concluded that "substantially none of the major innovations in semiconductors have been a direct result of defense sponsored projects."[5]

American dominance in semiconductors continued into the 1970s. American businesses created nearly all the pioneering advances, and as miniaturization advanced semiconductors became an increasingly important component of weapons systems. However, at the same time, defense applications became less important to advances in semiconductor technology. Until 1964, procurement of ICs for Air Force missile systems and NASA space programs accounted for more than 90 percent of U.S. and world IC production.[6] This figure has since dropped rapidly, as defense sales have consistently accounted for less than 10 percent of IC sales (and less than 5 percent by number of chips) since the 1970s.[7]

Even with a strong market position, U.S. firms began noting warning signs by the end of the 1970s as the Japanese semiconductor industry emerged as a major force in world markets.[8] In 1977, for the first time, Japanese exports of semiconductors to the United States exceeded American exports to Japan. In 1978, U.S. imports of metal oxide semiconductor (MOS) integrated circuits from Japan exceeded MOS exports to Japan. By 1979, three Japanese firms ranked among the top five world producers and accounted for one-third of the total world semiconductor market.[9]

By the early 1980s, the trickle of warnings turned into a flood of alarm.[10] Where U.S. firms faltered, Japanese businesses stepped in and became dominant market players. The decline of American firms culminated in the "semiconductor winter" of 1984 and 1985. During this fourteen-month period, Japanese dumping of 256K devices destroyed the remnants of the U.S. dynamic random access memory (DRAM) chip industry, securing 90 percent of the world DRAM market for Japan.[11] 1985 was also the year of the "crossover," where Japan's share of global market in DRAMs first surpassed that of the United States.

RESPONDING TO CRISIS: PROTECTION FOR CHIP PRODUCERS

As trends shifted to their disadvantage, American firms pressed for government action against Japan's "unfair" trading practices. Such lobbying represented a relatively new phenomenon for American firms. Unlike other industries, such as steel and automobiles, the U.S. semiconductor industry was weakly integrated and consisted of a few huge producers, such as IBM and Texas Instruments, along with hundreds of small, innovative firms based in California's Silicon Valley and elsewhere. These smaller firms long prided themselves on their entrepreneurial spirit, and felt confident that they could always "out-innovate" the competition. Thus, the industry was slow to organize in response to foreign challenges. Its trade association, the Semiconductor Industry Association (SIA), was not formed until 1977.[12]

Because of its weak organizational base, SIA was originally slow to respond. However, by the mid-1980s, under the leadership of SIA's trade lawyer, former Deputy U.S. Trade Representative Alan Wolff, American semiconductor firms began a more concerted push for government action. In a series of widely publicized reports, SIA claimed that the Japanese government was targeting the American chip industry for extinction.[13] These reports prompted Reagan administration officials to raise industry concerns in U.S.-Japan bilateral trade talks in the period from 1981 to 1983, but no concrete results followed.[14] Meanwhile, the U.S. market position eroded even further.

SIA soon backed its claims with action. On July 14, 1985, the industry filed an unfair trade petition against Japan under the provisions of Section 301 of the U.S. Trade Act of 1974.[15] Soon after, a number of individual firms filed suit charging Japan with dumping erasable programmable read-only memory (EPROM) chips on the U.S. market. After these cases were filed, the Department of Commerce, in an unprecedented move, followed suit by filing a claim itself, charging Japanese firms with dumping 256K and 1M DRAM chips.

In filing the petitions, U.S. industry did not ask for retaliation or protectionism. They instead called for an opening of Japanese markets to U.S. goods. The petitions, combined with significant congressional pressure, forced the Reagan administration to react to the erosion of the semiconductor industry. After months of tough negotiation, the U.S. and Japan eventually signed the Semiconductor Trade Agreement in August 1986. Under the terms of the agreement, Japan agreed to open its market to U.S. semiconductors and to monitor prices of products exported to the United States to prevent dumping.[16] In return, the U.S. agreed to drop the dumping cases and the 301 filing. Thus, the U.S. market remained unprotected. However, later in 1987, the United States did impose tariffs on Japanese products in response to Japan's failure to enforce the 1987 agreement.[17]

Helen Milner and David Yoffie argue that the semiconductor industry's actions were strategic; that is, the industry's drive to open foreign markets reflects an understanding that domestic capabilities cannot survive without such access.[18] Given the industry's strategic emphasis, we could speculate that policymakers supported the industry due to relative gains considerations. But such considerations played a minor role, as absolute gains concerns prevailed in the minds of American decisionmakers.[19] Indeed, the Reagan administration's unwillingness to sustain sanctions against Japan in April 1987 may indicate lessened emphasis on relative gains concerns.

The actions demanded by the industry, and supplied by policy makers, did not target Japan's exports into the United States and its growing dominance in semiconductors. It instead focused on specific trading practices that limited Japanese purchases of American semiconductors. Industry demands were couched in terms of creating a level playing field, a norm deeply embedded in U.S. trade law.[20]

Creating a level playing field did not address the real causes of defense dependence. This limitation was recognized at the time, and was one factor in the widespread criticism of the 1986 Semiconductor Agreement.[21] For many, the agreement was flawed because it contradicted America's traditional openness to foreign trade. For others, the agreement failed to address the real problems of the U.S. semiconductor industry and the ultimate cause of defense dependence—the weakness of its manufacturing and technology base. The agreement targeted semiconductor chips, which formed the end product of the production process. It did not address the health of the semiconductor manufacturing sector—those firms that produced the machinery and technologies needed to manufacture semiconductor chips. Trade protection could not solve those problems.

Improving Semiconductor Manufacturing

The critics were proved correct within months of the Semiconductor Agreement's signing. It soon revealed itself as an ineffective response to the issue of American dependence on Japanese semiconductors. The agreement actually raised costs for U.S. chip consumers,[22] and did little to stem Japanese market dominance or the erosion in U.S. market share. Between 1986 and 1989, Japanese imports as a share of total U.S. semiconductor consumption rose from 9.8 percent to 21.1 percent. U.S. exports as a percentage of total Japanese semiconductor consumption rose from only 5 percent to 7 percent over this same period.[23]

Even more worrisome for American leaders was the fact that Japanese market dominance was creating a situation of potentially dangerous defense dependence for semiconductors and semiconductor technology. Comprehensive figures on semiconductor dependence did not exist, but industry-level evidence,[24] combined with a declining market share for U.S. producers, raised many concerns over the national security implications of these trends. For example, a 1985 Production Base Analysis for the Air Force found that 90 percent of military semiconductors were assembled offshore.[25] A 1985 National Research Council study listed numerous components as potential danger points. Among the threatened sectors were silicon integrated circuits, robotics, ceramic packaging, fabrication of integrated circuits, and gallium arsenide technology.[26] Similarly, a Federal Interagency Task Force found the United States lagging Japan in fourteen semiconductor product and process areas. The United States led in just six categories, with its lead slipping in five of these sectors.[27]

Many officials feared that this continued Japanese dominance would lead to even more severe problems in the future. As Norman Augustine, CEO of Martin Marietta and chairman of the Defense Science Board (DSB) Task Force on Semiconductor Dependency noted,

If the present decline in . . . industrial vitality continues, there appears little question that defense manufacturers will have to turn to overseas suppliers and accept overseas dependence for these essential components. . . . We concluded that this option was unacceptable given the critical nature of semiconductors and of semiconductor technology.[28]

Table 5.1 summarizes the conclusions of these studies. This table, taken from the Defense Science Board's report, was circulated widely during 1987 debates on semiconductor dependency.

The failure of the Semiconductor Agreement led industry observers to examine another question: how to create a sustainable level of manufacturing and process expertise that matched Japanese performance and could be sustained over time. Industry leaders had recognized this problem for some time. As one industry leader argued, "The Semiconductor Agreement was a purely defensive response. We knew that we also had to combine it with an offensive response—something to strengthen the industry here at home."[29]

A number of potential alternatives existed, but all required one thing: a more active government role supporting domestic semiconductor manufacturers. Creating a more active role for government required breaching policymakers' traditional opposition to industrial policy. The machine tool industry's success indicated that this hurdle could be surmounted. However, making a case for government intervention still proved a difficult task. Sematech's creation is directly attributable to the reshaping of policy ideas that contributed to government concerns about industrial policy.

DEVELOPMENT OF THE SEMATECH IDEA

To support Sematech, policymakers had to be convinced of two things: (1) that semiconductor manufacturing was a critical industry worthy of government support, and (2) that government could create arrangements to successfully provide the needed support. To convince policymakers on these two counts required persuading them to alter their previous beliefs regarding the superiority of laissez faire.

Convincing policymakers that semiconductors represented a critical industry was the easiest task facing advocates of greater government activism. Nearly everyone agreed that semiconductor production produced significant spillover benefits for the economy while also contributing to a wide range of critical weapons systems. For example, the Congressional Office of Technology Assessment noted as far back as 1981 that "it is probably not an exaggeration to say that the semiconductor industry and particularly the application of semiconductor manufacturing technology, are now the future of an advanced industrial economy."[30]

In presenting their case, supporters of government intervention worked the "critical industry" definition from two fronts by stressing both military and economic factors. They faced few difficulties in convincing policymakers that semiconductors were important components in weapons systems.[31] After all, Pentagon investments

Table 5.1
The Shift in Semiconductor Technology—1987

	JAPAN LEAD	U.S.-JAPAN PARITY	U.S. LEAD
SILICON PRODUCTS			
DRAMs	✓ USPosition Declining		
SRAMs	✓ US Position Declining		
EPROMs		✓ US Position Steady	
Microprocessors			✓ US Position Declining
Custom Logic			✓ US Position Declining
Bipolar	✓ US Position Declining		
NONSILICON PRODUCTS			
Memory	✓ US Position Declining		
Logic	✓ US Position Declining		
Linear			✓ US Position Steady
Optoelectronics	✓ US Position Declining		
Heterostructures	✓ US Position Declining		
MATERIALS			
Silicon	✓ US Position Declining		

Table 5.1 Continued

Gallium Arsenide	✓ US Position Declining		
PROCESSING EQUIPMENT			
Optical Lithography		✓ US Position Declining	
E-Beam Lithography			✓ US Position Declining
X-ray Lithography		✓ US Position Declining	
Ion Implantaion Technonology			✓ US Position Declining
Chemical Vapor Deposition		✓ US Position Steady	
Deposition, Diffusion, Other		✓ US Position Steady	
Energy-Assisted Processing	✓ US Position Declining		
Assembly		✓ US Position Steady	
Packaging	✓ US Position Declining		
Test	✓ US Position Declining		
Computer-Aided Engineering		✓ US Position Steady	
Computer-Aided Manufacturing		✓ US Position Declining	

Source: Defense Science Board, *Report of the Defense Science Board Task Force on Semiconductor Dependency* (Washington, D.C.: Office of the Undersecretary of Defense for Acquisition, February 1987), p. 58.

had helped spur the industry's early development, and DoD continued to try to promote technological advances through such efforts as the VHSIC program (See Chapter Three).[32]

The more difficult argument required convincing policymakers that semiconductors were critical in the nonmilitary sense. This argument regarding semiconductors as "infrastructure" proved essential to Sematech's establishment. Indeed, a congressional report regarding Sematech noted that:

> The underlying premise of Sematech is that if the U.S. loses the point of the pyramid that everything rests on—the ability to manufacture the most technologically advanced and commercially successful semiconductors—the U.S.'s historically preeminent position in the whole electronics industry is sure to be eroded or destroyed. We are not alone in believing this. The belief in the importance of the point of the pyramid is precisely the rationale for Japan's multi-year, multi-billion dollar investment in semiconductors, a pattern that is now being copied in Korea and in Europe.[33]

As this excerpt indicates, government support for Sematech was premised on the belief that semiconductor manufacturing created significant externalities that would ripple through the entire U.S. economy, with especially strong impacts on key commercial sectors. These concepts were fully considered by DoD policymakers,[34] and played an especially important role in convincing Congress to support Sematech. As Alic et al. concluded, "National security provided no more than a secondary rationale for this decision (to fund Sematech); Congress, in particular, focused squarely on U.S.-Japan competition for commercial sales."[35]

Even the administration's most ardent "free traders" expressed few doubts about the economic importance of semiconductors. For example, while opposing federal support for Sematech, Lew Cramer, Acting Deputy Assistant Secretary of Commerce for Science and Electronics, conceded in 1987 that "I believe that semiconductors are the industrial rice, the crude oil of the future. . . . I would agree that [semiconductors are more important than the ball bearing or steel industries]."[36]

A Congressional Budget Office (CBO) study published immediately preceding the Congressional vote on Sematech also made a strong case for semiconductors as a critical industry.[37] The study highlighted the steep learning curves for semiconductor manufacturing as well as the substantial spillovers from the Sematech plan. Surprisingly, CBO downplayed the defense significance of Sematech.[38] Thus, a strong consensus supported designation of semiconductor manufacturing as a critical industry.

The next component involved persuading policymakers that government intervention could truly aid the domestic industry. It was on this question that traditional opposition to IP played an important role. The case against public funding was summarized by Dr. Thomas Dorsey, an OMB economist: "There is a real danger of politicization (with Sematech), a risk that this won't be done for scientific reasons, but instead evolve into a giant entitlement program. Government shouldn't be allocating resources and making priorities, the market should."[39]

Although Sematech was officially created in 1987, its genesis dates back to the early 1980s. The Pentagon had long feared the potential for defense dependence in the semiconductor industry; the VHSIC program was partly designed to address that threat. Industry had also discussed ideas for cooperation to solve common problems. Interest in such cooperation peaked in 1985—the period of intense public concern that eventually helped prompt the 1986 Semiconductor Agreement. At that time, several different groups, both inside and outside of government, began studying the competitiveness of semiconductor manufacturing, an industrial sector not affected by the 1986 agreement.[40] Most of these studies were based on the premise that government action was needed—their main focus involved the best way to expand the government role.

These panels met throughout 1986, and other groups also began undertaking similar analyses. In September 1986, the Semiconductor Industry Association created a task force to examine the semiconductor manufacturing sector. Finally, in 1986, as part of the government's effort to deflect domestic pressures for protection, the National Security Council commissioned an interagency study of the semiconductor industry.[41] As these studies progressed, the health of the U.S. semiconductor industry remained a front-burner issue in Washington.

The groundwork for Sematech was laid during this period in late 1985 and throughout 1986. As various studies progressed, the industry and its supporters also worked to educate policymakers in Washington. In September 1985, the industry helped establish the Semiconductor Congressional Support Group (SCSG), a bipartisan forum of twenty-eight House and Senate members who supported the semiconductor industry. The SCSG was designed to improve links between the industry and key members of Congress.

Even more important than the SCSG was the regular industry-held series of meetings where approximately 300 government officials and congressional staff members attended seminars on the industry and its current problems. All attendees also received a monthly newsletter that presented industry concerns in greater detail. Participants included key players from the White House, Congress, and the various executive departments.[42] These briefings presented a sophisticated analysis of the industry's plight; they made a similarly sophisticated case for government intervention to support the industry.[43]

Options for Reducing Dependence

A number of different proposals floated around Washington during this period. One industry-supported plan called for direct federal support for semiconductor firms who produced according to military specifications. These "captive"[44] firms would then use the funds to buy know-how and technology from throughout the industry.[45] In general, this option was similar to the VHSIC program, with its emphasis on limiting government support to firms producing for defense markets.

A second plan simply called for doing more of the same—increasing government funding for precompetitive R&D in semiconductor technologies. Spending increases were expected to average $60 million in the first year and to reach $250 million after four years.[46] A related program, suggested by the National Academy of Sciences, proposed using Department of Energy research laboratories as the main center for semiconductor R&D, but these efforts would remain limited to basic research work. Moreover, these programs envisioned limited industry-government cooperation.

A third option involved trade protection of the sort employed in the 1986 Semiconductor Agreement. This option was widely discussed but considered unattractive for several reasons.[47] Additional quotas offered only limited and indirect assistance to U.S. firms, as targeting semiconductor manufacturing technologies would prove much more complicated than targeting finished products, such as chips. Moreover, quotas might fail to work as in the case of the Semiconductor Agreement. Most importantly, U.S. firms viewed quotas as avoiding the real problem of strengthening domestic manufacturing capabilities.

A fourth proposal called for creation of a private consortium where firms would pool funds for joint R&D efforts. Various U.S. firms, led by Charles Sporck of National Semiconductor, had long entertained this option. Throughout early 1986, IBM circulated in both industry and government an internally developed study highlighting dangerous weaknesses in the industry and advocating creation of a private consortium. Sanford Kane, Vice-President of IBM, explained IBM's views by noting that "We thought the industry could do it alone and we were concerned about (government) strings attached to the money."[48]

Finally, the Sematech plan called for development of a public-private consortium. The idea for Sematech emerged publicly in early 1987 as the various study groups began to release their final reports. In February 1987, the DSB released its report supporting the establishment of a Semiconductor Manufacturing Technology Institute to be supported by DoD funding (approximately $200 million per year) and private industry. The DSB envisioned that government and industry would enter into a joint arrangement to manufacture DRAMs for the open market.

The DSB report is cited by nearly every source as the critical factor in expanding political support for government intervention. The DSB study group contained a number of high-level figures, including its chairman, Norman Augustine; R. Bobby Inman, the current Secretary of Defense, and William Perry, now serving as Secretary of Defense. The report's conclusions raised numerous concerns, especially concerning defense dependence. The report noted: "U.S. Defense will soon *depend on foreign sources* for state-of-the-art technology in semiconductors. The Task Force views this as an unacceptable situation."[49]

The task force's prestige, combined with its alarming message, spurred action both inside and outside of government. Soon after the DSB's report's release, on March 3, the SIA and the SRC announced their plan for Sematech, a proposal modeled on DSB's proposed institute. Within weeks, on March 27, 1987, legislation to provide government support for Sematech was introduced by Reps. James Florio (D-NJ) and Don Ritter (R-PA). As it developed the Sematech proposal, the SIA also committed its members to support 50 percent of the costs of the consortium. By May 12, fourteen firms had announced their intention to join Sematech.

REVIEWING THE OPTIONS: THE INTELLECTUAL
CASE FOR SEMATECH

Four potential options for strengthening semiconductor manufacturing were available to policymakers. However, the debate soon narrowed to consider only the two consortium plans. Nearly all of the various groups examining solutions to the domestic industry's problems saw consortia as the most attractive option.

As was the case with NCMS, a consortium offered a means to combine government support for critical industries with the market-led focus considered so crucial by policymakers. Because private investment represented at least 50 percent of Sematech's operating budget, the traditional concern about government picking winners and losers was lessened.[50] DoD involvement also helped weaken the case of industrial policy opponents and proved critical to swaying top Reagan administration officials. Rep. James Florio (D-NJ) expressed surprise when he described the public debate over Sematech: "Nobody has said anything about industrial policy. . . . about what seems to be, in some people's minds, an obvious change in the role of Government involvement in industrial concerns."[51]

Sematech was also viewed as a means to support U.S. industry without resorting to protectionism. Past experience with the Semiconductor Agreement and other VRAs had convinced policymakers that protection could not revitalize American industry.[52] For example, in announcing his plan, DSB Chairman Norman R. Augustine felt compelled to note: "The task force thought long and hard about many alternatives. By and large, we are not believers in subsidies and we are not believers in trade barriers. On the other hand, these are extraordinary circumstances."[53]

Most importantly, the Sematech plan offered a means to tackle the relative gains problem in a straightforward manner. Both Japan and various European states had employed government policy to promote industry integration and collaboration. These efforts culminated in systems like Japan's *keiretsu* and the tight linkages between banking and industry in Germany.[54] Consortia offered a means to create "home-grown" *keiretsu*. Indeed, the case for Sematech was based explicitly on this point. Robert Noyce, who subsequently became Sematech's first CEO, argued in June 1987 that: "We are asking that the government assume a role common for most of our industrial rivals and which gives our competitors a large advantage."[55] A 1990 industry-produced white paper echoed these points:

> Traditional economics has little to contribute to an American industry facing an entirely new world of brutal competition and foreign targeting. Facing these kinds of foreign practices, the U.S. has no choice but to respond with an industrial strategy of its own. . . . It is not appropriate to envision a large MITI-like government agency that would allocate capital to selected industries. The key, instead, is for U.S. companies to form consortia that enable them to combine their entrepreneurial strengths with the economy of scale needed to compete with their larger foreign counterparts.[56]

Beyond making a case for consortia, Sematech supporters also had to convince policymakers that government support was needed. The case for government intervention was based on three points: (1) the financial weakness of U.S. industry, (2) the industry's good faith efforts at self-help, and (3) the externalities generated by semiconductor manufacturing.

The case for the industry's financial weakness was fairly convincing. As many congressional witnesses noted, the U.S. semiconductor industry spent more on R&D than any other manufacturing sector.[57] Yet this high level did not compare to Japanese R&D spending. Without government support, the industry could not create a level playing field.

Advocates also warned that the semiconductor industry would soon disappear without outside assistance. Sen. Pete Domenici (R-NM) asked, "What will happen to the U.S. semiconductor industry without government support? Technological advances occur so fast. . . that if we do nothing. . . the Japanese will advance so far beyond us that we will not even be able to hold our current ground."[58]

Pursuing a consortium approach also strengthened the industry's argument that it was acting to help itself. By agreeing to share technology and contribute $100 million of their own funds, industry leaders convinced policymakers that they were not simply seeking a hand-out. This effort was further reinforced by SIA's unusual practice of lobbying by company chief executives, rather than by Washington staff. The personal entreaties of industry legends like Robert Noyce of Intel and Charles Sporck of National Semiconductor convinced policymakers that Sematech was a serious proposition.[59]

The case for Sematech was further bolstered by the critical nature of the industry. Strengthened semiconductor manufacturing capabilities would have numerous spillover effects, strengthening other industries. Moreover, because Sematech would focus on generic technologies, its benefits could not be appropriated by individual companies. Industry representatives argued that: "We are proposing a joint 50/50 industry/government funding, because it is really beyond the capacity of industry to do it alone. We feel that is well justified because the benefits will be far greater to the society than those that can be appropriated by the individual industrial sponsors."[60]

Finally, Sematech's passage was also eased by the experience of the machine tool industry one year earlier. Indeed, explicit comparisons between the two industries were common. For example, R. Bobby Inman, former deputy director of intelligence and a member of the DSB task force argued:

> Semiconductor processing equipment is as vital to a national capability in electronics as machine tools are to capability in automotive and industrial equipment. The Japanese subsidized both these enabling industries in various ways. . . . We must find ways to subsidize these same industries . . . One way is through consortiums fostered by and subsidized by the U.S. government.[61]

The importance of these arguments was made evident by Rep. Dave McCurdy (D-OK) in retrospective comments on Sematech's creation. In 1989, he commented:

> I guess philosophically why we in the Armed Services Committee . . . were involved in the development of Sematech was that this is a critical technology, not only for a commercial sector of our economy, but also in national security implications or

applications, and that we needed to prevent the further erosion of that technology and the dependence on potential foreign sources.[62]

The Creation of Sematech

The cumulative effect of these arguments proved quite powerful, creating a snowball effect that made government support for Sematech a fait accompli by summer 1987. The program proceeded on two tracks—through the Congress and through the executive branch. Sematech's passage through Congress was eased by intense public and congressional concern regarding record U.S. trade deficits.

The remarkable thing about the Congressional debates of 1987 is the lack of debate about Sematech. The path through the administration's top policymakers was much less smooth. The Pentagon originally had mixed feelings about Sematech. Staff involved in R&D work supported the concept; others, especially staffers in Office of the Secretary of Defense's (OSD) Acquisition office, were originally lukewarm toward Sematech. DoD officials, led by Robert Costello, were greatly concerned about DoD's limited funds. They argued that DoD simply could not support all industries and guarantee secure supplies of all defense-critical items. They instead determined to focus on only the most critical components. Convinced of the criticality of semiconductor manufacturing, DoD agreed to fund the consortium. By spring 1987, Secretary Weinberger agreed to support the proposal.[63]

DoD had few allies in the Cabinet. Commerce supported the plan,[64] but the rest of the government's economic agencies opposed it. The OMB, the Council of Economic Advisors (CEA), the Treasury Department, the president's science advisor, and the president himself all opposed federal funding for Sematech. According to a former DoD official, the White House Economic Policy Council (EPC) refused to support funding for Sematech on commercial grounds alone.[65]

As internal government debates progressed, Congress was acting. Its concerns over economic competitiveness took concrete form in the Omnibus Trade and Competitiveness Act. In 1987, the Trade Act became the vehicle for a whole range of efforts to restore American industrial preeminence.[66] It also became the focus of a rancorous partisan debate over the Reagan administration's trade policies. This debate created a window of opportunity for the semiconductor equipment industry.

The Sematech proposal originally emerged as an amendment to the Trade Act. The Reagan administration worked assiduously to defeat the bill, especially provisions calling for mandatory notification of plant closings. However, because the administration focused its lobbying on more objectionable provisions of the trade bill, they did not actively contest the Sematech provisions. Nonetheless, the administration succeeded in delaying final action on the Trade Act until August 1988.

Because of these delays with the trade bill, funding for Sematech was eventually approved in the fiscal year 1988/1989 defense authorization bill. This shift in Sematech's location within the U.S. government proved fortuitous. Given Sematech's focus on commercial competitiveness, many supporters argued that the Commerce Department should fund the program. However, in the end, supporters fell back on

DoD funding as the easiest route to guarantee support for Sematech.[67] Including Sematech in the massive annual defense bill had the effect of further insulating the proposal from administration opponents.

By late summer 1987, congressional actions had intensified pressure on the Reagan administration. Pressure further intensified when the results of a White House Council Panel on Semiconductors study were leaked in August. The study was never officially released, but reportedly supported public funding for Sematech.[68] The CBO study reaching similar conclusions was released in September.

Despite these pressures, the Cabinet remained divided. In the end, the administration reached the conclusion that they would not oppose the program. Sematech's opponents in the Cabinet agreed to acquiesce to the Pentagon's position. Tom Dorsey of OMB reflected the perspective of opponents when he argued, "If DoD says there is a national security problem, we can't argue with them."[69]

In September 1987, each house of Congress passed separate Sematech proposals, with the Senate authorizing $100 million per year and the House approving $25 million per year. The final package, which provided $100 million per year over five years, was signed into law on December 22, 1987. A unique confluence of events had helped ease the passage of Sematech without major public debate. As one Senate staffer concluded,

> Timing was critical for Sematech; they had three things going for them. The proposal came at a time when competitiveness was in vogue, it was a high-tech industry, and the trade bill was a major agenda item. Everyone wanted to be associated with doing something for American competitiveness, and then here comes the Sematech proposal. It fit the bill.[70]

Sematech in Action

Even with the approval of federal funding, Sematech faced many difficulties during its start-up phase.[71] Its original plan to create a manufacturing facility was scrapped in early 1988, when Sematech shifted its focus to serving as a provider of state-of-the art manufacturing equipment to its members. In keeping with this commitment, between 1988 and 1992 Sematech spent $990 million to develop manufacturing technologies, with a special focus on advanced lithography equipment. Sematech also built a model R&D facility in Austin, Texas.

Despite some difficult growing pains, Sematech is now widely hailed as a successful venture.[72] The consortium, with twelve current members, is still funded from the DoD budget at an annual rate of $100 million.[73] The bulk of its membership has expressed satisfaction with Sematech. Development times have been reduced and new production standards have been established. In addition, declines in U.S. world market share in semiconductor equipment have been reversed. Indeed, between 1988 and 1992, U.S. world market share rose slightly, from 45 percent to 48.8 percent.[74] While Sematech has not yet helped American industry surpass Japan in terms of semiconductor manufacturing equipment capability, it has helped the industry achieve its stated goals of arresting the decline of the mid-1980s and developing a capability to manufacture state-of-the-art semiconductors using only U.S. equipment.[75]

CONCLUSION: SEMATECH AS A WATERSHED

The decision to provide government support to Sematech was a seminal event in U.S. DIB policy. For the first time, significant government funding was employed to assist private industry in the pursuit of purely commercial goals. The program for Sematech was considerably more extensive than previous efforts to support American machine tool manufacturers.

Such a revolutionary step would have been inconceivable as recently as 1985. What made Sematech a reality was a change in the ideas of policymakers. These changes developed slowly over time, but were significantly strengthened by the power of new ideas developed by the strategic trade policy theorists. These concepts had become much more refined and better known to policymakers in the period between the machine tool decision of early 1986 and the 1987 Sematech episode. The debate over Sematech occurred at a much more sophisticated level, and included detailed discussions of externalities, spillovers, and the role of government in spurring technological innovation.

The Reagan administration supported funding of Sematech because it recognized that the semiconductor and semiconductor equipment sectors represented potentially strategic industries. Not only did these industries contribute greatly to defense systems, they also created the prospect of significant externalities for other sectors of the economy. While the externalities associated with semiconductor manufacturing had not been precisely measured, the industry did have the structural characteristics normally associated with strategic sectors. This recognition, combined with the industry's willingness to participate in a jointly funded consortium, helped tip the scales in support of the Sematech concept.

Tyson provided an apt summary of the Sematech episode when she noted:

> Ultimately, the justification for government support for Sematech depends on the national benefits resulting from securing more-competitive structures for the global semiconductor and semiconductor equipment industries and from maintaining American technological and production capabilities in both of them. . . . Because none of these benefits can be precisely specified or measured, some observers question their very existence. . . . [But] it is more prudent to err in the direction of supporting industry-specific programs, like Sematech, when they are not needed than in the direction of opposing them when they are needed.[76]

Recognizing the importance of this decision, other industry groups sought to emulate the SIA's initiatives. As we will see in Chapters Six and Seven, these efforts were rarely successful. Absorbing lessons from the Sematech episode, Reagan administration policymakers developed a more finely tuned set of criteria for determining an industry's strategic significance. By utilizing these criteria, they succeeded in defeating many subsequent proposals to create "new Sematechs" for other defense-critical industries.

NOTES

1. See, for example, Alic et al. (1992), p. 256; Tyson (1992), pp. 252-54; *Congressional Record*, September 24, 1987, pp. S12689-S12699; William H. Clinton and Albert Gore, "Technology: The Engine of Economic Growth," Campaign Position Paper, September 21, 1992.

2. For example, see Borrus (1988); Alic et al. (1992), pp. 255-82; Richard C. Levin, "The Semiconductor Industry," in Richard Nelson, ed., *Governments and Technical Progress* (New York: Pergamon Press, 1982), pp. 9-99; Slomovic (1991).

3. J. Nicholas Ziegler, "Semiconductors," *Daedalus*, vol. 120, no. 4 (Fall 1991), p. 157.

4. Levin (1982), pp. 9-10.

5. Cited in Slomovic (1991), p. 44.

6. Alic et al. (1992), p. 259, fn. 2.

7. Ibid.

8. On the development of the Japanese semiconductor industry, see Borrus (1988), pp. 139-90; and Thomas R. Howell et al., *The Microelectronics Race: The Impact of Government Policy on International Competition* (Boulder, Colo.: Westview Press, 1988), pp. 35-106.

9. These figures are cited in Levin (1982), p. 88.

10. The ultimate causes of Japan's ascendance and America's decline in semiconductors are complex and covered elsewhere in the literature. This study examines the responses to, not the causes of, these changes. For background, see Borrus (1988); Daniel J. Okimoto, *Between MITI and the Market* (Stanford, Calif.: Stanford University Press, 1991); Daniel J. Okimoto, T. Sugano, and F. Weinstein, eds., *Competitive Edge: The Semiconductor Industry in the U.S. and Japan* (Stanford, Calif.: Stanford University Press, 1985); Dertouzos et al. (1989), pp. 248-77.

11. The DRAM is the basic memory chip used in most microelectronic products. The speed of technological development in DRAMs has accelerated at enormous rates. Since the 1970s, the number of electronic functions that can be placed on a single chip has doubled every year. Over the same period, the cost per function has declined several thousandfold. Because DRAMs are so commonly used, their production creates significant scale economies. Howell et al. (1988), p. 30, fn. 53.

12. The SIA consisted of five firms at that time; its current membership is seventy firms. Even today, SIA maintains its main office in Cupertino, California; its Washington representatives are based in the law firm of Dewey, Ballantine, Bushby, Palmer & Wood. For background on the SIA, see Carol Matlack, "Shoestring Success," *National Journal*, May 20, 1989, p. 1239.

13. See Howell et al.,(1988). SIA distributed drafts of this text to policymakers during the debate over the Semiconductor Agreement and Sematech. Author interviews with SIA representatives.

14. Prestowitz (1989), pp. 151-59, provides an insider's look at these talks.

15. Section 301 authorizes the president to take any step necessary to prevent or retaliate against unfair trade practices that harm U.S. industry. SIA specifically requested that the Reagan administration negotiate for a commitment from Tokyo to pressure Japanese firms to increase their purchases of U.S. semiconductors and to observe U.S. and international antidumping laws.

16. The terms of the agreement are somewhat disputed. Contemporary news reports claimed that Japan committed itself to assisting U.S. firms in achieving a 20 percent market share in Japan within five years. See Prestowitz (1989), p. 172. For details on the agreement, see Tyson (1992), pp. 109-30.

17. These tariffs lasted only two months, as President Reagan removed most restrictions in June 1987.

18. Milner and Yoffie (Spring 1989), pp. 239-71.

19. Mastanduno (1991), pp. 100-101, makes a similar point regarding the use of Super 301 against the Japanese satellite industry. See also Krauss and Reich (Autumn 1992), pp. 857-98.

20. See, for example, Douglas Nelson (1989); Goldstein (1988).

21. Economic analysts have almost universally condemned the agreement. For example, Mowery and Rosenberg (Fall 1989, p. 113) bluntly note: "If the Semiconductor Agreement thus far is an example of successful 'managed trade,' it is hard to know what might constitute a failure." Tyson (1992, pp. 132-133) provides a more sanguine view of the agreement's effects.

22. In 1988, spot prices for 256K DRAMS tripled over a four-month period and American consumers reported difficulties in obtaining adequate supplies at any price. See Tyson (1992), pp. 114-15.

23. Ibid., pp. 128-30.

24. For example, the most comprehensive study of foreign dependence at that time, completed by DoD's Joint Logistics Commanders, cited semiconductors as a major problem area. The study is classified, but its findings are summarized in U.S. General Accounting Office (January 1991), pp. 4-6. Vawter (1986, pp. 26-29) reaches similar conclusions.

25. Cited in Vawter (1986), p. 5.

26. National Research Council, Committee on Electronic Components (1985), pp. 23-31.

27. Report of the Federal Interagency Staff Working Group, "The Semiconductor Industry" (Washington, D.C.: National Science Foundation, November 16, 1987). Cited in U.S. Congress, Office of Technology Assessment, *The Big Picture: HDTV and High-Resolution Systems*, OTA-BP-CIT-64 (Washington, D.C.: GPO, June 1990), p. 67.

28. Testimony of Norman R. Augustine before the Senate Committee on Armed Services, *Department of Defense Authorization for Appropriations for Fiscal Years 1988 and 1989*, 100th Congress, 1st Session, March 9, 1987, p. 3327. Also see reports cited in Glenn J. McLoughlin, *SEMATECH: Issues in Evaluation and Assessment* (Washington, D.C.: Congressional Research Service, October 1, 1992), pp. 5-6.

29. Author interview with industry official, 1993.

30. U.S. Congress, Office of Technology Assessment, *U.S. Industrial Competitiveness: A Comparison of Steel, Electronics and Automobiles* (Washington, D.C.: GPO, July 1981), pp. 103-4.

31. Dan Charles, "Keeping Semiconductors Safe for Democracy," *Bulletin of the Atomic Scientists*, vol. 45, no. 8 (November 1989), pp. 8-10.

32. Alic et al. (1992), pp. 257-261.

33. U.S. Congress, House Committee on Energy and Commerce, Subcommittee on Commerce, Consumer Protection, and Competitiveness, *Competitiveness of the U.S. Semiconductor Industry*, 100th Congress, 1st Session, June 9, 1987, p. 58.

34. Author interviews with former DoD officials. The Costello Report (DoD, July 1988, p. 6) specifically cites semiconductors as an example of a strategic industry.

35. Alic et al. (1992), p. 273.

36. Testimony, U.S. Congress, House Committee on Energy and Commerce, of Representatives Subcommittee on Commerce, Consumer Protection, and Competitiveness (June 9, 1987), p. 25.

37. U.S. Congress, Congressional Budget Office, *The Benefits and Risks of Federal Funding for Sematech* (Washington, D.C.: CBO, September 1987), pp. 44-46.

38. Ibid, p. 46.

39. Quoted in George C. Lodge, *Comparative Business-Government Relations* (Englewood Cliffs, NJ: Prentice-Hall, Inc., 1990a), p. 145.

40. In July 1985, the Semiconductor Research Corporation's Manufacturing Competitiveness Panel, began meeting to assess the impact of recent trends in the semiconductor industry. In December 1985, Donald Hicks, the deputy under Secretary of defense for research and engineering, requested that the Defense Science Board complete a similar analysis.

The SRC is a consortium of most U.S. semiconductor firms. It was formed in 1982 to improve basic research and training for young engineers. Four government agencies—DoD, NSF, NSC, and the National Bureau of Standards—have supported SRC's basic research activities. The Defense Science Board is an outside advisory body composed of business leaders and technical experts. Each year, the DSB completes a "summer study" of a technological issue of importance to the Pentagon. The DSB's work is directed by the Pentagon, but does not necessarily reflect DoD's official positions.

41. This maneuver failed to sidetrack supporters of the Semiconductor Agreement, and in early 1987 the NSC passed control over the study to the National Science Foundation. The report's findings were never officially published, but they were leaked to the press in August 1987.

42. Lodge (1990a), pp. 141-142; Author interviews with industry representatives, 1993.

43. SIA representatives presented policymakers with detailed briefing books on the industry and the impact of Japanese targeting. The briefing package was eventually published as Howell et al. (1988). Author Interviews with industry representatives, 1993.

44. The semiconductor industry is divided into two major segments. *Captive* firms produce chips for a single buyer for a specific purpose. Defense semiconductor producers, as well as those companies with in-house production capability (e.g. AT&T, IBM) fall in the captive category. All other firms, which produce for commercial markets, are referred to as *merchant* producers.

45. This proposal was first discussed by industry representatives at an October 1985 Diminishing Manufacturing Sources and Material Shortages Conference in Washington. See Glenn J. McLoughlin and Nancy R. Miller, "The U.S. Semiconductor Industry and the Sematech Proposal," CRS Report 87-354SPR (Washington, D.C.: Congressional Research Service, April 23, 1987), p. 11.

46. Ibid., p. 12.

47. Interviews with various industry officials, 1993.

48. Quoted in Lodge (1990a), p. 139.

49. Defense Science Board (1987), pp. 5-6. Emphasis in original.

50. See testimony by Norman Augustine and Ronald Kerber, deputy under Secretary of defense for research and advanced technology, in U.S. Congress, House Committee on Energy and Commerce, *Trade and Competitiveness (Part 2)*, 100th Congress, 1st Session, March 5, 10, 11, 1987, pp. 175-78.

51. Ibid., p. 185.

52. U.S. Congress, Congressional Budget Office (September 1987), pp. 53-54.

53. Testimony of Norman R. Augustine. U.S. Congress, Senate Committee on Armed Services, *Department of Defense Authorization for Appropriations for Fiscal Years 1988 and 1989*, 100th Congress, 1st Session, March 9, 1987, p. 3324.

54. See Hart (1993), pp. 41-45; 186-88.

55. See Noyce testimony in U.S. Congress, House Committee on Energy and Commrece, Subcommittee on Commerce, Consumer Protection, and Competitiveness (June 9, 1987). A similar argument is made in Tolchin and Tolchin (1992), p. 197.

56. "Consortia and Capital: Industry-Led Policy in the 1990s," White Paper released at "Wake-Up America" Conference in Washington, D.C., May 25, 1989. This paper is included in U.S. Congress, Joint Economic Committee (June 8, 1989), pp. 10-21.

57. See statement of Alexander Lidow, on behalf of SIA, in U.S. Congress, House Committee on Energy and Commerce (1987), pp. 187-91; Statement of Charles Sporck on behalf of SIA, in U.S. Congress, House Committee on Science, Space, and Technology, *The Role of Science and Technology in Competitiveness*, 100th Congress, 1st Session, April 28-30, 1987, pp. 656-59.

58. *Congressional Record*, September 24, 1987, p. S12693.

59. Author interviews with Congressional staff and industry representatives, 1993.

60. U.S. Congress, House Committee on Energy and Commerce (1987), p. 34.

61. Testimony by Admiral Bobby R. Inman, U.S. Congress, Senate Committee on Armed Services (March 9, 1987), p. 3336.

62. U.S. Congress, House Committee on Science, Space and Technology (November 8, 1989), p. 102.

63. Author Interviews.

64. However, Commerce Secretary Malcolm Baldridge did not publicly support the Sematech plan. See Lodge (1990a), p. 144.

65. Author interview.

66. For general background on debate over the 1988 Trade Act, see Pietro S. Nivola, *Regulating Unfair Trade* (Washington, D.C.: Brookings Institution, 1993), pp. 101-6.

67. Author interviews with industry officials, 1993; Lodge (1990a), pp. 146-47.

68. Author interview with industry officials, 1993; Lodge (1990a), p. 145.

69. Ibid.

70. Ibid., p. 144.

71. For background on Sematech's operations since 1988, see U.S. Congress, Congressional Budget Office (July 1990); and U.S. General Accounting Office, *Federal Research: Sematech's Technological Progress and Proposed R&D Program* (Washington, D.C.: GAO, July 1992).

72. See Ibid.; and Daniel Southerland, "Sematech's Critical Juncture," *Washington Post*, August 28, 1992, p. B1. For a more critical view of Sematech's results, see Charlotte Adams, "Was Sematech Worth DoD's $500 Million?" *Military and Aerospace Electronics* (March/April 1992), p. 10.

73. Sematech originally had fourteen members. LSI Logic and Micron Technology, Inc, withdrew from membership in 1992. DARPA funding was slated to end in 1992, but was authorized for an additional five years.

74. See Southerland, "Sematech's Critical Juncture" (August 28, 1992).

75. U.S. General Accounting Office (July 1992).

76. Tyson (1992), p. 154.

6

Yet Another Call to Arms: Revitalizing the Bearings Industry

In addition to crises affecting the machine tool and semiconductor industries, the mid-1980s also witnessed heightened concern in Washington about the condition of the U.S. ball and roller bearings industry. Such fears were not completely new as the competitiveness of this sector had long concerned defense planners. Government efforts to assist the industry on defense grounds date back to World War II and continued at intervals throughout the Cold War era. However, these efforts were ad hoc, and did not involve creation of a comprehensive government strategy for the bearings industry. Stimulated largely by recurrent crises in the industry, earlier government assistance efforts had done little to address the root causes of long-term decline.

By 1986, the situation facing the industry had worsened dramatically. A weakened bearings industry had now become enfeebled, forcing industry leaders to initiate a concerted push for government assistance. Working hand in hand with the Congressional Bearings Caucus and other supporters, the industry sought to follow the lobbying strategies employed by both the machine tool and semiconductor industries. Bearings lobbyists portrayed their industry as an essential building block for both national security and economic competitiveness. Without a government bailout, they argued, the United States would permanently lose this critical production capability. Given the importance of bearings to such critical military items as aircraft engines and heavy vehicles, the industry's decline could have profound repercussions for the U.S. defense posture.

While the bearing industry's strategy was similar to that employed by other sectors, bearing producers did not achieve similar results. Indeed, the push for a sector-specific industrial policy was a colossal failure. The only result of several years of effort was a limited Buy-American restriction enacted by Congress after several years of Pentagon delays.

The bearing industry's failure had several causes, but the most significant factor was the industry's inability to convince the Reagan administration that bearings were strategic on both commercial and national security grounds. Policymakers remained unconvinced about the industry's larger significance and its spillover benefits for the rest of the economy. Unlike semiconductor equipment and machine tools, ball bearings were viewed as an industrial input similar to steel, gears, or nuts and bolts. Even worse, bearings were a component produced more rapidly and inexpensively overseas. Close analysis of the industry's competitive condition and ability to recover convinced the Reagan administration to reject creation of a ball bearing rescue package similar to that developed for other defense-critical sectors.

NATURE OF THE BEARINGS INDUSTRY

Bearings, or antifriction bearings, as they are more formally described, reduce friction between any two moving surfaces. They exist in nearly every machine that contains moving parts, and are produced in two generic types: ball and roller. Each type accounts for approximately 50 percent of world output. Countless other classifications exist within these two broad categories. Overall, more than 200,000 different stock bearings are produced each year, accounting for 70 percent of world output. The remaining 30 percent of world output is based on custom designs. Manufacturing industries, especially automobile production, serve as the primary customers for bearings producers.[1]

Because of these numerous products, different sectors of bearings production face greatly differing competitive environments. Certain types of bearings, such as superprecision miniature bearings for use in guidance and control instruments, computer disk drives, and fire control mechanisms, are more complex and costly to produce. In contrast, bearings for turbine engines and gear boxes require low-cost, high-volume production. Learning economies characterize the superprecision sector, but play a limited role in high-volume production for engine bearings and other less sophisticated uses.

The defense dependency of various sectors also differs. Military purchases account for a large portion of the market in the superprecision and instrument bearing sectors.[2] For example, in 1987, defense shipments accounted for 53 percent of all U.S. superprecision bearing shipments.[3] Defense markets play a much less important role for other product types, such as tapered roller bearings and cylindrical bearings.[4]

World bearing production is highly concentrated. In 1986, the United States, Japan, and Germany accounted for 71 percent of world production.[5] Five firms, none based in the U.S account for more than 50 percent of world production.[6] Table 6.1 provides data on the performance and concentration of the world bearing industry in recent decades.

U.S. production is similarly concentrated.[7] Two firms, Timken and Torrington, dominate American production. In 1986, the Commerce Department estimated that only fifty American firms, with 140 U.S. facilities, produced complete bearings. An additional thirty-seven firms produced various parts and components.[8] Total industry

Table 6.1
World Bearings Industry: Company and World Market Share

Company World Market Share (%)

	1955	1970	1987
Japanese Firms			
NSK	1.4	4.8	10.0
NTN	1.6	5.7	9.8
Koyo	0.8	5.5	7.3
N-F	0..4	1.7	2.4
Minabea	0.0	0.3	3.3
	4.2	**18.0**	**32.8**
European Firms			
SKF	25.6	26.4	24.3
FAG	7.0	8.4	12.0
INA	2.5	2.1	6.0
SNR	2.5	2.2	1.4
RHP	3.8	3.5	1.5
	41.4	**42.6**	**45.2**
U.S. Firms			
Timken	15.6	9.7	7.7
Torrington	3.8	3.1	5.7
Federal Mogul	4.4	3.4	1.8
New Departure Hyatt	19.0	8.6	4.2
Kaydon	1.3	2.7	0.9
Fafnir	1.9	4.3	Not in existence
Other	8.3	7.1	1.8
	54.3	**39.3**	**21.5**

Source: Annual Reports, Company Estimates. Compiled in Collis (1991), p. 54.

employment for 1987 was 43,400.[9] Like the machine tool business, the U.S. bearing industry is small, highly specialized, and regionally concentrated.

INDUSTRY HISTORY

American firms were dominant players in world bearing markets for much of the twentieth century. This strong position derived from state-of-the-art technology, but it was also based on access to a large domestic market for both civilian and military goods. The U.S. automobile industry was an especially important customer for bearings producers, purchasing about 30-40 percent of the industry's output.[10]

Defense firms, and DoD itself, represented another major purchaser of bearings. The military uses enormous quantities and varieties of bearings. For example, the C-17 transport plane requires 10,000 bearings; the typical helicopter uses roughly 2,500 bearings.[11] In 1986, direct and indirect military consumption of bearings accounted for 19 percent of total U.S. consumption.[12] As we saw earlier, defense consumption plays an even more important role in the superprecision and instrument bearing sectors.

As American manufacturers prospered during the 1950s, both civilian and military bearing producers also enjoyed boom times. But as U.S. manufacturing industries began to be overtaken by foreign competitors, bearing producers were also hard-hit. In fact, problems in the U.S. bearing industry arose much earlier than in other sectors, such as machine tools or automobiles.

The beginning of the industry's decline dates back to the early 1960s, but accelerated most rapidly in the late 1970s and early 1980s. Table 6.2 provides some indications of the U.S.' relative performance during these years. The period from 1980 to 1987 was particularly difficult, as the industry as imports increased by 16.7 percent while exports declined by 28.5 percent (in constant dollars). During that same period, employment levels in the industry declined an average of 5.4 percent per year, compared to only 1.8 percent for all manufacturing industries.[13] Between 1978 and 1988, twenty-nine U.S. bearings plants were closed.[14] By 1986, most of the American bearing industry was in a state of virtual collapse.

The industry's deterioration had several causes. The rise of new competition certainly hurt U.S. firms, but foreign success in world markets was not a new phenomenon. After all, the world's largest firm, the Swedish conglomerate SKF, retained its position as the industry leader from the 1950s through the 1980s. The major shift came in the rise of Japanese firms, which captured market share at the expense of American businesses.

Japanese firms were relatively new players in world bearing markets, accounting for only 4.2 percent of global production in 1955. The rise of Japan's bearing industry resulted in part from close cooperation between individual firms and MITI.[15] In 1956, MITI helped organize Japanese producers into a cartel to help manage production and sell bearings through a jointly owned intermediary. Japanese firms were further assisted by *keiretsu* arrangements and long-term contracts with firms like Toyota, Nissan, and Mitsubishi. These ties provided Japanese bearing producers with access to long-term capital, and entree into the international market. They also served to restrict bearing imports into Japanese markets.

Table 6.2
World Bearing Industry Performance

Share of largest seven countries' production (%)

	US	Japan	Germany	UK	France	Italy	Sweden	Thai-land
1955	61.0	2.8	10.7	8.1	NA	NA	3.3	0.0
1960	53.5	8.1	12.6	8.1	8..3	NA	3.6	0.0
1965	53.4	9.1	13.7	8.4	6.6	NA	3.7	0.0
1970	41.8	19.1	17.6	7.6	5.5	5.4	3.0	0.0
1975	40.0	19.4	19.1	6.4	6.8	5.5	2.7	0.0
1980	39.0	19.3	20.2	6.2	6.9	5.8	2.6	0.0
1985	44.6	26.2	14.4	3.2	5.4	4.2	2.0	0..9
1988	30.1	32.8	19.0	3.9	7.1	4.3	2.0	0.6
Share of World Prod-uction (%)								
1988	24.4	25.9	15.0	3.1	5.6	3.4	1.6	0.5

Source: U.S. Bureau of Census, Japan Bearing Industry Association, Torrington, FAG. Compiled in Colllis (1991), p. 53.

U.S. industry representatives viewed this industrial targeting as the key to the success of Japanese firms such as Minabea and NMB. In their view, the Japanese system gave its firms an unfair advantage that U.S. businesses could never overcome. For example, one U.S. executive, referring to Japanese industrial policy, argued that "if these practices were done in the United States, the people involved would go to jail. . . . the Japanese businessmen now have carte blanche to avoid all the laws that we as American businessmen have to follow."[16]

While the rise of foreign competition was important, many of the industry's problems were self-induced. U.S. firms had done little to rationalize the industry in comparison to their Japanese and European competitors. As a result, U.S. firms were smaller and less integrated. Large size permitted the foreign firms to offer a full line of bearing products, contributed to more efficient production, and eased foreign producers' ability to continue investing in new plant and equipment. In comparison to foreign companies, many American firms devoted a much lower percentage of corporate income to R&D and investment.[17] Thus, the industry had done little to maintain its future technological and price competitiveness. As the domestic suppliers weakened, U.S. bearing customers turned to overseas producers, further reinforcing the vicious spiral affecting U.S. producers. Declining market share, neglect of reinvestment, and a host of other factors all coalesced to increase imports into the United States and decrease the ability of American firms to compete in global markets.

National Security Responses

Military officials had long recognized the national security importance of bearing production. For example, German bearing producers were a primary target of the Allied bombing campaign in World War II.[18] In addition to targeting foreign supplies, U.S. mobilization agencies also sought to guarantee secure bearing supplies at home by subsidizing nearly $100 million in bearing plant expansion and construction during the war.[19]

Although the industry reached its lowest point in 1986, its competitive weaknesses had concerned the Pentagon for many years. Periodically, DoD had supported modernization of bearing production through the Defense Production Act (DPA) and its MANTECH and IMIP programs.[20] The most dramatic step occurred in 1971 when DoD instituted Buy American regulations governing defense purchases of miniature and instrument bearings.

While these efforts provided some limited support, they did not constitute a defense industrial policy for the bearings sector. First, the restrictions applied only to precision bearings. Other types of bearings were exempt from the provisions. During the 1980s, industry representatives were most concerned about deterioration in these nonprecision sectors.

Secondly, the Buy-American regulations were subject to many exemptions. For example, as we saw in Chapter One, producers from MOU countries were often exempted from the restrictions. In addition, service procurement officers were also authorized to offer exemptions on a case-by-case basis.

Finally, procurement restrictions did little to address the primary causes of the industry's decline—its inability to invest in new plant and equipment and remain technologically competitive. Addressing these problems required a more activist government response.

A NEW PUSH FOR ACTION

By 1985, the industry was reeling and began a campaign seeking a government-led rescue. Working through their association, the Anti-Friction Bearing

Manufacturers of America (AFBMA)[21], U.S. producers enlisted the support of the Congressional Bearings Caucus, an informal group of approximately sixty senators and representatives headed by Rep. Nancy Johnson (R-CT) and Rep. John Spratt (D-SC).[22]

The Bearings Caucus and AFBMA began this effort by passing legislation that required the Pentagon to assess the impact of DOD's growing dependence on imported bearings. In response to this mandate, William Howard Taft IV, the deputy secretary of defense, directed the Joint Logistics Commanders (JLC) to conduct a study of the criticality of the bearing industry to the U.S. defense posture.

The JLC's study, released on June 18, 1986, painted an alarming picture of the industry's condition, describing "an industry on the precipice."[23] According to the JLC, foreign (i.e., Japanese) firms had specifically targeted high-volume bearing markets. Their success at the high-volume end forced U.S. producers into specialty niche (mainly defense) markets characterized by low profit, low volume, and high-cost production runs. Forced into these unprofitable niches, U.S. producers became increasingly unwilling to reinvest in modern capital equipment. This lack of investment created a vicious cycle, further weakening U.S. firms and opening up new markets to foreign competition.[24] As U.S. firms exited from profitable product lines, foreign businesses replaced them. The JLC report expressed strong fears about the potential national security ramifications of these trends. As the JLC noted,

> If this trend is permitted to continue, qualified domestic producers will be forced to shut down production lines. . . . Company officials estimate that it would take at least four years to rebuild capability to produce superprecision bearings. . . . As [U.S. manufacturers] increase their use of foreign bearings, additional limits are placed on domestic firms' ability to respond to surge and mobilization. . . . increased dependence on foreign sources can lead to interruption of supply during an emergency, placing our nation's defense posture in jeopardy.[25]

The JLC concluded with a series of policy recommendations quite similar to those developed by the DSB for semiconductor manufacturing and by the Manufacturing Studies Board for the machine tool industry. As short term remedies, the report called for a widening of the 1971 Buy American restrictions to cover all bearing types, expanding DoD funding for U.S. plant modernization, and restricting transfer of bearing technology to U.S. allies.[26] The JLC report also advocated more dramatic long-term measures. These remedies included quotas on bearing imports, tighter antidumping enforcement, antitrust exemptions to ease domestic mergers, low-interest loans, and a special investment tax credit for bearing producers.[27]

Industry officials were pleased with these findings and viewed the JLC report as a rallying point for action.[28] The far-reaching recommendations were also well received in Congress, especially by the Bearing Caucus members. Additional support came from the military services, who had participated in the study through membership on the JLC.

Unfortunately, this low-level support did little to convince skeptics. Inside the Pentagon, the higher levels of the Office of the Secretary of Defense were strongly opposed to the JLC recommendations. High-level DoD opposition was based on the fear that a bail-out for the bearing industry would encourage other industries to press for government intervention.[29] Moreover, if approved, trade protection would increase costs for the DoD, and, in many cases, provide the U.S. military with an inferior product.[30]

Even Malcolm Baldridge, traditionally a supporter of U.S. manufacturers, failed to weigh in on the industry's behalf. OSD's opposition, combined with that of OMB, Treasury, and other economic agencies, succeeded in postponing action on the JLC recommendations.

Fearing administration delays similar to those seen in the machine tool case, the AFBMA acted quickly. Eventually, the Congressional Bearing Caucus succeeded in inserting language into the fiscal year 1987 defense appropriations bill that required DoD to submit a Bearing Action Plan based on the JLC's conclusions. This plan, published in draft form in March 1987, accepted most of the JLC's recommendations for short-term remedies. Its centerpiece was a call for imposition of Buy American restrictions on *all* bearings purchased directly or indirectly by the DoD for use in military end-items or subassemblies.

Yet despite this tangible progress, business as usual continued. While DoD considered draft Buy American regulations, no additional initiatives were under consideration. The bearing industry's problems received limited attention, while the plight of machine tools, semiconductors, and other sectors took center stage.

Filing for Trade Restrictions

Government inaction caused endless frustration for the industry and its supporters. Moreover, many U.S. manufacturers felt that the JLC's recommendations would have little impact; a more comprehensive trade response was also required. As Joseph F. Toot, Jr., the President of Timken, noted:

> DoD actions alone will not resolve the problems facing the U.S. bearing industry. . . . It is caught in a battle for market share with foreign competitors—and many of our adversaries continue to compete unfairly. . . . [We must take] direct action to see that foreign producers no longer are allowed to flout the fair-trade regulations existing in America.[31]

The AFBMA eventually reached a decision to consider additional steps that might trigger a government response. However, creating industry consensus was a difficult task, as many AFBMA members opposed demands for trade protection. After much internal wrangling, the association ultimately decided to request quotas on bearing imports.[32]

On July 17, 1987, the industry filed a Section 232 petition for trade relief. The petition requested temporary quotas on seven categories of bearings. During the period of the quotas, the industry would "rebuild its severely deteriorated industrial base and, as necessary, expand capacity to the level required to meet the nation's need in a future national emergency."[33]

AFBMA chose this approach for several reasons.[34] First, the 232 petition kept the process "depoliticized." Because the 232 investigation process was highly technical, AFBMA hoped to avoid contentious political debates such as those surrounding the Omnibus Trade bill making its way through Congress at that time. Moreover, the 232 process did not require AFBMA to "name names." In contrast, antidumping petitions (another option considered by AFBMA) require petitioners to single out individual firms or countries as violators. Since the AFBMA included foreign firms as members, the association was reluctant to pursue that option.

Second, the 232 process's focus on national security proved politically attractive. Because protection would be based on military grounds, "free-traders" in the Reagan administration might be less likely to oppose the petition. Moreover, this national security emphasis also allowed the industry to use points raised in the JLC report. As one industry representative noted, "After all, we didn't have to do a lot of work in terms of making the case that the industry was critical to national security. The JLC had done the work for us, and the study was produced by the Department of Defense."[35]

Finally, the AFBMA was encouraged by the success of the NMTBA's petition in 1986. While the industry recognized that successful 232 petitions were rare, the machine tool industry's success raised hopes that the bearing industry might repeat that effort.

The industry's case was somewhat similar to that developed by NMTBA in its filing three years earlier. However, the AFBMA did little to emphasize the commercial significance of bearings. Its case rested on the impact of job losses in the bearings sector and the national security importance of the industry.

Job losses in the industry were indeed severe. For example, between 1980 and 1984, total bearing industry employment declined from 57,900 to 49,600,[36] with production jobs dropping 20.4 percent.[37] The high skill levels of these displaced workers made them difficult to replace. For example, the AFBMA noted that anywhere from six months to two years of training was required for the most critical functions in bearing manufacturing.[38]

This emphasis on job loss proved politically attractive at a time when competitiveness had become a buzzword in Washington. Nonetheless, the industry's case rested almost exclusively its the national security importance. Even AFBMA's arguments regarding job losses reflected national security concerns that the loss of skilled labor might inhibit mobilization in the event of a future conflict.

Ironically, the industry did not cite clear indicators of weakness in defense-critical bearing sectors.[39] After all, U.S. firms maintained technological superiority in the sector most critical to defense—superprecision bearings. However, imports in other sectors had increased significantly. According to AFBMA, overall import penetration threatened the entire bearing industry and its ability to continue supplying defense needs in key niche markets. The industry noted in a widely circulated brochure that "The present strength of our U.S. bearings industry is at the core of its vulnerability. Our uncommon capability for producing the full range of . . . highly specialized bearings . . . is a precious national resource. But unfairly priced imports of high-volume popular parts are eating the heart out of the bearings industry."[40]

The industry's national security claims rested on several points. First, AFBMA stressed the industry's importance in supporting surge mobilization, that is, the ability to quickly expand and accelerate production in the event of a crisis. In presenting its argument, the industry could point to recent history where bearing shortages had created significant bottlenecks in defense production. During the Vietnam conflict, for example, helicopters were grounded for long periods due to bearing shortages, and some U.S. bearings firms faced military order backlogs extending to two years.[41] More recently, during the Falklands War, bearings imports for use in U.S. production of the M1A1 tank were disrupted, shutting down manufacturing for two months.[42]

Second, the industry emphasized the pervasiveness of bearings in military products. This point was raised by the industry on nearly every occasion. For example, in a March 3, 1988, letter to Defense Secretary Frank Carlucci, the members of the Congressional Bearing Caucus noted: "Bearings are key components in almost all major military equipment, including aircraft, tanks, and submarines. If we lose our domestic bearing industry, our military would become dangerously dependent on foreign nations to supply us with these vital components."[43]

Few observers could question the industry on this point. In addition to the JLC report, AFBMA could point to reams of congressional testimony where Pentagon officials highlighted DoD's pervasive use of bearings.[44]

Finally, the AFBMA argued that previous Buy American restrictions had failed to preserve a domestic production base. They noted further that the draft restrictions announced in March 1987 would also prove ineffective. As one industry representative bluntly stated, "How effective can the FAR [Federal Acquisition Regulation] be when it only protects 15-20% of bearing production? . . . My personal view is that the FAR at best will only slow down the inevitable. . . . Only by the restriction of imports for *all* bearing uses can we insure an adequate industrial base.[45]

Based on all of these factors, the AFBMA felt it had devised an effective case for a government-led rescue package. Nonetheless, its efforts encountered extensive opposition from the outset. Much of the opposition arose from foreign bearing producers, many of which actually belonged to AFBMA. FAG, a German firm with production facilities in Joplin, Missouri, was especially active in opposing the AFBMA petition. Working with Rep. Gene Taylor (R-MO), FAG mounted a high-level campaign against quotas on imported bearings.

The AFBMA also faced opposition from other U.S.-based industries, especially vehicle, engine, and heavy equipment companies that purchased bearings in large quantities. These firms contended that U.S. bearing producers were incapable of meeting their current needs. They also noted that most U.S. bearing producers relied on foreign sources of bearing steel.[46] Fully addressing the problem of bearings dependence would thus require expansion of existing VRAs for specialty steel. As a representative of Caterpillar, Inc., argued, "Ball and roller bearings are industrial inputs. They appear in the middle of the production process between raw material and finished product. Attempting to assess the national security impact of ball and roller bearing imports in isolation is an exercise in futility."[47]

These engine and equipment manufacturers argued that bearing quotas would actually hurt the U.S. DIB by hampering industry's ability to supply key components like engines and turbines. Caterpillar's representative further argued: "If the assumption that foreign suppliers...are unreliable is correct, then restricting bearing imports, and thereby speeding up the relocation of the construction equipment and similarly situated industries to foreign locations will adversely affect national security. . . . It is a lot simpler to import ball bearings than D9 tractors!"[48]

Finally, AFBMA faced the expected opposition from free traders in the Reagan administration. Ironically, the success of the NMTBA's petition in 1986 worked against bearing producers. Many in the administration actively opposed the bearing petition out of fear that its approval might set a stronger precedent and trigger additional applications for protection based on national security grounds.[49]

Administration opposition was also strengthened by the industry's failure to implement extensive self-help measures. As we saw in the machine tool case, the industry's efforts to create NCMS and expand investment were critical to their petition's success. Commenting on the bearing petition and other industry requests for protection, DoD's undersecretary for acquisition, Robert Costello, noted: "Some would want us to subsidize obsolescence and we don't want to do that. . . . When [industries] lay out a plan to become world-wide competitive, then we'll be there to help."[50]

Unfortunately, U.S. bearing producers did little to initiate cooperative self-help efforts.[51] The industry had considered creating a consortium along the lines of Sematech and NCMS, but this effort ultimately collapsed. Thus, in contrast to the semiconductor manufacturing and machine tool industries, the AFBMA was simply requesting protection without initiating domestic-based efforts to revitalize production. A former DoD official was quite critical of the industry on these grounds, arguing that U.S. producers were "behind the power curve" and "resting on past laurels."[52] This official further noted that the industry "wanted Buy American and *then* they would re-invest in plant and equipment."[53]

Final Action on 232

The Commerce Department completed its 232 investigation on July 15, 1988. It concluded that the domestic bearings industry could meet most, but not all, national security requirements in the event of a major war. It postponed responding to the AFBMA's call for trade protection, arguing that it would first examine the effect of DoD's Bearing Action Plan. President Reagan accepted this finding on August 10, 1988, and directed DoD and the Commerce Department to complete their examination of the impact of ongoing administration initiatives by the end of 1988.

The joint DoD-Commerce study, completed on November 28, 1988, ultimately rejected the AFBMA petition. Commerce's analysis found that the likely impact of DoD's Bearing Action Plan, combined with improved economic conditions, were sufficient to maintain an effective domestic industrial base for bearings.[54] It recommended no other relief measures.[55]

In August 1988, after two years of delay, DoD finally published its Buy American restrictions for antifriction bearings.[56] These restrictions have not been effectively implemented. In addition to containing traditional exemptions for MOU countries, the restrictions were not regularly included in many DoD contracts. In fiscal year 1989, for example, DoD's inspector general found that 68 percent of awarded contracts did not contain the bearing restrictions.[57] The situation improved in fiscal years 1990 and 1991, but implementation still remained spotty.[58] A February 1993 Commerce Department study concluded that the restrictions had assisted the U.S. superprecision bearing sector, but had not had an appreciable effect on other sectors of the bearing industry.[59]

While the Buy American restrictions have had little impact,[60] the industry's condition has improved in the past five years.[61] Intense foreign competition forced many American firms to modernize manufacturing and enhance training for both management and labor. The period from 1988 to 1991 also saw significant increases in investment, R&D, and industry profitability.[62]

BACK TO THE FUTURE? BEARINGS AND
A RETURN TO LAISSEZ-FAIRE

Despite an intensive lobbying campaign and a clear indication of industrial decline, the AFBMA and its supporters failed to persuade the Reagan administration that extraordinary action was required to preserve a domestic ball and roller bearing capability. A similar fate awaited several other industries, including plastic injection molding machinery, gears, and industrial fasteners, which also filed for national security protection at roughly the same time.

Given the NMTBA's 1986 success in fostering an industrial policy for machine tools, the failure of the AFBMA may appear somewhat surprising. The machine tool case had set a precedent for government intervention based on national security grounds. Most importantly, from the AFBMA's perspective, it had also set the precedent for a positive ruling on a Section 232 petition.

The AFBMA's failure can be partially attributed to the industry's own internal weaknesses. The industry was small, and, as we saw above, it was not completely united behind the petition. In retrospect, AFBMA lobbyists described this lack of internal cooperation as a critical weakness. Without internal agreement, the industry's case was weak from the start. As one representative argued: "Basically, the debate came down to laissez-faire versus protection. In a Republican Administration, a small industry wasn't going to win—even if we were viewed as critical to defense."[63]

These limitations clearly impacted the AFBMA, but similar problems also affected the NMTBA. Like the AFBMA, the NMTBA was a small, geographically concentrated industry, with limited clout on Capitol Hill. The NMTBA also faced significant anti-protectionist pressures. Indeed, the pressure facing the NMTBA was probably more intense. Prior to 1986, there was no precedent for imposing national security-based trade quotas for manufacturing industries.

The real cause of the bearing industry's failure lies not in the political pressures cited so often by pluralist writers. Instead, it lies in the weakness of the AFBMA's case and the enhanced ability of policymakers to critically examine the industry's arguments.

The AFBMA clearly failed in its efforts to develop a compelling case for government intervention. Its arguments suffered from several critical weaknesses. First, the industry failed to present any evidence for its commercial criticality. It presented no evidence that improvements in bearing manufacturing would spill over into other sectors of the economy. AFBMA's case rested almost exclusively on the fact that bearings had been critical in past wars and that nearly all major weapons systems contained bearings. As we saw in the two previous chapters, industrial policy was likely only in cases where industries were considered critical on both military and commercial grounds.

Second, the industry sought trade protection for the entire bearing industry based on the national security importance of only one sector—the precision bearing industry. However, the precision bearing sector remained relatively competitive in comparison to other sectors.[64] Thus, the most defense-critical sector was also the sector least impacted by imports.

Finally, the AFBMA did not initiate self-help efforts through industry-wide consortia or other means. Industry involvement was viewed as critical by Pentagon officials. For example, Deputy Assistant Secretary of Defense Robert McCormack offered a veiled hint to the industry when he noted in 1988: "I must reiterate the need for action by the bearing community. The continuation of this [Buy American] restriction will largely depend on a positive response by industry. We must see a measurable difference in industry commitment to improve product quality and to lower costs."[65] Because it was viewed as requesting a government "hand-out," the bearing industry's plight generated little sympathy from the Reagan administration.

While the AFBMA's case was relatively weak, another important factor in the industry's failure was the improved analytical ability resident in top policymaking circles in Washington. The Reagan administration's decision to reject the bearing petition rested on several factors. For one thing, DoD was determined that it would not provide the sole support for an industry.[66] In comparison to the semiconductor manufacturing and machine tool industries, bearing companies appeared unwilling to cooperate in collaborative research or other joint ventures. Most importantly, bearing producers were unwilling to contribute their own funds to R&D and investment. In the eyes of many government officials, the industry had not tried to help itself and, as one DoD representative noted, "they were looking for a government bail-out."[67]

In addition to highlighting the industry's failure to help itself, government officials also pointed out that bearings were simply not a strategic industry. While bearings did exist in many weapons systems, their production did not generate externalities that offered economic benefits to other industrial sectors. In the words of one DoD official, bearings were not "wealth generators" like machine tools and semiconductors.[68] They were simply a component that happened to be used in a wide variety of weapons systems.

CONCLUSIONS

Based on this analysis, the Reagan administration responded to a national security problem with a national security solution. Facing intense congressional pressure, it imposed limited Buy American restrictions on bearings. It did not expand R&D funding for bearings producers or consider other remedies for the industry's plight. In sum, it continued with existing DIB policy toward U.S. bearing producers.

While the bearing case concluded with a status quo response, this decision was not reached via a status quo process. Instead of simply rejecting industry's pleas at the outset, administration officials did attempt to analyze the industry's claims in a rigorous manner. The bearing case offers a clear indication that the Pentagon, the Commerce Department, and other relevant agencies were searching for means to discriminate between "worthy" industries and those that did not warrant government support. While one cannot claim that a completely rational and scientifically rigorous review process was in place, the Administration's recognition of the bearing industry's plight and its full review of potential options represented a dramatic change from previous DIB policies. In the bearings case, the public policy debate proceeded outside of the glare of the media spotlight. In Chapter Seven, we analyze a similar debate which occurred amidst great media and public attention: the effort to support the development of high-definition television.

NOTES

1. See David J. Collis, "A Resource-Based Analysis of Global Competition: The Case of the Bearings Industry," *Strategic Management Journal* Vol. 12 (1991), p. 53. For background on U.S. industry, see U.S. Department of Commerce, International Trade Administration, *A Competitive Assessment of the U.S. Ball and Roller Bearings Industry* (Washington, D.C.: Department of Commerce, February 1985). Hereafter referred to as ITA Bearings Study.

2. DoD directly purchases very few bearings; most demand is indirect, generated by the purchase of end items containing bearings. Donna J. S. Peterson, Gerald T, Kelley, and Myron G. Myers, *An Assessment of the Economic Status of the Antifriction Bearing Industry* (Bethesda, Md.: Logistics Management Institute, October 1991), pp. 2-2, A-3.

3. U.S. Department of Commerce, Bureau of Export Administration, *National Security Assessment of the Antifriction Bearings Industry* (Washington, D.C.: Department of Commerce, February 1993), pp. 19-20.

4. Peterson et al (1991), pp. A3-A4.

5. France and the United Kingdom also maintain large domestic production capacity; they account for an additional 8 percentof world bearing production. See U.S. Department of Commerce, Bureau of Export Administration, *The Effect of Imports of Anti-Friction Bearings on the National Security* (Washington, D.C.: Department of Commerce, July 1988), p. II-1. Hereafter referred to as Bearings 232 Study.

6. Ibid.., p. II-3.

7. Although a few U.S. firms dominate the American market, the U.S. bearings industry is much less concentrated than its foreign counterparts. In 1986, the top eight U.S. firms produced 58 percent of completed bearings. In Europe and Japan, the top eight firms controlled more than 90 percent of production. Moreover, concentration in U.S. industry declined in the 1980s as foreign competition has displaced U.S. firms from high-volume markets. Bearings 232 Study, p. III-4.

8. Ibid.., p. II-9.

9. Ibid., p. II-11.

10. Collis (1991), p. 53.

11. Bearings 232 Study, p. I-4.

12. Ibid., p. I-4.

13. Peterson et al (1991), pp. 3-2, 3-5.

14. Bearings 232 Study, p. VI-18.

15. Ibid., pp. III-2 - III-4.

16. Statement of Augustine Sperrazza, in U.S. Congress, Joint Economic Committee, *Impact on the U.S. Economy of Imbalanced and Unfair Trade Relations-The Case of Japan*, 99th Congress, 1st Session, August 22, 1985, p. 38.

17. Bearings 232 Study, pp. III-10 - III-12.

18. For background, see Milward, pp. 49-57. This episode was widely cited by the bearing industry in Congressional testimony and formal requests for trade relief. For example, see the remarks of Augustine Sperazza, CEO of Kubar Bearings, in U.S. Congress, Joint Economic Committee (August 22, 1985).

19. Bearings 232 Study, p. VI-17.

20. For example, in the early 1980s, DPA funds were utilized to support Barden's production of "noise quiet" submarine bearings. Similarly, IMIP funds supported modernization of Torrington's Fafnir facility in 1987. Author interviews with Defense Department officials, 1993.

21. Now known as the American Bearing Manufacturers Association (ABMA). Based in Washington, the ABMA includes foreign firms as members. However, these companies must maintain manufacturing facilities in the United States.

22. The caucus was established at the suggestion of the AFBMA, led by Torrington Bearings. Torrington, based in Rep. Johnson's Connecticut district, is one of the largest U.S. bearing manufacturers. Author interviews with industry and Congressional officials, 1993.

23. U.S. Department of Defense, Joint Bearing Working Group, *Joint Logistics Commanders Bearing Study* (Washington, D.C.: JLC, June 18, 1986). Hereafter referred to as JLC Bearing Study.

24. Ibid., p. ii.

25. Ibid., p. iii.

26. Ibid., pp. 68-69.

27. Ibid., pp. 69-71.

28. Author interview with industry representatives, 1993.

29. Author interviews with DoD and Commerce Department representatives, 1993.

30. For background on the DoD perspective, see U.S. Department of Defense (July 1989).

31. Joseph F. Toot, Jr., "Defense Dept. Alone Can't Save U.S. Bearing Industry," *Industry Week*, January 26, 1987, p. 14.

32. The industry had considered requesting trade relief on national security grounds for some time. Indeed, the AFBMA had formally begun considering a 232 petition as far back as February 1983. Author interviews with industry officials, 1993.

33. Bearings 232 Study, p. A4.

34. The following points are based on author interviews with industry representatives, 1993.

35. Author interviews with industry representatives, 1993.

36. AFBMA petition.

37. "A Strategic Industry at Its Turning Point," Brochure distributed by AFBMA.

38. Bearings 232 Study, Tab A, p. 2.

39. However, DoD did estimate that 35 percent of bearings used by the Pentagon were procured from foreign sources. See U.S. Congress, Senate Committee on Small Business, *Problems Affecting the Domestic Ball and Roller Bearing Industry*, 100th Congress, 2nd

Session, September 8, 1988, p. 252.

40. See "A Strategic Industry at its Turning Point."

41. ITA Bearings Study, p. 59.

42. Bearings 232 study, p. III-19.

43. Letter from Congressional Bearing Caucus to the Honorable Frank C. Carlucci, III. Mimeo.

44. For example, see statement of Robert McCormack, Deputy Assistant Secretary of Defense for Production Support, in U.S. Congress, Senate Committee on Small Business (September 8, 1988), p. 234. In this testimony, McCormack describes bearings "to be as critical to our military readiness as munitions or weapon systems."

45. Statement of Donald K. Brush, vice president and general manager, Bearing Product Operations, The Barden Corporation, in U.S. Congress, Senate Committee on Small Business (September 8, 1988), pp. 137-138.

46. Bearings require high-quality specialty steel. Steel is the most expensive input in bearing production and accounts for roughly 15-20 percent of shipment value. Bearings 232 Study, p. III-14.

47. Comments of Stephen C. Hoffman, Caterpillar, Inc. in U.S. Congress, Senate Committee on Small Business (September 8, 1988), p. 57. Caterpillar's position prompted Sen. Alan Dixon (D-IL), long identified for his efforts to strengthen the U.S. DIB, to oppose the AFBMA petition.

48. Ibid., p. 57.

49. Author interviews with industry officials and Department of Commerce representatives, 1993.

50. Quoted in Tim Carrington, "Military's Dependence on Foreign Suppliers Causes Rising Concern," *Wall Street Journal*, March 24, 1988, p. 1.

51. Although industry-wide cooperation never proceeded, many individual firms had initiated major investments in R&D and new plant and equipment. For background on the efforts of one successful U.S. firm, the Canton, Ohio-based Timken, see Ralph King, Jr., "You Do the Job or You're Dead," *Forbes*, October 3, 1988, pp. 56-58.

52. Author interview with Defense Department officials, 1993.

53. Ibid. Emphasis added.

54. "Statement by Secretary of Commerce C. William Verity on Anti-Friction Bearings," U.S. Department of Commerce News, November 28, 1988.

55. While the AFBMA's petition was rejected, several U.S. firms did succeed in winning anti-dumping cases against individual foreign producers. These filings were unconnected to the AFBMA Section 232 petition. See Peterson et al (1991), pp. 4-2 - 4-3. This study found that the anti-dumping duties provided significant economic benefits to American firms.

56. Publication of the final rule resulted from yet another legislative provision inserted in the DoD appropriations bill by members of the Congressional Bearings Caucus.

57. U.S. Department of Defense, Office of the Inspector General, *Quick-Reaction Report on the Review of the Restrictive Contract Clause on Antifriction Bearings*, Report No. 92-067 (Washington, D.C.: DoD, April 3, 1992).

58. Ibid. In FY1990 and FY1991, 40 percent of army and navy contracts still omitted the Buy American restrictions. However, nearly all Air Force and Defense Logistics Agency contracts contained the clause.

59. U.S. Department of Commerce, Bureau of Export Administration, (February 1993), pp. 75-76.

60. Peterson et al. (1991), pp. 5-10—5-11.

61. The most recent study of the U.S. bearing industry is U.S. Department of Commerce, Bureau of Export Administration, (February 1993).

62. Ibid., pp. 36-47.
63. Author interview with industry representatives, 1993.
64. See 232 Bearing Study, pp. II-14; V9-V10.
65. U.S. Congress, Senate Committee on Small Business (September 8, 1988), p. 239.
66. Author interviews with DoD representatives; Costello Report (DoD, July 1988).
67. Ibid.
68. Author interview with DoD officials, 1993.

7

HDTV: A Strategic Industry at Risk?

Undeterred by the failure of the ball bearing and other sectors and emboldened by the example of Sematech, other industries began to emphasize their strategic nature. Prominent among these was the U.S. consumer electronics industry, especially those firms interested in high-definition television, better known as HDTV. As the Bush administration entered office in 1989, HDTV advocates were ready, touting HDTV as a strategic industry that could help restore American dominance in consumer electronics.

This initiative provoked a heated public policy debate[1] much more intense than that found in our other case studies. It appeared for a short time that HDTV advocates might succeed in creating a mini-industrial policy for this sector. Indeed, both the Commerce Department and DARPA originally approved such an effort. In the end, however, a closer analysis of the industry and the case for intervention revealed a sector of limited strategic importance on both commercial and national security grounds. This analysis doomed HDTV to defeat.

WHAT IS HDTV?

HDTV is not simply better television.[2] HDTV does provide a better television picture comparable to a movie and twice as clear as conventional televisions, but HDTV also lies at the heart of the next generation in communications technology. Combined with other technologies such as computers and interactive video, HDTV could serve as a vital link in the creation of a whole range of new information services.

The potential market for HDTV was considered huge. Forecasts in the late 1980s projected U.S. sales of HDTVs at ten to fifteen million sets annually within fifteen years. By 2003, the projected market value of HDTV ranged between $5 billion and $12 billion.[3] A report prepared for the National Telecommunications and Information

Administration (NTIA) went even further, arguing that the advanced television (ATV) market could be worth up to $144 billion in twenty years.[4] Potential market value grew even more rapidly if other high resolution systems were included.

The vast potential for this market made it an especially attractive candidate for government intervention. As one advocate, Rep. Don Ritter (R-PA) argued: "For America to miss out on HDTV is to miss out on the 21st century. It's as simple as that."[5]

However, market considerations were not the only factors driving interest in HDTV. HDTV advocates also raised concerns about the dangers of dependence on foreign producers of HDTV and related products. Such concerns permeated congressional debates of 1989. Ishiharo's *The Japan that Can Say No* was cited on numerous occasions, raising the specter of Japanese control of critical electronics markets. Alfred Sikes, assistant secretary of commerce for communications and information, noted that U.S. weakness in HDTV-related markets had forced American firms to purchase critical parts from their foreign competitors, making them dangerously dependent on the Japanese supply of "'choke point' components and technologies."[6]

U.S. weaknesses in HDTV also raised the potential for commercial dependence which created dangerous problems of its own.[7] First, American firms would not control patent rights. As a result, profits would flow overseas and be used to spur innovation and develop new technologies outside the U.S. These impacts would be felt in HDTV and the whole range of spin-off technologies affected by HDTV. Second, job growth would be impacted. Valuable, high-technology jobs in R&D and engineering would be lost, replaced by jobs in service and assembly that offered fewer benefits to the economy. In the eyes of its advocates, HDTV offered the means to avoid such dependence and also ensure American dominance in the critical technology areas of the future.

The Development of HDTV

One must return to the rise and decline of the American consumer electronics industry to fully understand the enthusiasm for HDTV.[8] Consumer electronics offers the paradigmatic example of an innovative, high-technology industry originally developed in the United States and later decimated by foreign competition. Between 1976 and 1986, the U.S. domestic consumer electronics market grew 15 percent annually, totalling approximately $30 billion in factory sales by 1986.[9] Yet U.S. firms controlled a minuscule share of this market. American firms controlled close to 100 percent of the domestic market in the 1950s; this share shrunk to 5 percent by the late 1980s and contributed $11 billion to the 1986 U.S. trade deficit.[10]

As the U.S. market presence in consumer electronics declined, Japanese and European firms expanded their market control. This market dominance provided Japanese and European firms (and governments) with a head start on the next generation of HDTV technology.

Japan had long expressed interest in HDTV.[11] Initial research by NHK, Japan's state-owned broadcasting corporation, began in 1964 and a formal research program was established in 1970. These efforts expanded over time, and by the late 1970s the Japanese government was providing a web of direct and indirect supports for HDTV. These programs included R&D funding, subsidies and loans for interested firms, and market promotion. Such efforts bore fruit in the late 1980s, as Sony began marketing HDTV production equipment in 1984 and NHK began experimental HDTV broadcasts by 1988. By 1989, it was estimated that NHK had spent almost $500 million on HDTV research alone, and private Japanese firms had expended an additional $400 million.[12]

European firms were also active in HDTV development.[13] However, the Europeans were late starters in comparison to Japan, beginning comprehensive HDTV programs in 1986. At that time, European firms began a two-pronged strategy based on creation of EC-wide technical standards, and expanded financial support for cooperative R&D programs through the Eureka 95 HDTV consortium.[14] European governments also aggressively enforced antidumping laws and imposed stringent domestic content requirements in their consumer electronics sectors.

U.S. HDTV programs paled in comparison to the efforts of its trading partners. The Federal Communications Commission (FCC) was working to create new technical standards, but little direct support existed. Even private firms did little to promote HDTV. For example, total private expenditures on HDTV R&D were roughly $70 million as of early 1988.[15] This picture had changed somewhat by 1989, when DARPA announced a three-year, $30 million program to support basic research into projection display technology. However, Congress blocked release of these funds until the administration developed a comprehensive program for HDTV.[16]

THE DRIVE FOR GOVERNMENT SUPPORT

These disparities in government initiatives drove industry and policymakers to promote U.S. initiatives of their own. Here, a clear relative gains problem arose in stark detail.[17] Foreign governments had intervened to spur HDTV development. Could the United States simply sit back and not create similar programs of its own?

An activist government program was considered attractive not only because it would involve U.S. firms in HDTV, but also because it would help restore American preeminence in consumer electronics. For many, the history of consumer electronics served as a parable for the decline of American industry. HDTV offered the promise of "leapfrogging" the current state of the art and restoring American dominance in the consumer electronics sectors of the future. As the American Electronics Association noted: "The stakes are too high—economically, job-impact, national security, defense, and technological leadership—for us not to proactively seek an American best interest solution. ATV (advanced television) represents the opportunity, the point of entry, probably the 'last chance,' for the United States electronics industry to be a significant player in consumer electronics again."[18]

These relative gains concerns came to the forefront in May 1989 when the AEA unveiled its comprehensive plan designed to assist American firms in entering the

HDTV market.[19] The goal of this effort was to develop "a U.S. owned and controlled HDTV industry that ensures that such HDTV components as chips and displays, and such related HDTV products as VCRs and computer monitors are manufactured here by U.S.-owned companies."[20]

The AEA plan was breathtaking in scope, calling for government spending of more than $1.3 billion.[21] The AEA plan contained several parts, all of which envisioned HDTV receiving "national champion" treatment from the government. Its centerpiece was the Advanced T.V. Corporation, a federally chartered development corporation designed to steer public and private investment toward the HDTV industry. The ATV Corporation would pursue these objectives by managing funds based on local content, R&D, and performance requirements, stimulating demand, and overseeing licensing, standards, and import activities.

Many members of Congress responded enthusiastically to the AEA proposals. By early 1990, seven HDTV-related bills had been introduced, ten committees had held hearings,[22] and a bipartisan congressional HDTV Caucus had been formed.

The Bush administration seemed similarly supportive of an HDTV-related initiative. DARPA had already backed up this commitment with its $30 million program for HDTV research and DARPA Director Craig Fields strongly supported wider efforts. HDTV also found a strong supporter in Robert Mosbacher, President Bush's new secretary of commerce. Indeed, Mosbacher came to be known in the press as the "High Definition Commerce Chief."[23]

Mosbacher entered office strongly committed to government support for HDTV. He viewed HDTV as "the first step in a whole new generation of technology."[24] He also directly referred to the relative gains problems facing the United States:

> Our companies face foreign competitors which often enjoy the benefits of heavy support for their governments and access to markets that we are denied. Simply put, there are serious implications for our balance of trade if the U.S. fails to participate fully in the development of HDTV.
>
> The efficiencies U.S. industry could gain through having a domestic capability [in HDTV] could go far in maintaining our strength and competitiveness in world markets. Dependency by U.S. industry upon our competitors for key components and technologies poses very real risks.[25]

Such full participation required direct government assistance. In March 1989, Mosbacher committed the Commerce Department to support the formation of HDTV consortia, the provision of seed capital, expansion of R&D support, and the removal of legal obstacles that blocked U.S. industry cooperation on HDTV R&D. Mosbacher also created an Advisory Committee on Advanced Television to examine other means for spurring business-government cooperation in this area. A White House Economic Policy Council working group, chaired by Commerce, was also examining options for assisting the industry.

Such high-level commitment was a heady experience for the AEA and other HDTV advocates. Unlike the machine tool and semiconductor cases, government officials appeared willing to help from the outset. However, not all administration officials supported Mosbacher's and Fields's views. For example, Michael Boskin,

Chairman of the Council of Economic Advisors, argued in early 1989 that "The 'industrialized policy' approach, by which Washington picks out a favored industry to subsidize, is neither fiscally or economically sensible. Instead of providing special benefits to the private sector, Washington simply should get out of the way, removing federal impediments to new products and services."[26]

The Intellectual Case for HDTV

Thus, advocates still had to convince skeptics like Boskin that HDTV was an industry worthy of support. As in our other cases, support depended on convincing policymakers that HDTV was a critical industry on both commercial and military grounds, and that government support could help the industry.

Advocates sought to paint HDTV as a critical industry for both defense and commercial purposes. Richard Elkus, chairman of the Prometrix Corporation and a key figure in AEA's HDTV initiative, offered a typical argument. Comparing electronics to oil, he argued that "many [electronics] markets will in their own way become just as strategic as oil. Lack of access to these markets will quickly destroy the viability of products and technologies that support these markets and finally the industrial infrastructure of an entire economy. At the very least, a nation's control of its destiny will be negatively affected."[27]

Unlike our other cases, most HDTV advocates did not place heavy emphasis on the national security rationale for the industry.[28] Commercial criticality was deemed more important. However, industry advocates still recognized that HDTV would contribute to improvements in existing military systems as well as future weapons systems designs.

HDTV was considered relevant to a number of DoD's future needs. In particular, HDTV would be employed in various video applications in battle management, command and control, training and simulation, and intelligence analysis.[29] The primary use for HDTV technology was in airplane cockpits and command centers. A McDonnell Douglas study of future display technology found that it contributed to significant improvements in combat capabilities.[30] The technology was also considered potentially relevant to video-controlled guided weapons.[31] Finally, in addition to these combat applications, potential non-combat applications included video conferencing, reconnaissance photo transmissions, and electronic data transmissions.

In examining these uses, one quickly reaches the conclusion that only one important direct defense application for HDTV existed: airplane cockpits. Moreover, the technology to be employed in cockpits was centered in display technology, only one component considered essential for HDTV. DARPA clearly recognized this fact, as the bulk of its HDTV funding went to funding display R&D.[32]

These relatively limited defense uses put DARPA officials in a bind. Instead of portraying HDTV as critical for military uses, defense officials emphasized HDTV's importance as a driver for semiconductor technology. As Acting DARPA Director Fields candidly acknowledged,

If HDTVs were not rich in semiconductors, this would not be a national security issue in any way. If the semiconductors in HDTV were in some way technologically unique and unrelated to the larger semiconductor market elsewhere, this would not be of interest. If there was not such a huge economy of scale in producing semiconductors, this would not be of interest.[33]

Thus, the direct military rationale for HDTV was fairly weak. The case for government intervention rested largely on the commercial criticality of the industry.[34] Advocates asserted that competitive strength in HDTV would contribute to strength in related industries and also improve overall U.S. manufacturing competitiveness. Three types of effects were considered most important: upstream effects, downstream effects, and manufacturing effects.[35]

Upstream effects refers to the role of HDTV as a source of demand for inputs, particularly for displays, semiconductors, and computers. These upstream effects were the most widely cited argument in favor of HDTV support. As we saw above, these upstream effects were deemed important for both military and commercial reasons.

This argument was based on the concept of an electronics "food chain."[36] The food chain argument views all electronic components as tightly linked, with semiconductors as the enabling industry or "technology driver." Figure 7.1 presents a version of this argument as portrayed by the National Advisory Committee on Semiconductors' report, "A Strategic Industry at Risk."

Figure 7.1
The Electronics "Food Chain"

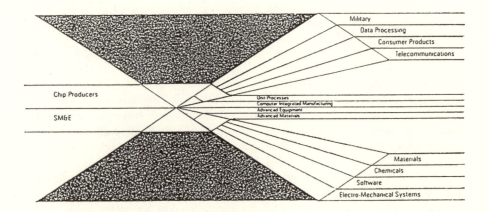

Source: National Advisory Committee on Semiconductors.

According to this argument, success in one industry, such as telecommunications, depends on competitive strengths in other parts of the food chain. Rep. Don Ritter (R-PA) summarized the food chain concept in his advocacy for HDTV: "If the U.S. does not compete in consumer electronics, it will not have a semiconductor industry. Without a semiconductor industry, we will not have a state of the art computer industry or a military electronics industry."[37] Thus, HDTV's spin-off effects on other industries were the most commonly cited argument in favor of creating an HDTV-specific industrial policy.

Based on the market projections for HDTV cited earlier, advocates developed their own projections for HDTV's impact on related industries. The impact on semiconductors received the greatest attention. Much of the weakness in the U.S. semiconductor industry was attributed to the lack of markets for U.S. firms. This had a variety of causes, including Japanese preference for Japanese semiconductors and U.S. firms' inability to rapidly produce low-cost, high-quality chips.[38] The development of HDTV offered a chance to address the latter problem.

By guaranteeing a new and expanding market for semiconductors, HDTV could help provide the economies of scale needed to produce semiconductors in a cost-effective manner. The AEA argued that HDTV units were significantly more semiconductor-intensive than current television sets. According to some projections, by 2005, the use of DRAMs in HDTVs could alone account for up to five times the *total* 1987 DRAM market.[39] If U.S. firms controlled 50 percent of U.S. HDTV sales, this effort would create sufficient economies of scale to maintain existing domestic semiconductor production capability. If U.S. firms controlled less than 10 percent of the domestic HDTV markets, AEA projected that the U.S. share of the global semiconductor market would be cut in half.[40]

During the Congressional debates of 1989, DARPA circulated two graphs that captured the upstream arguments (See Figures 7.2 and 7.3). In addition to improving DRAM capability, HDTV was also expected to drive advances in new chip technologies, such as gallium arsenide semiconductors and digital signal processor chips.[41]

While the upstream impact of HDTV on semiconductors received the greatest level of public attention, advocates also emphasized its impact on downstream sectors, such as the U.S. personal computer, display, and television industries.[42] U.S. firms in these sectors were often forced to purchase chips from Japanese suppliers. As HDTV helped improve the quality and lower the cost of domestically produced chips, the benefits of higher quality, lower cost chips would trickle down to strengthen computer and television firms. For example, the AEA estimated that the U.S. personal computer industry world market share would decline in half by 2007 without the incentive of large HDTV markets. If the government stepped in to support HDTV, AEA projected that current market shares would be retained.[43]

Finally, HDTV was expected to have a profound effects in improving the generic manufacturing skills and technologies of American industry. A widely circulated study prepared for the Electronics Industries Association (EIA) argued that the production of HDTV receivers would increase the contribution of television manufacturing to total GNP by $6 billion morethan would be the case if HDTV were not

Figure 7.2
DARPA Comparison of Worldwide DRAM Usage in Computers and HDTV

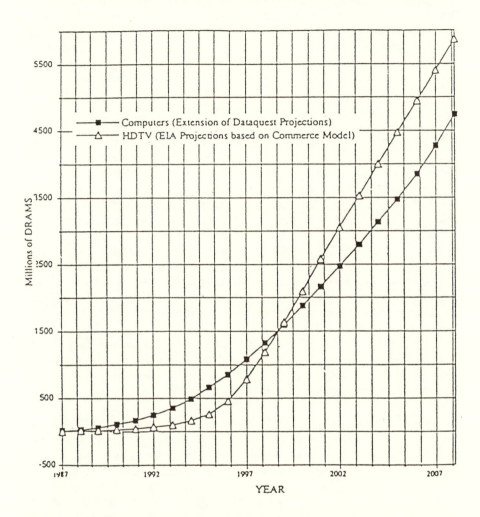

Source: Statement of Craig Fields, Director, Defense Advanced Research Projects Agency, in U.S. Congress, Senate Committee on Commerce, Science, and Transportation, 101st Congress, 1st Session, March 26, 1989, p. 17.

Figure 7.3
DARPA Comparison of Worldwide HDTV and Computer Sales

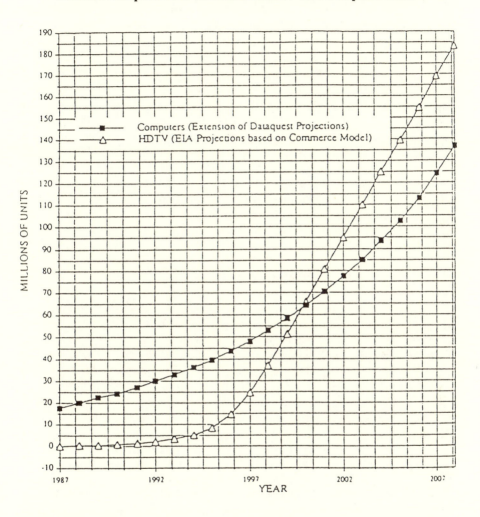

Source: Statement of Craig Fields, Director, Defense Advanced Research Projects Agency, in U.S. Congress, Senate Committee on Commerce, Science, and Transportation, 101st Congress, 1st Session, March 26, 1989, p.. 18.

commercialized.[44]   Advocates also noted that HDTV manufacturing would help
disseminate the skills and technologies used in advanced manufacturing and help to
maintain high-skill jobs in the United States.[45]

In the minds of HDTV supporters, all of these factors coalesced to make HDTV
an opportunity that could not be missed. However, industry was both unwilling and
incapable of rising to this challenge alone. For this reason, HDTV advocates also
faced a second hurdle: convincing policymakers that government support for HDTV
could help solve this problem.

HDTV advocates enjoyed a number of advantages in making the case for
government support. First, America's trading partners clearly viewed HDTV as a
critical industry. Both Japan and the EC had extensive HDTV R&D programs. For
example, a Japanese Foreign Ministry official argued in September 1989 that Japanese
firms considered HDTV technology "too strategic" to share with other countries.[46]
According to this view, if Japan and Europe saw HDTV as critical, the United States
should also follow suit.

Second, advocates could point to previous precedents for government
intervention.   After all, DoD had intervened to support the machine tool and
semiconductor industries, Indeed, Sematech was consistently cited as an example for
HDTV advocates to emulate.[47]

Supporting HDTV: Policy Options

Armed with these advantages, HDTV supporters aimed to convince policymakers
that the United States would "miss out on the twenty-first century" without government
intervention to bolster this sector. A two-pronged effort followed. A public-private
consortium modeled on Sematech would be pursued. HDTV advocates also sought
more dramatic types of support—envisioned in the AEA's proposal of May 1989.

The road to developing support for an HDTV consortium began quite smoothly.
In late 1988, AEA organized seventeen companies in a consortium (based on the
Sematech precedent) that was expected to receive 49% of its funding from the
Department of Commerce.[48]

This concept received strong initial support from the Commerce Department and
key members of Congress.[49] However, extensive federal support faced some obstacles.
Unlike the Sematech R&D effort, the HDTV consortium was proposed as a
manufacturing consortium. At that time, manufacturing consortia were restricted on
antitrust grounds. As a result, many congressionally sponsored efforts to support
HDTV called for amended antitrust laws to permit joint HDTV production ventures.[50]

Over the early months of 1989, momentum favoring a government role in HDTV
grew. A number of government studies were examining how to structure government
support for HDTV, ignoring the previously thorny issue of creating a justification for
government intervention. This shift in emphasis represented a major change from the
policy debates highlighted in previous chapters.

At the same time, many industry representatives grew increasingly confident that
HDTV would signal the creation of a broader industrial policy and closer cooperation

between business and government. One outside analyst quipped that the administration, "won't use the IP word, [but the progress of industrial policy] is probably going at a faster pace than it would have had Dukakis been elected."[51] The hopes of IP advocates reached their crescendo with the publication of the AEA's May 1989 plan for the Advanced Television Corporation.

These initial hopes for government support of HDTV were very short-lived. In fact, the May 1989 proposal can be seen as a high-water mark. The boldness of the AEA proposal shocked Mosbacher and he began retreating almost immediately. In an interview soon after the AEA announcement, he decried the plan: "Frankly, the problem is they're hoping that . . . Uncle Sugar will fund it. I don't think they should depend on that."[52] On the same day, Assistant Secretary of Commerce Sikes cautioned that "the government not get ahead of the private sector in (HDTV)."[53]

However, Mosbacher and Sikes were not simply responding to the AEA plan. After all, other proposals to support HDTV were under consideration. HDTV was strongly opposed in the Cabinet, led by OMB Director Richard Darman and White House Chief of Staff John Sununu. Moreover, government analyses provided analytical backing for this position, questioning industry market projections as well as the strategic importance of HDTV. The most damning analysis was found in a Congressional Budget Office report released in July 1989.[54] In later congressional testimony, CBO Director Robert Reischauer summarized the report's conclusions: "It seems implausible to suggest that such a small and uncertain future market will be more important as a driver of technology, as a provider of economies of scale, or as a determiner of competitive success than will be the growth of present markets. . . . it is not at all clear that HDTV will act to drive or significantly spur [technological] advances."[55]

By September 1989, Mosbacher had retreated even further from his initial position, arguing that the government should provide general R&D support for a broad range of technologies instead of targeting certain critical industries.[56] The final blow came in November 1989, when the Bush administration announced plans to severely cut DARPA's HDTV project, even going so far as to block several previously awarded contracts.

In response, acting DARPA Director Craig Fields later decided in April 1990 to fund HDTV projects with DARPA's discretionary funds. This action, along with another controversial decision to invest government funds in a gallium arsenide chip manufacturer, directly led to Fields's firing by the White House.[57] The firing was covered widely in the national media, and produced a flurry of interest in HDTV. Nonetheless, the HDTV proposals were not resurrected. In retrospect, the ouster of Fields—an outspoken HDTV advocate—marked the end of any possibility for an active government role in HDTV.

WHY DID HDTV FAIL?

As the preceding section indicates, HDTV advocates began their efforts with a whole host of apparent advantages. They created a sophisticated case for their industry, replete with extensive facts and figures detailing its strategic nature. The case for HDTV was much more sophisticated than the arguments developed to support programs for the machine tool and semiconductor industries. At the outset, these arguments were effective, creating a groundswell of support for HDTV and linking the cause with a high-ranking political figure—Commerce Secretary Mosbacher.

Nonetheless, this extensive effort was insufficient, because the industry also started from a position of irreversible weakness. HDTV was not a strategic industry, and despite their best efforts, the AEA and its supporters could not convince policymakers otherwise. As the EIA acknowledged, "HDTV, by itself, cannot make or break the electronics complex or turn the tide in U.S. electronics competitiveness, but it can make a contribution to what has to be a larger national effort."[58]

What is surprising about the HDTV episode is that administration officials defeated this program by using arguments based on strategic trade theory. In effect, the theories came back to haunt those who hoped to use them in support of a comprehensive American industrial policy. In the past, the anti-industrial policy argument was based almost exclusively on the ideological belief that "government can't pick winners and losers." This argument did not disappear in the HDTV case, but it was augmented by a sophisticated argument questioning HDTV's "winner" status.

In analyzing the case for HDTV, opponents proved conclusively that HDTV was not a strategic industry. This sophisticated use of strategic trade concepts offers a clear example of learning at work. The arguments against HDTV rested on several key points. First, HDTV was shown to contain few unique qualities, thus questioning the industry's claim that HDTV was the critical technology of the digital revolution. For example, the CBO found that, outside of display and imaging technology, HDTV was not unique. Moreover, even this display and imaging technology was not limited to HDTV. Computer workstations, already being manufactured, used similar items.[59]

Second, analysts found little proof of pent-up demand for HDTV.[60] Even the most optimistic scenarios found that demand for HDTV would be dwarfed by demand for a whole range of other consumer electronics products. If demand was limited, the learning economies associated with HDTV production would be similarly limited. Thus, the spillover impact of HDTV was greatly exaggerated.

Third, analysts also found few linkages between HDTV and the semiconductor industry. For example, Brookings Institution analyst Kenneth Flamm, who later served at DoD, testified before Congress regarding extensive errors in DARPA's analysis of the DRAM demand generated by HDTV.[61] Most importantly, analysts questioned the entire rationale for supporting the semiconductor industry through development of HDTV. Several studies had indicated that consumer electronics products did little to spur DRAM demand. In Japan, for example, computer and office automation accounted for 80 percent of DRAM demand in 1989, far outstripping any market demand based on television.[62]

The case against employing HDTV as a driver for semiconductors was succinctly criticized by Brookings' analyst Kenneth Flamm: "If we are talking about doing something for the semiconductor industry, we ought to be analyzing the concrete problems of the semiconductor industry and trying to do something about it."[63]

Finally, the administration noted that the industry itself was divided on appropriate steps for promoting HDTV. In addition to disputes between U.S. and foreign business regarding an industrial policy targeting U.S.-based firms, the industry was also divided over appropriate transmission standards for HDTV.[64] These internal industry disputes further convinced policymakers to take a "hands-off" approach.

CONCLUSIONS

Based on these analyses, policymakers concluded that the case for an industrial policy for HDTV was weak. In fact, HDTV met none of the criteria associated with strategic industries. It would not drive other technologies, it would have limited spillover effects, and it would not promote learning economies in the manufacture of electronics components. Ultimately, policymakers concluded that HDTV was an important technology, but not one that warranted a sector-specific industrial policy. Wayne Berman, Counselor to Commerce Secretary Mosbacher, offered a fitting conclusion to this episode. When asked about the lessons of HDTV, he stated: "What we've learned in the last six months is that there are a lot of technologies that are equally important . . . the federal government is hardly in the best position to predict which technologies will or will not succeed in the marketplace."[65]

With the defeat of an HDTV industrial policy, policymakers returned to a more traditional policy line. Some funds for basic research were approved, and DARPA continued some programs for display technologies.[66] However, the bulk of the U.S. effort in HDTV devolved to the FCC and its efforts to define industry-wide technical standards for HDTV. This effort was significantly smaller than the comprehensive industrial policies established in Japan and Europe.

For HDTV, the absence of an industrial policy has proved beneficial. Because of their significant head starts in HDTV, Japanese and European firms had produced systems based on analog standards. As these ventures proceeded, the FCC continued to solicit ideas for U.S.-wide HDTV production standards. It ultimately approved digital standards—a technology significantly more advanced than analog. Because they produced according to these digital standards, U.S. firms were able to regain a significant technological advantage over the Japanese and European analog systems. Indeed, this U.S. success in HDTV has been widely cited by IP opponents as a case study in the hazards of government intervention.[67]

This fortuitous turn of events might not have resulted had policymakers not become more sophisticated in their analysis of industry's arguments for intervention based on strategic grounds. Despite its powerful political connections, the industry presented a weak case for HDTV as a strategic industry. Utilizing similar analytical tools, policymakers were successful in exposing the limitations of these arguments.

The defeat of HDTV also indicates the continuing relevance of lingering policy ideas regarding the appropriate roles of business and government. The AEA and its supporters explicitly linked support for HDTV to calls for a broader government industrial policy. This linkage hurt the cause of HDTV, sparking especially strong opposition in the White House. Indeed, in his 1988 campaign, President Bush took a very strong stand against IP, stating in September 1988. "I oppose the federal government's picking winners and losers in the private sector. That's known as 'industrial policy.'"[68]

As we have seen, overcoming American policymakers' traditional opposition to IP is a difficult task. Successful efforts by industries are quite rare, and result only when a given industry is viewed as important on both military and commercial grounds. HDTV met neither of these criteria. Unable to surmount these intellectual hurdles, the industry effort was easily defeated.

NOTES

1. Much of the analysis in this chapter is based on the excellent case study by Cynthia A. Beltz, *High-Tech Maneuvers: Industrial Policy Lessons of HDTV* (Washington, D.C.: AEI Press, 1991).

2. For background on the technology of HDTV, see U.S. Congress, Office of Technology Assessment, *The Big Picture: HDTV and High Resolution Systems*, OTA-BP-CIT-64 (Washington, D.C.: GPO June, 1990); "Super Television: The High Promise—and High Risks—of High-Definition TV," *Business Week*, January 30, 1989, pp. 56-63.

3. U.S. Congress, Office of Technology Assessment (June 1990), pp. 9-10.

4. Larry F. Darby, "Economic Potential of Advanced Telecommunications Products," National Telecommunications and Information Administration, April 7, 1988, p. ii. Hereafter referred to as the Darby Report. The Darby report is reprinted in U.S. Congress, Senate Committee on Governmental Affairs, *Prospects for Development of a U.S. HDTV Industry*, 100th Congress, 1st Session, August 1, 1989.

5. Quoted in Beltz (1991), p. 60.

6. Statement of Alfred Sikes, in U.S. Congress, House Committee on Armed Services, Subcommittee on Research and Development, *High Definition Television*, 101st Congress, 1st Session, May 10, 1989, pp. 55-56.

7. See American Electronics Association, *High Definition Television: Economic Analysis of Impact* (Washington, D.C.: AEA, November 1988), pp. i-iii.

8. For background, see U.S. Congress, Office of Technology Assessment (June 1990); Dertouzos et al.(1989), pp. 217-31.

9. Dertouzos et al. (1989), p. 217.

10. Ibid.., p. 217. In 1986, imports from Japan were responsible for 74 percent of the consumer electronics trade deficit.

11.For background on Japanese programs, see Leland L. Johnson, *Development of High Definition Television: A Study in U.S.-Japan Trade Relations* (Santa Monica, Calif.: RAND Corporation, July 1990); U.S. Congress, Office of Technology Assessment (June 1990), pp. 27-32.

12. U.S. Department of Commerce, National Telecommunications and Information Administration, *Advanced Television, Related Technologies and the National Interest* (Washington, D.C.: NTIA, 1989), p. 21. This NTIA report is reprinted in U.S. Congress, House Committee on Energy and Commerce, *High Definition Television*, 100th Congress, 1st Session, March 8-9, 1989.

13. On Europe, see Tyson (1992), pp. 217-50; U.S. Congress, Office of Technology Assessment (June 1990), pp. 32-34.

14. The Eureka 95 consortium, which included all of the leading European-owned television companies, was designed to develop European HDTV capabilities in production, transmission, display, recording standards, and equipment. The project was originally funded at approximately 400 million ecu, with 50 percent of the costs contributed by the involved national governments. Participating firms contributed the remaining 50 percent. E u r e k a Project 95 is part of the much larger Eureka program. Eureka was begun in 1985 by nineteen19 European nations and is designed to support collaborative multinational efforts on R&D, manufacturing, and services.

15. Darby Report, pp. 39-41.

16. U.S. Congress, Office of Technology Assessment (June 1990), pp. 36-37. The report was never formally submitted. In addition, DARPA funds were later cut and employed for other purposes including foreign aid and a study of streamlining the Pentagon's acquisition system. See John Markoff, "High-Detail TV Faces Fund Cuts," *New York Times*, April 6, 1990, p. D1.

17. Mastanduno (1991) analyzes the HDTV case from a similar perspective.

18. Statement by AEA in U.S. Congress, House Committee on Energy and Commerce, Staff Report, *Public Policy Implications of Advanced Television Systems*, 101st Congress, 1st Session, March 1989, p. 34.

The AEA was the major industry advocate for HDTV. It is composed of approximately 3,500 member companies and forty-five engineering universities. Its members design, manufacture, or conduct research in electronics, electronics components, and related information technologies. Unlike the Electronics Industries Association (EIA), AEA membership is limited to 100 percent U.S.-owned firms.

19. AEA had long planned this initiative on HDTV. In June 1988, it created an ATV Task Force. The task force developed AEA's November 1988 review of the ATV market as well as the May 1989 proposal.

20. Statement of Fred Branfman in *High Definition Television*, U.S. Congress, House Committee on Energy and Commerce (March 8-9, 1989), p. 205.

21. For background on the AEA plan, see Beltz (1991), pp. 54-57; Statement of Pat Hill Hubbard, AEA, in U.S. Congress, Senate Committee on Commerce, Science, and Transportation, *Hearings on High Definition Television*, 101st Congress, 1st Session, May 16, 1989, pp. 42-46.

22. Beltz (1991), p. 39.

23. Stuart Auerbach, "High-Definition Commerce Chief," *Washington Post*, April 28, 1989, p. A23.

24. See statement of Robert A. Mosbacher, in *High Definition Television*, U.S. Congress, House Committee on Energy and Commerce (March 8-9, 1989), pp. 12-16.

25. Ibid., p. 12, 14.

26. Quoted in Alvin F. Lindsay, "Tuning into HDTV: Can Production Joint Ventures Improve America's High-Tech Picture?" *University of Miami Law Review*, vol. 44 (1990), p. 1188-89, fn. 173.

27. Richard J. Elkus, Jr., "Toward a National Strategy: The Strategy of Leverage," Economic Strategy Institute Occasional Paper (Washington, D.C.: Economic Strategy Institute, 1991), p. 34.

28. Most outside analysts also place little emphasis on military arguments. For example, Beltz (1991) examines only the economic case for strategic industry promotion of HDTV. Sternberg's study of U.S. policy toward the photonics industry also argues that Bush administration officials, including DARPA representatives, downplayed the industry's military impact. See Ernest Sternberg, *Photonic Technology and Industrial Policy*, (Albany: State University of New York Press, 1992), pp. 211-13.

29. Statement of William Ronald Young, Harris Corporation, in U.S. Congress, House Committee on Armed Services (May 10, 1989), p. 64.

30. Ibid., p. 109.

31. Johnson (1990), p. 41.

32. For background, see Sternberg (1992), pp. 213-17.

33. U.S. Congress, Senate Committee on Commerce, Science, and Transportation, *High Definition Television*, 101st Congress, 1st Session, March 26, 1989, p. 20.

34. The most compelling case for HDTV as a strategic industry is: Jeffrey A. Hart and Laura D'Andrea Tyson, "Responding to the Challenge of HDTV," *California Management Review*, vol. 31, no. 4 (Summer 1989), pp. 132-45. Beltz (1991), esp. pp. 38-59, and U.S. Congress, Office of Technology Assessment (June 1990) also offer excellent reviews of these arguments.

35. Hart and Tyson (Summer 1989), p. 137; Electronics Industries Association, *Consumer Electronics, HDTV, and the Competitiveness of the U.S. Economy* (Washington, D.C.: EIA, 1989), pp. 31-35.

36. Speaking in more critical terms, *The Economist* referred to this argument as the industrial domino theory. "High-Definition Television: The World at War," *The Economist*, August 4, 1990, pp. 58-61. The food chain argument is considered by many analysts to be one of the weaker arguments in support of assisting strategic industries. For example, see Richardson's (1990) review of the strategic industry literature.

37. Quoted in Beltz (1991), p. 50. See also Statement of the AEA, in U.S. Congress, House Committee on Energy and Commerce, Subcommittee on Telecommunications and Finance, *Public Policy Implications of Advanced Television Systems*, March 1989.

38. See Howell et al. (1988).

39. U.S. Congress, Office of Technology Assessment (June 1990), p. 66.

40. See U.S. Congress, Congressional Budget Office, *The Scope of the High-Definition Television Market and Its Implications for Competitiveness* (Washington, D.C.: CBO, July 1989), p. 21. Hereafter referred to as CBO HDTV study.

41. U.S. Congress, Office of Technology Assessment (June 1990), pp. 63-66.

42. See American Electronics Association (1988); Electronics Industries Association, (February 1, 1989).

43. CBO HDTV Study, pp. 26-27.

44. Electronics Industries Association (1989), p. 42.

45. Hart and Tyson (1989), p. 138.

46. Quoted in Mastanduno (1991), p. 105.

47. Several congressional hearings were held on Sematech as a model for HDTV programs. Robert Noyce, the CEO of Sematech, was brought before Congress to discuss Sematech as a model for an HDTV consortium. See U.S. Congress, House Committee on Energy and Commerce, *High Definition Television (Part 2)*, 101st Congress, 1st Session, September 13, 1989.

48. Alan Hall and Otis Port, "Why High-Tech Teams Just Aren't Enough," *Business Week*, January 30, 1989, p. 63.

49. See *High Definition Television*, U.S. Congress, House Committee on Energy and Commerce (March 8-9, 1989).

50. Lindsay (1990), pp. 1188-98. Antitrust restrictions on joint production ventures were eliminated in early 1993.

51. Jeff Faux, president of the Economic Policy Institute, quoted in Paul Blustein and Evelyn Richards, "U.S. Weighs Industrial Policy Shift," *Washington Post*, May 7, 1989, pp. A1, A8.

52. Carl T. Hall, "Feds Say Their Funding of HDTV to Be Modest," *San Francisco Chronicle*, May 10, 1989, p. C1.

53. Sikes testimony, in House Committee on Armed Services, Subcommittee on Research and Development (May 10, 1989), p. 57.

54. CBO HDTV Study.

55. Statement of Robert Reischauer, U.S. Congress, Senate Committee on Government Affairs, *Prospects for Development of a U.S. HDTV Industry*, 101st Congress, 1st Session, August 1, 1989, p. 10.

56. John Burgess and Evelyn Richards, "Commerce to Drop Role in HDTV," *Washington Post*, September 13, 1989, pp. C1, C4.

57. Bob Davis, "Ouster of Defense Aide Craig Fields Sparks Discord, Congressional Criticism," *Wall Street Journal*, April 25, 1990, p. A4.

58. Electronics Industries Association (1989), p. 44.

59. Reischauer testimony, U.S. Congress, Senate Committee on Government Affairs (August 1, 1989), p. 10.

60. AEA's market projections were considered especially suspect. See U.S. Congress, Senate Committee on Government Affairs (August 1, 1989).

61. See, especially, Statement of Kenneth Flamm, Brookings Institution, in Ibid., pp. 496-99.

62. Ibid.

63. See U.S. Congress, Senate Committee on Commerce, Science, and Transportation (March 26, 1989), p. 142.

64. See U.S. Congress, Office of Technology Assessment (June 1990), pp. 56-59.

65. See Andrew Pollack, "The Setback for Advanced TV," *New York Times*, September 30, 1989, p. Y1.

66. After the collapse of the HDTV initiative, DARPA did spend significant sums on R&D for advanced displays—a precompetitive technology critical to HDTV development. In 1991 and 1992, DARPA allocated roughly $75 million annually for its advanced displays project. See Sternberg (1992), pp. 215-16.

67. See, for example, Robert L. Rose, "How U.S. Firms Passed Japan in Race to Create Advanced Television," *Wall Street Journal*, July 20, 1992, pp. A1, A2; Cynthia Beltz, "The Big Picture," *Reason*, August/September 1993, pp. 58-59.

68. Quoted in Blustein and Richards. *Washington Post*, (May 7, 1989).

8

Conclusions

The cases examined in the four previous chapters tell a story of gradual yet dramatic policy change. Between the 1983 machine tool case and the 1989 policy debate over HDTV, policy makers in Washington discovered the growing potential dangers of defense dependence and sought new remedies to counter them. In some instances, new policy responses such as industry-led consortia were created. In others, efforts to create new institutional mechanisms were rejected.

Despite these differences in outcomes, the episodes also highlighted another consistent trend: learning by policymakers as they sought to address the problem of defense dependence. In the past, policy toward ailing U.S. industries veered between extremes of laissez-faire or blanket protectionism. And, in most cases, trade protection was based on the political power, not the national security significance, of ailing industries.

By the 1980s, many observers reached the conclusion that this stark "either-or" choice was no longer sufficient. Advocates of government intervention sought new methods to justify public action and to develop rigorous criteria for determining industries worthy of support. They also sought new means to support industry without resorting to protectionism. At the same time, many free market advocates realized that sole reliance on market forces could not always offer sufficient protection from potential security threats.

This search for solutions coalesced with the development of industrial policy concepts and strategic trade theory by economists and public policy experts. These concepts offered a potential third path which helped transform U.S. defense industrial base policy.

To put it differently, the 1980s witnessed the collapse of an existing DIB policy monopoly based on the concepts of free trade and nonintervention at home. New ideas have been injected into the policy debate. However, a new institutional structure has not yet replaced the understandings that underpinned earlier policies. The result has been the gradual emergence of a new DIB policy, combined with episodic returns to the laissez-faire policies of the past.

LEARNING BY DOING?

As our case studies have shown, policymakers' response to industry demands for protection was transformed over the course of the 1980s. In our first case, the machine tool industry spent three years pursuing protection and finally succeeded in obtaining Reagan administration approval of VRAs in 1986. This trade policy response was largely attributable to significant pressures from Congress, which in turn based its arguments on the strategic significance of machine tools. At the same time, policymakers developed a new mechanism for supporting defense critical industries through the Machine Tool Domestic Action Plan and federal funding for NCMS.

The machine tool industry's success was soon followed by a more dramatic departure in government policy toward the semiconductor industry. While supporting trade protection for semiconductor chips through the 1986 Semiconductor Agreement, the Reagan administration also agreed to provide substantial support to the Sematech consortium for semiconductor manufacturing. Pentagon support continues today, and Sematech is widely considered as a model for effective U.S. DIB policies.[1]

In our final two cases—the ball bearing and HDTV industries—policymakers rejected calls for direct support for ailing industries. An interesting facet of these cases concerns the arguments utilized by policymakers in rejecting industry's call for action. In both cases, the arguments of strategic industry's advocates were absorbed by the government and turned on their heads to provide a sophisticated justification *against* government intervention.

These four policy debates did not occur in isolation; they were part of a larger transformation of U.S. DIB and technology policy throughout the 1980s. During this period, policymakers experimented with a number of new initiatives to support critical industries. Policy toward the semiconductor and semiconductor manufacturing industries since the 1987 creation of Sematech offers a useful illustration of these efforts to develop new approaches both domestically and internationally.

In terms of international trade in semiconductor chips, U.S. trade officials recognized flaws in the 1986 Semiconductor Agreement soon after its signing.[2] According to many observers, the 1986 agreement helped create a Japanese producer cartel, resulting in higher chip prices and supply shortages.[3] Even worse, the agreement did little to open the Japanese market to U.S. producers. In 1991, Japanese and U.S. negotiators revisited the agreement. Working closely with U.S. industry, American negotiators succeeded in tightening the agreement's market access provisions and eliminating the antidumping provisions that had contributed to Japan's cartelization.[4] While it is premature to assess the final results of these revisions, both industry and government view the 1991 agreement as a significant improvement on its predecessor.[5]

Washington also revised its programs toward domestic promotion of semiconductor production. While maintaining funding for Sematech, it rejected government support for other ambitious consortia to restore American predominance in chip production. In 1989, American computer and semiconductor makers suggested creation of U.S. Memories, a consortium designed to establish a world-class factory for memory chip production.[6] At the same time, the National Advisory Committee on Semiconductors released a report calling for a new Consumer Electronics Capital Corporation (CECC) to support the semiconductor and electronics industries.[7]

For a number of reasons, neither U.S. Memories nor the CECC succeeded in attracting federal support. This failure resulted to a large extent from Washington's recognition that industry cooperation was insufficiently advanced and that foreign supplies in these industries were sufficiently secure.[8] This situation contrasts sharply with the circumstances surrounding Sematech's creation. In that case, DoD officials greatly feared potential supply disruption and capitalized on close industry cooperation along with extensive private financial support.

Government DIB policy has shifted in other areas as well. For instance, after rejecting support for HDTV, ARPA has funded a number of innovative efforts to develop flat-panel displays.[9] Such focused efforts have been widely cited as superior to the grandiose HDTV plans originally discussed in 1989.[10]

Similarly, the Commerce Department has also begun to revise its Section 232 program to emphasize domestic remedies for affected industries. Such remedies were recently implemented to support U.S. manufacturers of ceramic packages for semiconductor chips.[11] In the past, the use of domestic action plans was quite rare, as Section 232 was interpreted only as a trade statute. Today, the consideration of domestic remedies has become relatively common.

In addition to these sector-specific responses, the Reagan and Bush administrations also experimented with the creation of broad guidelines for steering U.S. DIB policy across the entire range of U.S. industry. In early 1987, Presidential Science Advisor William Graham presented one of the first efforts to develop criteria for determining levels of government R&D support. Graham's criteria included the state of the particular technology area, the amount of potential progress relative to the investment level, the leverage of the technology on achievement of mission objectives, and the availability of competent technical teams.[12] Similar efforts continued throughout the late 1980s and proceed today with efforts to develop various Critical Technology lists.[13] As we will see below, these initial efforts form the foundation for the Clinton administration's DIB policies.

THE FINDINGS AND INTERNATIONAL RELATIONS THEORY

Much of the contemporary debate in the international relations (IR) field has concerned itself with this issue of the importance of the relative gains problem and its impact on the prospects for international cooperation.[14] This debate has largely focused on the importance of relative gains considerations on state preferences, and the impact of these concerns on multilateral cooperation. This discussion has lately become embedded in a larger debate regarding the relative benefits of liberalism and realism as guides for IR theory.

Throughout this research, my inclination has been to focus on middle-range theory and to avoid this broader debate.[15] A far more fruitful approach seeks to explain the conditions under which relative gains considerations prove most important as well as the factors that influence political leaders' understanding of these concepts. Finally, IR theory must also examine the impact of relative gains seeking on the subsequent behavior of states.

This study sought to help answer these questions by explaining why the United States did not respond to the relative decline of several defense-related industries and the growing evidence of dependence on Japan and other nations for important components of critical weapons systems. As we have seen, structural realism suggests that these external conditions would induce policymakers to respond aggressively by creating policies that would counter the trend toward growing defense dependence.

Our case studies highlighted mixed results. Government officials did respond to problems facing the machine tool and semiconductor manufacturing industries. They rejected intervention to support the ball bearing and HDTV sectors. While relative gains considerations appear to influence policymakers' preferences, their impact is not uniform and remains largely subject to situational variables.

Efforts to understand these situational variables produced several interesting results. In every case, advocates for government intervention faced high hurdles to success. When intervention did occur, it often took novel forms, such as industry-led consortia, and government funds were normally expended to support initiatives led by the private sector. Rarely did Washington create a government-led industrial policy such as those often utilized in Western Europe and Asia. In sum, government intervention was rare, restricted, and unique when compared to efforts in other states.

How can we explain these results? Our case studies offered some support for the utility of an approach that emphasizes the impact of policy ideas on government responses. In particular, we found that the presence and persistence of certain ideas, often embodied in policy monopolies, served to prevent policymakers from considering options viewed as "illegitimate."[16] In the DIB issue area, concern over the propriety of government picking winners and losers served to block active consideration of industrial policy solutions for many years.

An important finding of our case studies concerns the linkage between the concepts of learning and the policy monopolies. The literature on learning has often failed to fully account for the policy environment in which policymakers act. For example, Tetlock has described how learning theories often assume a causal logic where, for a variety of reasons, policymakers come to question their fundamental beliefs and then develop a more complex framework for future policy.[17] An approach based on the policy monopoly concept may better capture the often random "garbage can" process whereby thorny problems, new ideas, and windows of opportunity combine to produce policy change.

At the same time, the concept of policy monopolies has downplayed the process by which policymakers come to question existing understandings of a given issue. Current research implicitly postulates a random process of search by policymakers combined with the generation of new ideas by policy entrepreneurs and others. It does not explain how and why decisionmakers come to consider and reject certain new ideas. Learning concepts may better capture the individual dynamics of the search for and acceptance of new concepts.

A closer melding of policy monopoly and learning approaches could help eliminate some of the weaknesses suffered by each concept. By combining learning theory's emphasis on individual cognitive change with the policy monopoly approach's emphasis on political dynamics, we can gain a much richer picture of the causes and effects of policy change.[18]

A second important finding concerns the linkage between domestic and international politics. Our case studies indicated that systems-level theories offer an incomplete explanation for U.S. DIB policy in the 1980s. Given Waltz's own recognition that structural realism does not explain domestic politics, such a conclusion is not startling.[19] However, our conclusions do provide further support for efforts to expand and develop alternative approaches that combine insights from various theoretical traditions.

One potentially fruitful approach might examine how international changes open up domestic windows of opportunity for policy entrepreneurs. This research program could also examine different types of external changes and their impact on the reception for certain types of new policy ideas. For example, relative economic decline appears to foster enhanced interest in the economic policies of a state's leading competitors. Our cases highlighted American interest in Japanese economic approaches. In the early 1900s, British elites showed a similar interest in German economic policies.[20] This research program might add useful insights to recent theorizing on epistemic communities and learning.

One must turn to domestic level explanations to obtain a full picture of U.S. DIB policy. Domestic factors, such as the existence of policy monopolies and learning by policymakers, can have profound repercussions on a state's international behavior.

Such a process offers a useful perspective for understanding American DIB policies in the 1980s. Throughout most of the Cold War, American DIB policy was characterized by two main thrusts: support for free trade within the alliance and an opposition to activist industrial policy at home. America's continued economic and military hegemony led few to question this approach, creating a strong policy monopoly.

By the late 1970s and early 1980s, the relative decline of American industry and the rise of Japan and other economic competitors led many outside analysts to argue in favor of a more activist government industrial policy toward defense-related industries. Systemic changes opened up a window of opportunity for new policy ideas. Industrial policy advocates presented a structural realist challenge to the Reagan administration, arguing that dependence on foreigners for defense systems was inherently risky and required government action to prevent exploitation of this foreign advantage.

The Reagan Administration rebuffed these initiatives, arguing that existing policies offered sufficient insurance against foreign dependence. In effect, the administration's initial response was to deny that a relative gains problem existed. It even rejected efforts to gather data on the extent of the potential defense dependence problem.[21]

The United States did not respond as system level approaches would suggest, constantly adjusting national policy in response to changes in relative power. Friedberg's study of Britain's response to industrial decline reached similar conclusions, arguing that this "calculative model" does not offer a complete explanation of British government policy.[22] Friedberg also postulated a second approach—the "perceptual model"—based on the importance of policy beliefs and images.[23] Because these beliefs are "sticky," policy change is likely to be sharply discontinuous, with periods of relative quiescence followed by crises which often produce dramatic policy change. While Friedberg also found limits to the perceptual model, he concluded that it did help explain British leaders' failure to develop accurate data sources on Great Britain's relative economic position.[24]

Friedberg's perceptual model offers a useful first cut at explaining the lag in America's response to defense dependence. This lag occurred for two reasons. Initially, policymakers remained uncertain that a problem existed. They had simply failed to collect data on the problem—much as the British lacked effective economic data at the turn of the century.[25] Even today, the Pentagon does not collect data on the economic performance and health of various sectors of the defense industrial base.[26]

After confirming that dependence was growing, policymakers also questioned the propriety of many suggested responses. Many top level Reagan and Bush administration officials viewed this trend as part of a process of growing interdependence. This perspective was captured in 1985 comments that Prestowitz has attributed to then-Deputy Treasury Secretary Richard Darman. Asked for his views on enforcing anti-dumping laws against Japanese semiconductor producers, Darman reportedly quipped: "Why do we want a semiconductor industry? We don't want some kind of industrial policy in this country. If our guys can't hack it, let 'em go."[27]

This perception of growing interdependence was widely shared. However, not all administration officials were as fatalistic as Darman, Sununu, and others. Other top administration officials, such as Weinberger and Baldridge, recognized the potential dangers of dependence. They were willing to act, but did not want to embrace an activist industrial policy.

Thus, the perceptual model helps explain why policymakers first doubted that defense dependence presented a potential national security threat. It offers a less complete explanation for the failure to respond after problems were uncovered. Furthermore, it does not explain why policies change or the form that these new policies might take. The concepts of policy ideas, policy monopolies, and policy learning offer a useful complement to these other analytical tools.

These concepts help us answer several important questions. First, after finally recognizing that a problem existed, why did the United States lag in its response to defense dependence? This lag is largely attributable to the presence of a strong policy monopoly that viewed industrial policies as an inappropriate solution to economic problems.

Second, why did policy begin to change in the mid-to-late 1980s? Policy change, as seen in the machine tool and semiconductor cases, resulted from a growing realization by policymakers that existing policies were not working. As they searched for new solutions, they found that strategic trade theory concepts could offer a potential model for effectively supporting defense-critical industries. These theories helped create a new alternative to existing policy options that had failed to resolve the dependence problem. In his discussion of Soviet economic reform, Moltz introduces the concept of "borrowing," which he defines as "the process by which political leaders derive new knowledge from the international arena—and adopt new policy positions based on that information—in order to increase their political efficacy."[28] As we have seen, a similar type of borrowing process emerged in the transformation of American DIB policy.

Third, why did the new policies assume the form they did? In contrast to what Friedberg's perceptual model might predict, the new DIB policy represented incremental change, not a government-directed industrial policy similar to some efforts in Japan or France. U.S.-style industrial policy relies on funding industry-led consortia and fostering closer government-business cooperation.

The literature on policy learning offers some illuminating ideas on why policy change proved so gradual. Heclo and others have noted that policymakers tend to frame new problems in terms that rely heavily on preexisting policy frameworks and concepts.[29] Indeed, incremental change often remains the norm until existing policy monopolies are completely replaced by new understandings of the issues.[30] For example, U.S. policy on child abuse did not change dramatically until policymaking authority shifted from Washington to the states.[31]

Such incremental change describes the present state of U.S. DIB policy. Although many industrial policy advocates, including presidential candidate Bill Clinton, called for creation of a MITI-like agency, these efforts were never implemented. In its place, the United States has created an "industrial policy by proxy," which relies on private sector leadership and minimal government intervention.

Future Research Challenges

This research highlighted several shortcomings in existing theoretical approaches and also pointed to several areas for future research. Because this study restricted its focus to U.S. policy in one issue area, one must remain cautious about the generalizability of my conclusions—a shortcoming in much of the existing literature.

In general, most research on the impact of policy ideas and policy learning has examined the American case.[32] More cross-national comparisons are needed. For example, Western European states have faced similar issues regarding dependence on Japanese weapons systems components.[33] A comparison of U.S. and Western European policy responses might offer useful insights.

In addition to further cross-national studies, future research must also apply these theoretical tools to other issue areas. In particular, foreign and national security policy has been neglected in the literature on policy ideas and policy monopolies. Existing research on policy monopolies has tended to focus on purely domestic issues such as nuclear power, transportation policy, and health care.[34] This research, as well as the work of Shafer, Goldstein, and others, has begun to expand the range of policy issues examined using these approaches.

Such efforts should help address a major shortcoming in the existing literature on policy ideas: its inability to specify the conditions under which policy monopolies form or collapse.[35] As our case studies indicated, existing policy monopolies tend to collapse when old understandings and institutions fail to offer solutions to pressing social problems. Yet, we remain unable to predict which situations are most conducive to policy learning or which types of policy monopolies are most unstable. Addressing these important issues must be the central focus of future research; this effort will require careful research designs that compare different types of policies in different types of decision making environments.

Several recent studies have presented a number of interesting questions that warrant further study.[36] First, what factors prompt policymakers to search for new understandings of policy problems? In other words, how do political leaders define policy failure?

Second, under what conditions are foreign ideas and concepts considered most attractive to political leaders? Answers to this question would offer a useful complement to the growing literature on the impact of epistemic communities.

Third, what types of policy monopolies or decision-making venues are most resistant to change? This research indicated that national security-related policy monopolies may prove more resistant to change than domestic policy monopolies. While the pace of change may differ, the study also indicated that the actual process of change may be similar across issue areas.[37]

IMPLICATIONS FOR POLICY

As we noted in Chapter Two, policy monopolies have two primary characteristics: powerful supporting ideas and an institutional framework that supports them. The 1980s witnessed the creation of new policy ideas in the DIB area. However, new institutions to support these ideas have not yet been established. We now face a period of instability in U.S. DIB policy. The existing policy monopoly has been toppled, but a new institutional framework to replace it does not yet exist in final form.

The ascendance of new policy ideas was fairly well solidified by 1991. While continuing to oppose industrial policy on ideological grounds, the Bush administration implemented a number of activist programs as part of its technology policy.[38] These included increased funding for R&D programs operated by the Department of Commerce as well as new initiatives to support the National Research and Education Network (NREN), one of the precursors to today's information superhighway.

Such efforts were accelerated with the election of Bill Clinton, who ran on a platform of expanding government efforts to support critical industries. Clinton campaigned on the promise to create a technology policy that went "beyond support for basic research and a reliance on 'spin-offs' from defense R&D."[39] Upon entering office, he soon followed up on this promise by announcing an across-the-board plan to enhance U.S. competitiveness.[40]

In addition to this activist policy agenda, Clinton also promoted into office those individuals who had long criticized U.S. DIB policies. The Clinton administration's top ranks read like a "Who's Who" of strategic trade policy and industrial policy supporters. For example, both Labor Secretary Robert Reich and Council of Economic Advisors Chair Laura Tyson were widely known for their advocacy of industrial policy. At the Pentagon, Defense Secretary Les Aspin and Deputy Secretary William Perry, later appointed to replace Aspin, sought to completely reverse the Bush administration's market-driven approach to the DIB.[41] In an interview published in August 1992, Perry described the Clinton Administration's new perspective: "We're willing to commit to a defense industrial policy. In fact, not only are we willing, we think it's a necessity. We're therefore willing to consider options that I don't believe the previous administration seriously considered."[42]

While change in policy ideas has been dramatic, institutional change has been less sweeping. As we have seen, institutional change was purposely restricted by the Reagan and Bush administrations. In several cases, however, the Congress was able to enact new programs over administration objections. For example, the 1988 Omnibus Trade and Competitiveness Act altered the mission of the National Bureau for Standards.[43] Now known as the National Institute for Standards and Technology (NIST), the agency provides funding for commercial R&D, supports manufacturing extension services, and provices a range of other services.

Despite this success, administration opposition succeeded in defeating most other institutional changes. In addition to the efforts described in this study, the Bush administration succeeded in blocking creation of a civilian DARPA and also weakened congressional proposals to establish an independent Critical Technologies Institute.[44]

This situation has changed under the Clinton Administration. In less than one year, it has developed a number of new institutions that may help solidify this new approach to DIB policy. First, it has reoriented DARPA's mission to expand its support for dual-use research. In addition, ARPA now manages a new program, the Technology Reinvestment Project (TRP), to support dual-use R&D and to promote defense conversion.[45]

Second, the administration has created a new National Economic Council (NEC) as a counterpart to the National Security Council. Designed to ensure high-level White House attention to the economic dimensions of all issues (including those related to national security), the NEC has become the central coordinating mechanism for economic policy under Clinton.[46]

Finally, the Pentagon has created a new position, the Assistant Secretary of Defense for Economic Security, to focus on the DIB and the economic impacts of U.S. military policies. In addition, U.S. national security policy now clearly identifies economic security as a central part of the DoD mission.[47]

Policy Prescriptions

As these examples indicate, major changes in U.S. DIB policy are underway. These policy changes represent an impressive effort, especially when compared to past inaction. Building on preliminary efforts in the last half of the Bush administration, the Clinton administration has begun to shift policy toward a greater concern with relative gains and has initiated a series of efforts to insure against potential dependence.

While the direction of policy is appropriate, there are a number of potential dangers associated with these ongoing initiatives. Hubris is certainly the most serious pitfall. Strategic trade concepts offer general guidelines for determining the criticality of key industries, but developing rigorous measurements of learning-by-doing and externalities has proved next to impossible.[48] These limitations raise the potential for abuse of the strategic industry label.

Because of these practical difficulties, some observers reject any government effort to support strategic industries.[49] However, such a blanket response is both politically impractical and potentially dangerous on national security grounds. The best alternative is to continue employing general guidelines from strategic trade theory. This assessment would then be combined with analyses of a given sector on both technical and military grounds.[50] The HDTV episode provides some evidence that rigorous analysis could help prevent misuse of the strategic industry label.

A second potential danger concerns the possibility of political capture of DIB policy. The Pentagon's recent decision to produce a third Seawolf submarine on defense industrial base grounds indicates the potential for intrusion of pork barrel concerns.[51] These political pressures have plagued U.S. R&D policies for many years,[52] and can never be fully eliminated. The most effective means for reducing these pressures has already been implemented in a number of programs operated by ARPA and NIST. Current procedures require a peer review of proposals by an independent panel of technical experts, and 51 percent cost-sharing by private industry. Both of these requirements help reduce the potential for a government bail-out of industry on purely political grounds.

A third danger involves the potential for overreaction to defense dependence. As we saw in Chapter One, globalization has become a way of life in both defense and commercial businesses. Given the inevitability of growing interdependence, the U.S. cannot simply ban foreign procurement or foreign investment in American industries. Autarky no longer represents a feasible policy option. At the same time, the potential dangers of defense dependence require insurance against future threats.

Moran has developed an effective middle ground approach that applies antitrust concepts to DIB policy.[53] His approach applies antitrust concentration rules to determining the potential for defense dependence. The application of concentration rules is employed as an additional screening device to supplement more traditional analyses of the defense dependence problem.[54] Analysts would continue to examine the criticality of threatened industries, the potential for supply disruption, and the adequacy of surge capabilites. Reviews of global supply concentration and the availability of alternative supply sources would be added under this new model.

According to Moran's perspective, the extent of dependence does not matter. What does matter, however, is the concentration of dependence on a few suppliers.[55]

Based on Moran's guidelines, defense officials must attack areas where DoD or U.S. private firms rely on highly concentrated sources of foreign supply. In general, intervention to support strategic defense-related industries should occur only when three conditions concurrently exist: (1) when the concentration of the critical product in the international economy is such that there are few substitutes, (2) when the lead time to develop alternative sources or products is long, and (3) when the cost of doing without the critical product is substantial.[56]

This model offers many benefits. It helps create relatively rigorous criteria for analyzing the case for government intervention. Moreover, it helps further narrow the range of industries requiring government support. Very few industries meet these criteria.[57]

Finally, although DIB policy is evolving, the United States still lacks the ability to predict potential danger points in advance. Although the government can initiate investigations of the competitiveness of strategic industries on its own, that step rarely occurs in practice. Instead, as all of our case studies indicated, Washington tends to respond to industry cries for action. Unfortunately, it is often too late to reverse downward trends by the time companies approach the government for subsidies or trade protection.

This reactive approach could be transformed through the creation of a new system of early warning that tracks the likely course of American industries, as well as the activities of foreign firms and governments in similar sectors. This new system is also essential to the success of the above-outlined DIB policy based on concentration rules.

Creating this system requires better data collection and stronger analytical capabilities within the Pentagon, the Commerce Department, and other relevant agencies. In addition, the system requires closer cooperation and information exchange between industry and government.

Multiple benefits would arise from this mechanism. With a proactive system of early warning in place, both government and industry would enjoy a considerably wider range of options for reducing defense dependence. At the same time, early warning could encourage responses prior to the arrival of full-blown industry crises as we saw in the machine tool, semiconductor, and ball bearing cases.

FINAL THOUGHTS

This study described a painful and tortuous process whereby American defense policymakers gradually adjusted to a new national security environment that required new ways of thinking and new ways of doing business. International relations theorists are now stumbling through a similarly difficult adjustment process.

Defense policymakers have responded to these changes by turning to new policy instruments derived from academia, from other countries, and from other government departments. Over time, Pentagon officials reached the conclusion that a military problem—defense dependence—was not amenable to a military solution alone. This recognition prompted a whole range of new policies, many of which are being institutionalized and expanded today.

International relations theorists have begun and must continue a similar process. This research, along with countless other studies, has indicated both the strengths and weaknesses of our most commonly utilized explanatory tool---the theory of structural realism. Moving beyond the insights of structural realism requires examination of concepts from other areas of political science, as well as insights from other disciplines. My discussion of policy ideas and policy monopolies is only one modest part of this effort. Continued work in this vein is essential to promoting further progress and development in international relations theory.

NOTES

1.   Katie Hafner, "Does Industrial Policy Work? Lessons from Sematech," *New York Times*, November 7, 1993, p. F5.

2.   For background, see Hart (1993), pp. 269-77; Tyson (1992), pp. 106-33.

3. Council on Competitiveness, *Roadmap for Results: Trade Policy, Technology, and American Competitiveness*, (Washington, D.C.: Council on Competitiveness,1993), p. 51.

4. See Tyson (1992), pp. 130-33; Council on Competitiveness (1993), pp. 51-54.

5. Council on Competitiveness (1993), p. 42. The evolution of U.S. negotiating strategies in the U.S.-Japan semiconductor talks represents another case that might be fruitfully explained using insights from the literature on policy ideas and learning.

6. See Evelyn Richards, "High-Tech Strategy Struggle: U.S. Firms Seek a New Direction for 1990s," *Washington Post*, November 20, 1989, pp. A1, A30.

7. National Advisory Committee on Semiconductors, *A Strategic Industry at Risk*. (Washington, D.C.: NACS, November 1989).

8.   See Evelyn Richards, "High-Tech Strategy Struggle," and "The Future of Silicon Valley," *Business Week*, February 5, 1990, pp. 54-60.

9.   For background, see Arielle Emmett, "Pentagon Pledges Resources for Flat-Panel Displays," *Federal Computer Week*, September 27, 1993, pp. 22-25.

10. Council on Competitiveness (1993), pp. 160-61.

11. Among the remedies proposed were creation of a new manufacturing center for ceramic packages, expanded R&D funding, and establishment of a new government-industry working group to monitor the industry's condition on a regular basis. For background, see U.S. Department of Commerce, Bureau of Export Administration, Office of Industrial Resource Administration, *The Effect of Imports of Ceramic Semiconductor Packages on the National Security*. (Washington, D.C.: Department of Commerce, August 1993; Erik R. Pages, "Coming to Terms with Foreign Dependence: Proactive Alternatives to Cold War Trade Laws." (Washington, D.C.: Business Executives for National Security, July 1993).

12.   See U.S. Congress, House Committee on Armed Services, *Hearings on the National Defense Authorization Act for Fiscal Years 1988/1989: Research, Development, Test, and Evaluation*. 100th Congress, 1st Session, February/March 1987, p. 133.

13.   For a discussion of additional list-making efforts, see Sternberg (1992), pp. 217-22. For criticisms of this approach, see Branscomb (1993), pp. 36-60; Moran (1993), pp. 30-34.

The Commerce Department's Advanced Technology Program (ATP) now provides R&D support based on four criteria: (1) Potential for U.S. economic benefit, (2) Presence of good technical ideas, (3) Strong industry commitment, and (4) The opportunity for ATP funds to make a significant difference. See U.S. Department of Commerce, Technology Administration, *Advanced Technology Program: A "How-To" Guide for Submitting Program Ideas* (Washington, D.C.: Department of Commerce, October 1993).

14. For a flavor of this debate, see the exchange in "The Relative Gains Problem for International Cooperation," *The American Political Science Review,* vol. 87, no. 3 (September 1993), pp. 729-43.

15. In this sense, I agree with Duncan Snidal, who describes this debate as largely "phony," urging that IR theory avoid "mutual assured destruction." See Ibid., pp. 740-1.

16. To some extent, these policy monopolies operate in a manner similar to "epistemic communities," defined as networks of knowledge-based experts. However, the epistemic communities approach stresses the role of transnational groups of experts who introduce new ideas into the policy process. The policy monopoly concept is somewhat different, with its emphasis on the role of ideas becoming embedded in domestic institutions. For background on epistemic communities, see the Special Issue of *International Organization* entitled "Knowledge, Power, and International Policy Coordination," *International Organization,* vol. 46, no. 1 (Winter 1992). For a discussion comparing epistemic community and agenda-setting approaches, see Checkel (January 1993), p. 299.

17. See Tetlock (1991), pp. 49-50.

18. Mendelson utilizes a similar approach in her discussion of the Soviet withdrawal from Afghanistan.

19. Kenneth N. Waltz, "Reflections on *Theory of International Politics:* A Response to My Critics," in Robert O. Keohane, ed., *Neorealism and its Critics* (New York: Columbia University Press, 1986), p. 339.

20. See Friedberg (1988).

21. As we saw in Chapter One, the government did sponsor a number of studies of defense dependence in selected industries, but it opposed comprehensive data gathering efforts. For example, a Defense Intelligence Agency (DIA) effort to gather such data, known as Project Socrates, was shut down by the Bush Administration in the aftermath of the HDTV debate. See Richard McCormack, "Socrates on Execution Block," *New Technology Week,* April 9, 1990, p. 4.

22. Friedberg (1988), pp. 279-91.

23. Ibid., pp. 14-19.

24. Ibid. p. 279.

25. Ibid., pp. 282-88.

26. See U.S. Congress, Office of Technology Assessment, *Redesigning Defense: Planning the Transition to the Future U.S. Defense Industrial Base,* OTA-ISC-500, (Washington, D.C.: GPO, July 1991), pp. 115-17.

27. Quoted in Clyde Prestowitz, "America Without Tools," *Washington Post,* January 12, 1991, pp. C1-C2.

28. James Clay Moltz, "Divergent Learning and the Failed Politics of Soviet Economic Reform," *World Politics,* vol. 45 (January 1993), p. 308.

29. See Hugh Heclo, *Modern Social Politics in Britain and Sweden* (New Haven, Conn.: Yale University Press, 1974); Paul Pierson, "When Effect Becomes Cause: Policy Feedback and Political Change," *World Politics,* vol. 45, no. 3 (July 1993), pp. 595-628.

30. Baumgartner and Jones (1993), pp. 9-12.

31. See Barbara J. Nelson, *Making an Issue of Child Abuse: Political Agenda Setting for Social Problems,* (Chicago: University of Chicago Press, 1984).

32. Some prominent exceptions that examine the impact of policy ideas in non-U.S. settings include Hall (1989), Sikkink (1991), and Breslauer and Tetlock (1991). The literature on the impact of policy monopolies in non-U.S. settings is even more sparse. One exception

is Frank R. Baumgartner, "Parliament's Capacity to Expand Political Controversy in France," *Legislative Studies Quarterly,* vol. 12 (1987), pp. 33-54.

33. See, for example, Martin Edmonds, "United Kingdom National Security and Defence Dependence: The Technological Dimension," *Government and Opposition,* vol. 26, no. 4 (Autumn 1991), pp. 427-48.

34. See Kingdon (1984); Baumgartner and Jones (1993).

35. See Pierson (1993), pp. 615-17

36. See, for example, Ibid., pp. 624-28; Baumgartner and Jones (1993), pp. 237-43.

37. This result differs from Mastanduno's (1991) conclusions in his study of U.S. policy in the HDTV, FSX, and satellite trade cases.

38. For background, see Executive Office of the President, Office of Science and Technology Policy, *U.S. Technology Policy,* September 26, 1990; Branscomb (1993); Michael Schrage, "Bush's Record Beats His Rhetoric on Technology," *Washington Post,* October 2, 1992, p. D3.

39. Clinton and Gore (1992).

40. For background, see Branscomb (1993); Executive Office of the President, "Technology for America's Economic Growth: A New Direction to Build Economic Strength," Background Paper, February 22, 1993.

41. For background on Aspin's views, see Les Aspin, "Tomorrow's Defense from Today's Industrial Base: Finding the Right Resource Strategy for a New Era," House Armed Services Committee Background Paper, February 26, 1992. Perry chaired a number of blue-ribbon panels on the DIB and also served on the DSB study group that first suggested the creation of Sematech. For insight into his views, see Carnegie Commission on Science, Technology, and Government (August 1990). Perry chaired this task force and is widely credited with drafting the report.

42. "William Perry: Guarding the Base," (Interview), *Government Executive,* August 1993, p. 40.

43. For background, see Branscomb (1993), pp. 91-92.

44. The Critical Technologies Institute (CTI) was designed to compile lists of critical technologies and to develop national strategies for enhancing competitiveness in these sectors. Branscomb (1993), pp. 50-51. In 1993, the RAND Corporation won a contract to operate and manage CTI.

45. For background on the TRP, see U.S. Congress, Congressional Budget Office, *The Technology Reinvestment Project: Integrating Military and Civilian Industries* (Washington, D.C.: CBO, July 1993).

46. For background on the NEC, see "National Economic Council Emerges as Key Player in U.S. Trade Policy," *Bureau for National Affairs-Daily Report for Executives,* April 7, 1993, pp. C1-C3.

47. For example, see U.S. Department of Defense, *Report on the Bottom-Up Review,* (Washington, D.C.: DoD, October 1993), p. 10.

48. Moran (1993), pp. 32-33.

49. See Beltz (1991), pp. 104-6.

50. See Branscomb (1993), pp. 58-59, for a discussion of various criteria. NIST has also developed a useful series of criteria for industries worthy of R&D support. One of the more sophisticated efforts to determine the impact of defense dependence is Lois Lembo et al., *Foreign Vulnerability of Critical Industries* (Arlington, Va.: Analytical Sciences Corporation, March 1990).

51. For a useful discussion of these issues, see Steven Kelman, "The Pork Barrel Objection," *American Prospect,* no. 11 (Fall 1992), pp. 88-90.

52. See, for example, Linda Cohen and Roger Noll, *The Technology Pork Barrel* (Washington, D.C.: Brookings Institution, 1991).

53. See Moran (1990); Moran (1993), pp. 41-69; Graham and Krugman (1991).

54. See U.S. General Accounting Office, *Industrial Base: Assessing the Risk of DoD's Foreign Dependence* (Washington, D.C.: GAO, April 1994).

55. Moran postulates the 4/50 rule as a useful rule of thumb for determining concentration. The 4/50 rule states that when four nations or companies control more than 50 percent of the market in a given product, there is a potential that the suppliers might collude to control prices or supply. See Moran (1990), p. 83. More recent research has indicated that the 4/50 rule might be too stringent, as most high technology sectors are highly concentrated. Leech, for example, suggests that a 2/41 rule might provide a more effective and discriminating measure. David P. Leech, "Conversion, Integration, and Foreign Dependency: Prelude to a New U.S. Economic Security Strategy," Unpublished Manuscript, May 1993.

56. Moran (1993), pp. 43-46.

57. In a recent study, the Commerce Department did find that the U.S. ceramic packages industry met these criteria. U.S. Department of Commerce, Bureau of Export Administration, Office of Industrial Resource Administration, (August 1993).

Bibliography

Achen, Christopher H. and Duncan Snidal. "Rational Deterrence Theory and Comparative Case Studies," *World Politics*. Vol. 41, No. 2 (January 1989), pp. 143-69.

Adams, Charlotte. "Was Sematech Worth DoD's $500 Million?" *Military and Aerospace Electronics*, March/April 1992, p. 10.

Adams, Gordon. *Arms Exports and the International Arms Industry: Data and Methodological Problems*. Washington, D.C.: Defense Budget Project, December 1991.

———. *The Politics of Defense Contracting: The Iron Triangle*. New Brunswick, NJ: Transaction Books, 1982.

Adams, Gordon, and David Gold. *Defense Spending and the Economy: Does the Defense Dollar Make a Difference?* Washington, D.C.: Defense Budget Project, July 1987.

Adams, Gordon, and Eric Munz. *Fair Shares: Bearing the Burden of the NATO Alliance*. Washington, D.C.: Defense Budget Project, March 1988.

Air Force Association. *Lifeline Adrift: The Defense Industrial Base in the 1990's*. Arlington, Va.: Air Force Association, September 1991.

———. *Lifeline in Danger: An Assessment of the U.S. Defense Industrial Base*. Arlington, Va: Air Force Association, September 1988.

Alexander, Arthur J. *Adaptation to Change in the U.S. Machine Tool Industry and the Effects of Government Policy*. Santa Monica, Calif.: RAND Corporation, 1990.

Alic, John A., Lewis Branscomb, Harvey Brooks, Ashton Carter, and Gerald Epstein. *Beyond Spinoff: Military and Commercial Technologies in a Changing World*. Cambridge, Mass.: Harvard Business School Press, 1992.

Allison, Graham T. *Essence of Decision: Explaining the Cuban Missile Crisis*. Boston: Little, Brown and Co., 1971.

Almond, Gabriel A. "The Return to the State" *American Political Science Review*, Vol. 82, No. 3 (September 1988), pp. 853-73.

Almond, Gabriel A. and Stephen J. Genco. "Clocks, Clouds and the Study of Politics." *World Politics*, Vol. 29 (July 1977), pp. 489-522.

American Electronics Association. *High Definition Television: Economic Analysis of Impact*. Washington, D.C.: AEA, November 1988.

Art, Robert J. "Bureaucratic Politics and American Foreign Policy: A Critique." *Policy Sciences,* Vol. 4 (1973), pp. 467-90.

Art, Robert J., Vincent Davis, and Samuel P. Huntington, eds. *Reorganizing America's Defense.* Washington, D.C.: Pergamon-Brassey's, 1985.

Ashburn, Anderson. "The Machine Tool Industry: The Crumbling Foundation." In Donald A. Hicks, ed., *Is New Technology Enough?* (Washington, D.C.: American Enterprise Institute, 1989, pp. 19-85.

————— . "Is There a Place for Joint Research?" *American Machinist,* Vol. 138, No. 1 (January 1984), p. 5.

—————. "Machine Tools and National Security II."*American Machinist,* Vol. 127, No. 5 (May 1983), p. 5.

—————. "Machine Tools and National Security I." *American Machinist,* Vol. 127, No. 4 (April 1983), p. 5.

Aspin, Les. "Tomorrow's Defense from Today's Industrial Base: Finding the Right Resource Strategy for a New Era," House Armed Services Committee Background Paper, February 26, 1992.

Axelrod, Robert. *The Evolution of Cooperation.* New York: Basic Books, 1984.

Bachrach, Peter and Morton S. Baratz. "Two Faces of Power." *The American Political Science Review,* Vol. 56, No. 4 (December 1962), pp. 947-52.

Baily, Martin N. and Alok K. Chakrabati. *Innovation and the Productivity Crisis.* Washington, D.C.: Brookings Institution, 1988.

Baldwin, David A. *Economic Statecraft.* Princeton, N.J.: Princeton University Press, 1985.

—————. "Interdependence and Power: A Conceptual Analysis." *International Organization,* Vol. 34, No. 4 (Autumn 1980), pp. 471-506.

Baldwin, Robert. *The Political Economy of U.S. Import Policy.* Cambridge,Mass.: MIT Press, 1985.

Ball, Alan R., and Frances Millard. *Pressure Politics in Industrial Societies.* Atlantic Highlands, N.J.: Humanities Press International, 1986.

Banting, Keith, ed. *State and Society: Canada in Comparative Perspective.* Toronto: University of Toronto Press, 1986.

Barfield, Claude E., and William A. Schambra, eds. *The Politics of Industrial Policy.* Washington, D.C.: American Enterprise Institute, 1986.

Barnett, Michael. "High Politics is Low Politics: The Domestic and Systemic Sources of Israeli Security Policy, 1967-1977." *World Politics,* Vol. 42, No. 4 (July 1990), pp. 529-62.

Baumgartner, Frank R. "Parliament's Capacity to Expand Political Controversy in France." *Legislative Studies Quarterly,* Vol. 12 (1987), pp. 33-54.

Baumgartner, Frank R., and Bryan D. Jones. *Agendas and Instability in American Politics.* Chicago: University of Chicago Press, 1993.

—————. "Agenda Dynamics and Policy Subsystems." *Journal of Politics,* Vol. 53, No. 4 (November 1991), pp. 1044-74.

Beam, David R., Timothy J. Conlan, and Margaret T. Wrightson. "Solving the Riddle of Tax Reform: Party Competition and the Politics of Ideas." *Political Science Quarterly,* Vol. 105, No. 2 (1990), pp. 193-217.

Beltz, Cynthia A. "The Big Picture." *Reason,* August/September 1993, pp. 58-59.

—————. *High-Tech Maneuvers: Industrial Policy Lessons of HDTV.* Washington, D.C.: AEI Press, 1991.

Bennett, Andrew Owen. *Theories of Individual, Organizational, and Governmental Learning and the Rise and Fall of Soviet Military Interventionism, 1973-1983.* Ph.D.

dissertation, Harvard University, February 1990.

Bergsten, C. Fred. "Economic Imbalances and World Politics." *Foreign Affairs*, Vol. 65 (Spring 1987), p. 784-95.

Berry, F. Clifton, Jr. "British Offset Policy." *National Defense*. Vol. 73, No. 448 (May/June 1989), pp. 31-33.

Bhagwati, Jagdish. *Protectionism*. Cambridge, Mass.: MIT Press, 1988.

Blackwell, James A., Jr. "The Defense Industrial Base." *Washington Quarterly*, Vol. 15, No. 4 (Autumn 1992), pp. 189-206.

Blinder, Alan S. *Hard Heads, Soft Hearts*. Reading, Mass.: Addison-Wesley, 1987.

Bluestone, Barry, and Bennett Harrison. *The Deindustrialization of America*. New York: Basic Books, 1982.

Boger, Dan C., Willis R. Greer, and Shu S. Liao. "Competition in Defense Acquisition: Myths and Facts" *Defence Analysis*, Vol. 5, No. 3 (1989), pp. 245-55.

Borrus, Michael. *Competing for Control: America's Stake in Microelectronics*. Cambridge, Mass.: Ballinger, 1988.

Borrus, Michael, Laura D'Andrea Tyson, and John Zysman. "Creating Advantage: How Government Policies Shape International Trade in the Semiconductor Industry." In Paul Krugman (ed.), *Strategic Trade Policy and the New International Economics*. Cambridge, Mass.: MIT Press, 1986.

Branch, Christopher I. *Fighting a Long Nuclear War*. Washington, D.C.: National Defense University Press, 1984.

Branscomb, Lewis M., ed. *Empowering Technology*. Cambridge, Mass.: MIT Press, 1993.

Breslauer, George W., and Philip E. Tetlock, eds. *Learning in U.S. and Soviet Foreign Policy*. Boulder, Colo.: Westview Press, 1991.

Brown, Harold. *U.S.-Japan Relations: Technology, Economics and Security*. Washington, D.C.: US/Japan Economic Agenda, 1987.

Callaghan, Thomas A., Jr. *Pooling Allied and American Resources to Produce a Credible, Collective Conventional Deterrent*. Report prepared for the U.S. Department of Defense, August 1988.

———. "A Common Market for Atlantic Defense," *Survival*, Vol. 17, No. 3 (May/June 1975), pp. 129-32.

———. *U.S. Economic Cooperation in Military and Civil Technology*. Washington, D.C.: Center for Strategic and International Studies, 1975.

Calleo, David P. *Beyond American Hegemony: The Future of the Western Alliance*. New York: Basic Books, 1987.

Campbell, Colin. *Governments Under Stress*. Toronto: University of Toronto Press, 1983.

Campbell, Colin, and B. Guy Peters, eds. *Organizing Governance, Governing Organizations*. Pittsburgh, Pa.: University of Pittsburgh Press, 1988.

Caporaso, James A., ed. *The Elusive State: International and Comparative Perspectives*. Newbury Park, Calif.: Sage, 1989.

Carnegie Commission on Science, Technology, and Government. *New Thinking and American Defense Technology*. New York: Carnegie Corporation, August 1990.

Carnoy, Martin. *The State and Political Theory*. Princeton, N.J.: Princeton University Press, 1984.

Center for Strategic and International Studies. *The Atlantic Partnership: An Industrial Perspective on Transatlantic Defense* Cooperation, Washington, D.C.: CSIS, May 1991.

———. *Deterrence in Decay: The Future of the U.S. Defense Industrial Base*. Washington, D.C.: CSIS, May 1989.

————. *U.S. Defense Acquisition: A Process in Trouble*. Washington, D.C.: CSIS, March 1987.

Charles, Dan. "Keeping Semiconductors Safe for Democracy." *Bulletin of the Atomic Scientists*, Vol. 45, No. 8 (November 1989), pp. 8-10.

Checkel, Jeff. "Ideas, Institutions, and the Gorbachev Foreign Policy Revolution." *World Politics*, Vol. 45, No. 1 (January 1993), pp. 271-300.

Clinton, William H., and Albert Gore. "Technology: The Engine of Economic Growth." Campaign Position Paper, September 21, 1992.

Cobb, Roger W., and Charles D. Elder. *Participation in American Politics: The Dynamics of Agenda Building*, 2d ed. Baltimore, Md.: Johns Hopkins University Press, 1983.

Cobb, Roger W., Jennie-Keith Ross, and Marc Howard Ross. "Agenda Building as a Comparative Political Process." *American Political Science Review*, Vol. 70 (1976), pp. 126-38.

Cohen, Stephen D. *The Making of U.S. International Economic Policy*. 2d ed. New York: Praeger, 1988.

Cohen, Linda, and Roger Noll. *The Technology Pork Barrel*. Washington, D.C.: Brookings Institution, 1991.

Coker, Christopher. *British Defence Policy in the 1990's*. London: Brassey's Defence Publishers, 1987.

Collis, David J. "A Resource-Based Analysis of Global Competition: The Case of the Bearings Industry." *Strategic Management Journal*, Vol. 12 (1991), pp. 49-68.

————. "The Machine Tool Industry and Industrial Policy, 1955-1982." In A. Michael Spence and Heather A. Hazard, *International Competitiveness*. Cambridge, Mass.: Ballinger., 1988), pp. 75-114.

Cooper, Richard N. *The Economics of Interdependence* New York: McGraw-Hill, 1968.

Corcoran, William J. "The Machine Tool Industry Under Fire." In Donald L. Losman and Shu-Jan Liang, *The Promise of American Industry*. New York: Quorum Books, 1990, pp. 227-47.

Correll, John T., and Colleen A. Nash. "The Industrial Base at War." *Air Force*, December 1991, p. 52-55.

Cothier, Phillipe, and Andrew Moravscik. "Defense and the Single Market." *International Defense Review*, September 1991, pp. 949-63.

Council on Competitiveness. *Roadmap for Results: Trade Policy, Technology, and American Competitiveness*. Washington, D.C.: Council on Competitiveness, 1993.

————. *Gaining New Ground: Technology Priorities for America's Future*. Washington, D.C.: Council on Competitiveness, 1992.

Cox, Andrew, and Stephen Kirby. *Congress, Parliament and Defence: The Impact of Legislative Reform on Defence Accountability in Britain and America*. New York: St. Martin's Press, 1986.

Cox, David. "Sovereignty and Security: New Defence Policy." Interview with Perrin Beatty. *Canadian Business Review*, Vol. 14, No. 3 (Autumn 1987), pp. 8-15.

Cowhey, Peter F. "States and Politics in American Foreign Economic Policy." In John Odell and Thomas D. Willett, *International Trade Policies: Gains from Exchange between Economics and Political Science*. Ann Arbor, Mich.: University of Michigan Press, 1990, pp. 225-32.

Crain, Robert, Elihu Katz, and Donald Rosenthal. *The Politics of Community Conflict: The Fluoridation Decision*. Indianapolis, In.: Bobbs-Merrill, 1969.

Creasy, Pauline, and Simon May. *The European Armaments Market and Procurement Cooperation*. London: Macmillan, 1988.

Cypher, James M. "Military Spending, Technical Change and Economic Growth: A Disguised Form of Industrial Policy?" *Journal of Economic Issues*, Vol. 21, No. 1 (March 1987), pp. 33-59.

Dahl, Robert. *Who Governs?* New Haven, Conn.: Yale University Press, 1963.

Davey, Michael E. "Managing Defense Department Technology Base Programs." Report No. 88-310. Washington, D.C. : Congressional Research Service, 1988.

Defense Forecasts, Inc. *Foreign Investment in the U.S. Defense Industrial Base: A Sound National Strategy for America's Future*. Washington, D.C.: Defense Forecasts, Inc., May 1992.

Derian, Jean-Claude. *America's Struggle for Leadership in Technology*. Cambridge, Mass.: MIT Press, 1990.

Dertouzos, Michael L. et al. *Made in America*. Cambridge, Mass.: MIT Press, 1989.

Dery, David. *Problem Definition in Policy Analysis*. Lawrence: University Press of Kansas, 1984.

Destler, I. M. *American Trade Politics: System Under Stress*. Washington, D.C.: Institute for International Economics, 1986.

———. *Presidents, Bureaucrats and Foreign Policy*. Princeton, N.J.: Princeton University Press, 1974.

Destler I. M., and John Odell. *Anti-Protection: Changing Forces in U.S. Trade Politics*. Washington, D.C.: Institute for International Economics, 1987.

Deutsch, Karl W. *The Analysis of International Relations*. Englewood Cliffs, N.J.: Prentice Hall, 1978.

Dickson, Keith. "The Influence of Ministry of Defence Funding on Semiconductor Research and Development in the United Kingdom." *Research Policy*, Vol. 12 (1983), pp. 113-20.

Diehl, Paul F. "Ghosts of Arms Control Past." *Political Science Quarterly*, Vol. 105, No. 4 (Winter 1990-91), pp. 597-615.

Dietrich, William S. *In the Shadow of the Rising Sun: The Political Roots of American Economic Decline*. University Park, Pa.: Pennsylvania State University Press, 1991.

DiFilippo, Anthony. *From Industry to Arms: The Political Economy of High Technology*. New York: Greenwood Press, 1990.

———. *Military Spending and Industrial Decline: A Study of the American Machine Tool Industry*. New York: Greenwood Press, 1986.

Dillon, Patricia, James Lehman, and Thomas D. Willett. "Assessing the Usefulness of International Trade Theory for Policy Analysis." In John S. Odell and Thomas D. Willett, eds. *International Trade Policies: Gains from Exchange Between Economics and Political Science*. Ann Arbor, Mich: University of Michigan Press, 1990, pp. 21-54.

Domke, William K., Richard C. Eichenberg, and Catherine M. Kelleher. "The Illusion of Choice: Defense and Welfare in Advanced Industrial Democracies, 1948-1978." *American Political Science Review*, Vol. 77, No. 1 (1983), pp. 19-35.

Dosi, Giovanni, Laura D'Andrea Tyson, and John Zysman, "Trade, Technologies and Development: A Framework for Discussing Japan." In Chalmers Johnson, Laura D'Andrea Tyson, and John Zysman, eds. *Politics and Productivity: The Real Story of Why Japan Works*. New York: Harper Business, 1989.

Downs, George W. "The Rational Deterrence Debate." *World Politics*, Vol. 41, No. 2 (January 1989), pp. 225-37.

Drifte, Reinhard. *Arms Production in Japan*. Boulder, Colo.: Westview Press, 1986.

Drown, Jane Davis, Clifford Drown, and Kelly Campbell, eds. *A Single European Arms Industry?* London: Brassey's, 1990.

Dyson, Kenneth H. F. *The State Tradition in Western Europe*. New York: Oxford University Press, 1980.

Earle, Edward Mead. "Adam Smith, Alexander Hamilton, Friedrich List: The Economic Foundations of Military Power." In Peter Paret, ed. *Makers of Modern Strategy*. Princeton, N.J.: Princeton University Press, 1986, pp. 217-61.

Eckstein, Harry. "Case Study and Theory in Political Science." In Fred Greenstein and Nelson W. Polsby, eds. *Handbook of Political Science*. Vol. 3. Reading, Mass.: Addison-Wesley, 1975, pp. 79-137.

Edelman, Murray. *The Symbolic Uses of Politics*. Urbana: University of Illinois Press, 1964.

Edmonds, Martin. "United Kingdom National Security and Defence Dependence: The Technological Dimension." *Government and Opposition*, Vol. 26, No. 4 (Autumn 1991), pp. 427-48.

Elder, Charles, and Roger Cobb. *The Political Use of Symbols*. New York: Longman, 1983.

Electronics Industries Association. *Consumer Electronics, HDTV, and the Competitiveness of the U.S. Economy*. Washington, D.C.: EIA, February 1, 1989.

Elkus, Richard J., Jr. "Toward a National Strategy: The Strategy of Leverage." Economic Strategy Institute Occasional Paper. Washington, D.C.: Economic Strategy Institute, 1991.

Ellison, John N., Jeffrey W. Frumkin, and Timothy W. Stanley. *Mobilizing U.S. Industry: A Vanishing Option for National Security?* Boulder, Colo.: Westview Press, 1988.

Enthoven, Alain C., and K. Wayne Smith. *How Much is Enough: Shaping the Defense Program, 1961-1969*. New York: Harper and Row, 1971.

Etheredge, Lloyd S. *Can Governments Learn?*. New York: Pergamon Press, 1985.

Etheredge, Lloyd S., and James Short, "Thinking About Government Learning." *Journal of Management Studies*, Vol. 20, No. 1 (1983), pp. 41-58.

Evangelista, Matthew. "Sources of Moderation in Soviet Security Policy." In Philip E. Tetlock et al., eds. *Behavior, Society and Nuclear War*. Vol. 2. New York: Oxford University Press, 1991, pp. 254-354.

Evans, Peter, Dieter Rueschemeyer, and Theda Skocpol, eds. *Bringing the State Back In*. New York: Cambridge University Press, 1985.

Executive Office of the President. *Technology for America's Economic Growth: A New Direction to Build Economic Strength*. Background Paper, February 22, 1993.

Executive Office of the President, Office of Science and Technology Policy. *U.S Technology Policy*. Background Paper, September 26, 1990.

Fagen, Richard R., ed. *Capitalism and the State in U.S.-Latin American Relations*. Stanford, Calif.: Stanford University Press, 1979.

Feldman, Jan. "Collaborative Production of Defense Equipment Within NATO." *Journal of Strategic Studies*, Vol. 7, No. 3 (1984), pp. 282-300.

Ferguson, Yale H., and Richard W. Mansbach. *The State, Conceptual Chaos, and the Future of International Relations Theory*. Boulder, Colo.: Lynne Reinner Publishers, 1989.

Fong, Glenn R. "State Strength, Industry Structure and Industrial Policy: American and Japanese Experiences in Microelectronics." *Comparative Politics*, Vol. 22, No. 3 (April 1990), pp. 273-99.

Freedman, Lawrence. *The Evolution of Nuclear Strategy*. 2d ed. New York: St. Martin's Press, 1989.

————. "The Case of Westland and the Bias to Europe." *International Affairs*, Vol. 63,

No. 1 (Winter 1986/87), pp. 1-19.

Friedberg, Aaron L. "Why Didn't the United States Become a Garrison State?" *International Security*, Vol. 16, No. 4 (Spring 1992), pp. 109-42.

———. "The Changing Relationship Between Economics and National Security." *Political Science Quarterly*, Vol. 106, No. 2 (1991), pp. 265-76.

———. "The End of Autonomy." *Daedalus*, Vol. 120, No. 4 (Fall 1991), pp. 69-90.

———. "The Strategic Implications of Relative Economic Decline." *Political Science Quarterly*, Vol. 104, No. 1 (1989), pp. 401-31.

———. *The Weary Titan: Britain and the Experience of Relative Decline, 1895-1905*. Princeton, N.J.: Princeton University Press, 1988.

Fullerton, Lawrence R. "Exon-Florio as an Anti-Trust Enforcement Tool," *Antitrust*, Vol. 4, No. 2 (Spring 1990), pp. 28-32.

Gansler, Jacques S. *Affording Defense*. Cambridge, Mass.: MIT Press, 1989.

———. "Needed: A U.S. Defense Industrial Strategy." *International Security*, Vol. 12, No. 2 (Fall 1987), pp. 45-62.

———. *The Defense Industry*. Cambridge, Mass.: MIT Press, 1980.

———. *The Diminishing Economic and Strategic Viability of the U.S. Defense Industrial Base*. Ph.D. Dissertation, American University, Ann Arbor, Mich.: University Microfilms, 1978.

Gansler, Jacques, and Charles Paul Henning. "European Acquisition and the U.S." *Defense and Diplomacy*, Vol. 7, No. 6 (June 1989), pp. 29-35, 62.

Garrett, Geoffrey, and Barry R. Weingast. "Ideas, Interests, and Institutions: Constructing the European Community's Internal Market." In Judith Goldstein and Robert O. Keohane, eds., *Ideas and Foreign Policy: Beliefs, Institutions, and Political Change*, Ithaca, N.Y.: Cornell University Press, 1993.

George, Alexander L. "Ideology and International Relations: A Conceptual Analysis." *Jerusalem Journal of International Relations*, Vol. 9, No. 1 (1987), pp. 1-21.

———. "The `Operational Code': A Neglected Approach to the Study of Political Leaders and Decision Making." In Erik P. Hoffmann and Frederic J. Fleron, Jr., *The Conduct of Soviet Foreign Policy*. New York: Aldine Publishing, 1980.

———. "Case Studies and Theory Development: The Method of Structured, Focused Comparison." In Paul Lauren, ed. *Diplomacy: New Approaches in History, Theory and Policy*. New York: Free Press, 1979a.

———. "The Causal Nexus Between Cognitive Beliefs and Decision-Making Behavior: The Operational Code Belief System." In Lawrence Falkowski, ed. *Psychological Models in International Politics*. Boulder, Colo.: Westview Press, 1979b.

George, Alexander L., and Robert Keohane. "The Concept of National Interests: Uses and Limitations." In Alexander L. George, *Presidential Decisionmaking in Foreign Policy: The Effective Use of Information and Advice*. Boulder, Colo.: Westview Press, 1980.

Gibson, David R. "High Definition Television, Joint Production Ventures, and the Antitrust Barrier." *Cornell International Law Journal*, Vol. 24 (1990), pp. 325-55.

Gilder, George. "How Computer Companies Lost their Memories." *Forbes*, June 13, 1988, pp. 79-84.

Gold, David A., Clarence Y. H. Lo, and Erik Olin Wright. "Recent Developments in Marxist Theories of the State." *Monthly Review*, Vol. 27, Nos. 5&6, pp. 29-43, 36-51.

Goldstein, Judith. "The Impact of Ideas on Trade Policy: The Origins of U.S. Agricultural and Manufacturing Policies." *International Organization*, Vol. 43, No. 1 (Winter 1989), pp. 31-71.

———. "Ideas, Institutions and American Trade Policy." *International Organization*, Vol.

42, No. 1 (Winter 1988), pp. 179-217.

―――. "The Political Economy of Trade: Institutions of Protection." *American Political Science Review*, Vol. 80, No. 1 (March 1986), pp. 161-84.

Goldstein, Judith, and Robert O. Keohane, eds. *Ideas and Foreign Policy: Beliefs, Institutions, and Political Change*. Ithaca, N.Y.: Cornell University Press, 1993.

Goldstein, Judith, and Stefanie Ann Lenway. "Interests or Institutions: An Inquiry into Congressional-ITC Relations." *International Studies Quarterly*. Vol. 33 (1989), pp. 303-27.

Gourevitch, Peter. *Politics in Hard Times*. Ithaca, N.Y.: Cornell University Press, 1986.

―――. "The Second Image Reversed: International Sources of Domestic Politics." *International Organization*, Vol. 32, No. 4 (Autumn 1978), pp. 881-912.

Gowa, Joanne. "Public Goods and Political Institutions: Trade and Monetary Policy Processes in the United States." *International Organization*, Vol. 42, No. 1 (Winter 1988), pp. 15-32.

Graham, Edward M., and Paul R. Krugman. *Foreign Direct Investment in the U.S.* 2d ed. Washington, D.C.: Institute for International Economics, 1991.

Graham, Otis L. *Losing Time: The Industrial Policy Debate*. Cambridge, Mass.: Harvard University Press, 1992.

Grant, Wyn. *Government and Industry: A Comparative Analysis of the U.S., Canada and the U.K.* Hants, U.K.: Edward Elgar Publishers, 1989.

Greenberg, Edward S., and Thomas F. Mayer, eds. *Changes in the State: Causes and Consequences*. Newbury Park, Calif.: Sage, 1990.

Grew, Raymond, ed. *Crises of Political Development in Europe and the United States*. Princeton, N.J.: Princeton University Press, 1978.

Grieco, Joseph. *Cooperation Among Nations: Europe, America and Non-Tariff Barriers to Trade*. Ithaca, N.Y.: Cornell University Press, 1990.

Grossman, Gene M. "Strategic Export Promotion: A Critque." In Paul R. Krugman, ed., *Strategic Trade Policy and the New International Economics*. Cambridge, Mass.: MIT Press, 1986, pp. 48-68.

Guertner, Gary L. "Machine Tools: Imports and the U.S. Industry, Economy, and Defense Industrial Base." Report No. 86-762E. Washington, D.C.: Congressional Research Service, July 17, 1986.

Gummett, Philip, and Judith Reppy. "Military Industrial Networks and Technical Change in the New Strategic Environment." *Government and Opposition*, Vol. 25, No. 3 (Summer 1990), pp. 287-303.

Gusfield, Joseph. *The Culture of Public Problems: Drinking-Driving and the Symbolic Order*. Chicago: University of Chicago Press, 1981.

Haas, Peter M. "Introduction: Epistemic Communities and International Policy Coordination." *International Organization*, Vol. 46, No. 1 (Winter 1992), pp. 1-36.

Haggard, Stephen. "The Institutional Foundations of Hegemony: Explaining the Reciprocal Trade Agreements Act of 1934." *International Organization*, Vol. 42, No. 1 (Winter 1988), pp. 91-119.

Haglund, David G., ed. *The Defense Industrial Base and the West*. London: Routledge, 1989.

―――. *Canada's Defence Industrial Base*, Kingston, Ont.: Ronald P. Frye, 1988.

Haglund, David G., and Joel J. Sokolsky, eds. *The U.S.-Canada Security Relationship*. Boulder, Colo.: Westview Press, 1989.

Hall, John A., and G. John Ikenberry. *The State*. Minneapolis: University of Minnesota Press, 1989.

Hall, Peter A., ed. *The Political Power of Economic Ideas: Keynesianism Across Nations*.

Princeton, N.J.: Princeton University Press, 1989.

————. *Governing the Economy: The Politics of State Intervention in Britain and France.* New York: Oxford University Press, 1986.

Halperin, Morton H. *Bureaucratic Politics and Foreign Policy.* Washington, D.C.: Brookings Institution, 1974.

Hammond, Thomas H. "Agenda Control, Organizational Structure and Bureaucratic Politics." *American Journal of Political Science,* Vol. 30, No. 2 (May 1986), pp. 379-420.

Hampson, Fen Osler. *Unguided Missiles: How America Buys Its Weapons.* New York: W. W. Norton, 1989.

Hart, Jeffrey A. *Rival Capitalists: International Competitiveness in the United States, Japan, and Western Europe.* Ithaca, N.Y.: Cornell University Press, 1993.

Hart, Jeffrey A., and Laura D'Andrea Tyson, "Responding to the Challenge of HDTV." *California Management Review,* Vol. 31, No. 4 (Summer 1989), pp. 132-45.

Hartley, Keith. "Defense Procurement and Industrial Policy." In John Roper, ed. *The Future of British Defence Policy.* Aldershot: Gower Publishing, 1985.

————. *NATO Arms Cooperation.* London: Allen and Unwin, 1983.

Hartley, Keith, Farooq Hussain, and Ron Smith. "The UK Defence Industrial Base." *Political Quarterly,* Vol. 50, No. 1 (1987), pp. 62-81.

Hartz, Louis. *The Liberal Tradition in America.* New York: Harcourt, 1955.

Hawes, Michael K. "The Swedish Defense Industrial Base: Implications for the Economy." In David G. Haglund, ed. *The Defense Industrial Base and the West.* London: Routledge, 1989.

Heclo, Hugh. "Issue Networks in the Executive Establishment." In Anthony King, ed. *The New American Political System.* Washington, D.C.: American Enterprise Institute, 1978.

————. *Modern Social Politics in Britain and Sweden.* New Haven, Conn.: Yale University Press, 1974.

Helpman, Elhanan, and Paul R. Krugman. *Trade Policy and Market Structure.* Cambridge, Mass.: MIT Press, 1989.

Hermann, Charles F., Charles W. Kegley, Jr., and James N. Rosenau. *New Directions in the Study of Foreign Policy.* Boston: Allen and Unwin, 1987.

Hermann, Margaret G., and Charles F. Hermann, "Who Makes Foreign Policy Decisions and How: An Empirical Inquiry." *International Studies Quarterly,* Vol. 33 (1989), pp. 361-87.

Higgs, Robert, ed. *Arms, Politics, and the Economy: Historical and Contemporary Perspectives.* New York: Holmes & Meier, 1990.

————. "Beware the Pork Hawk." *Reason,* Vol. 21 (June 1989), pp. 28-34.

Hirschman, Albert O. *National Power and the Structure of Foreign Trade.* Berkeley: University of California Press, 1980. (original edition 1945)

————. "Beyond Assymetry: Critical Notes on Myself as a Young Man and on Some Other Old Friends." *International Organization,* Vol. 32, No.1 (Winter 1978), p. 45.

Hobkirk, Michael D. *The Politics of Defense Budgeting: A Study of Organization and Resource Allocation in the United Kingdom and the United States.* Washington, D.C.: National Defense University Press, 1983.

Holland, Max. *When the Machine Stopped: A Cautionary Tale from Industrial America.* Boston: Harvard Business School Press, 1989.

Holsti, K. J. "Politics in Command: Foreign Trade as National Security Policy." *International Organization,* Vol. 40, No. 3 (Summer 1986), pp. 643-72.

Holsti, Ole, and James Rosenau. *American Leadership in World Affairs: Vietnam and the Breakdown of Consensus.* Boston: Allen and Unwin, 1984.

Hooks, Gregory. "The Rise of the Pentagon and U.S. State Building: The Defense Program as Industrial Policy." *American Journal of Sociology,* Vol. 96, No. 2 (September 1990), pp. 358-404.

Hooley, Richard. *Protection for the Machine Tool Industry: Domestic and International Negotiations for Voluntary Restraint Agreements.* Pew Case Study in International Affairs, Case 120, Pittsburgh, Pa.: University of Pittsburgh Graduate School of Public and International Affairs, 1989.

Howell, Thomas R., Brent L. Bartlett, and Warren Davis. *Creating Advantage: Semiconductors and Government Industrial Policy in the 1990s.* Washington, D.C.: Semiconductor Industry Association, 1992.

Howell, Thomas R., William A. Noellert, Janet H. MacLaughlin, and Alan William Wolff. *The Microelectronics Race: The Impact of Government Policy on International Competition.* Boulder, Colo.: Westview Press, 1988.

Huntington, Samuel P. "The U.S.: Decline or Renewal?" *Foreign Affairs,* Vol. 67 (Winter 1988-1989).

Ikenberry, G. John. "Conclusion: An Institutional Approach to American Foreign Economic Policy." *International Organization.* Vol. 42, No. 1 (Winter 1988), pp. 219-43.

————. *Reasons of State: Oil Politics and the Capacities of American Government.* Ithaca, N.Y.: Cornell University Press, 1988.

————. "The Irony of State Strength: Comparative Responses to the Oil Shocks in the 1970's." *International Organization,* Vol. 40, No. 1 (Winter 1986), pp. 105-37.

————. "The State and Strategies of International Adjustment." *World Politics,* Vol. 39, No. 1 (1986), pp. 53-77.

Ikenberry, G. John, David A. Lake, and Michael Mastanduno. "Introduction: Approaches to Explaining American Foreign Economic Policy." *International Organization,* Vol. 42, No. 1 (Winter 1988), pp. 1-14.

"Interview with James A. Lyons, Jr.." *U.S. Naval Institute Proceedings,* Vol. 113 (July 1987), p. 67.

Jacobs, Lawrence R. "Institutions and Culture: Health Policy and Public Opinion in the U.S. and Britain." *World Politics,* Vol 44 (January 1992), pp. 179-209.

Janis, Irving L., and Leon Mann. *Decisionmaking: Choice and Commitment.* New York: Free Press, 1977.

Jervis, Robert. *Perception and Misperception in International Politics.* Princeton, N.J.: Princeton University Press, 1976.

Jessop, Bob. *The Capitalist State: Marxist Theories and Methods.* New York: New York University Press, 1982.

Johnson, Chalmers. *MITI and the Japanese Miracle: The Growth of Industrial Policy.* Stanford, Calif.: Stanford University Press, 1982.

Johnson, Chalmers, Laura D'Andrea Tyson, and John Zysman, eds. *Politics and Productivity: The Real Story of Why Japan Works.* New York: Harper Business,   1989.

Johnson, Leland L. *Development of High Definition Television: A Study in U.S.-Japan Trade Relations.* Santa Monica, Calif.: RAND Corporation, July 1990.

Johnston, William. "Canadian Defence Industrial Policy and Practice." *Canadian Defence Quarterly,* Vol. 18, No. 6 (June 1989), pp. 21-28.

Jordan, A. Grant. "Iron Triangles, Woolly Corporatism and Elastic Nets: Images of the Policy Process." *Journal of Public Policy,* Vol. 1, No.1 (1981), pp. 95-123.

Kaldor, Mary. "The Weapons Succession Process." *World Politics,* Vol. 38, No. 4 (1986), pp. 577-95.

Kapstein, Ethan B. "International Collaboration in Armaments Production: A Second Best Solution." *Political Science Quarterly*, Vol. 106, No. 4 (Winter 1991-92), pp. 657-75.

———. "Losing Control: National Security and the Global Economy." *National Interest*, Winter 1989-90.

Katzenstein, Peter. *Small States in World Markets*. Ithaca, N.Y.: Cornell University Press, 1985.

———, ed. *Between Power and Plenty*. Madison: University of Wisconsin Press, 1978.

Kelman, Steven. "The Pork Barrel Objection." *The American Prospect*, No. 11 (Fall 1992), pp. 88-90.

Kennedy, Paul. *The Rise and Fall of Great Powers*. New York: Random House, 1987.

Kennedy-Wallace, Geraldine A., and J. Fraser Mustard. "From Paradox to Paradigm: The Evolution of Science and Technology in Canada." *Daedalus*, Vol. 117, No. 4 (1988), pp. 191-214.

Keohane, Robert O., and Joseph S. Nye. *Power and Interdependence: World Politics in Transition*. Boston: Little, Brown, 1977.

Kettl, Donald F. *Government By Proxy*. Washington, D.C.: Congressional Quarterly Press, 1988.

King, Anthony, ed. *The New American Political System*. Washington, D.C.: American Enterprise Institute, 1978.

Kingdon, John W. *Agendas, Alternatives and Public Policies*. Boston: Little Brown, 1984.

Kirk, Elizabeth J., and Robert Goldberg. "U.S. and European Defense Industries: Changing Forces for Cooperation and Competition." AAAS Issue Paper No. 91-13S. Washington, D.C.: American Association for the Advancement of Science, 1991.

Kirkpatrick, D.L.I. "The Rising Unit Cost of Defence Equipment." *Journal of Cost Analysis*, Vol. 5, No. 1 (1987), p. 39-58.

Knoll, David D. "Section 232 of the Trade Expansion Act of 1962: Industrial Fasteners, Machine Tools and Beyond." *Maryland Journal of International Law and Trade*, Vol. 10 (1986), pp. 55-88.

Knorr, Klaus. *The Power of Nations*. New York: Basic Books, 1975.

Kolodziej, Edward A. *Making and Marketing Arms: the French Experience and its Implications for the International System*. Princeton, N.J.: Princeton University Press, 1987.

Kotz, Nick. *Wild Blue Yonder: Money, Politics and the B-1 Bomber*. Princeton, N.J.: Princeton University Press, 1988.

Krasner, Stephen D. "Sovereignty: An Institutional Perspective." *Comparative Political Studies*, Vol. 21, No. 1 (April 1988), pp. 66-94.

———. "Approaches to the State: Alternative Conceptions and Historical Dynamics." *Comparative Politics*, Vol. 16, No. 2 (January 1984), pp. 223-46.

———. *Defending the National Interest: Raw Materials Investments and U.S. Foreign Policy*. Princeton, N.J.: Princeton University Press, 1978.

———. "U.S. Commercial and Monetary Policy: Unravelling the Paradox of External Strength and Internal Weakness." *International Organization*, Vol. 31, No.4 (Autumn 1977), pp. 635-72.

Krauss, Ellis S., and Jon Pierre, "Targeting Resources for Industrial Change." In R. Kent Weaver and Bert A. Rockman, eds. *Do Institutions Matter?: Government Capabilities in the United States and Abroad*. Washington, D.C.: The Brookings Institution, 1993, pp. 151-87.

Krauss, Ellis S., and Simon Reich. "U.S. Policy and International Competition." *International*

Organization, Vol. 46, No. 4 (Autumn 1992), pp.857-98.

Krugman, Paul R. "Is Free Trade Passe?" *Economic Perspectives*, Vol. 1, No. 2 (Fall 1987), p. 131-44.

———. "Introduction: New Thinking About Trade Policy." In Paul R. Krugman, ed. Strategic Trade Policy and the New International Economics. Cambridge, Mass.: MIT Press, 1986a, pp. 5-10.

———, ed. Strategic Trade Policy and the New International Economics. Cambridge, Mass.: MIT Press, 1986b.

———. "Targeted Industrial Policies: Theory and Evidence." In *Industrial Change and Public Policy*. Kansas City, Mo.: Federal Reserve Bank of Kansas City, August 1983, pp. 123-34.

Kuhn, Thomas L. *The Structure of Scientific Revolutions* Chicago: University of Chicago Press, 1962.

Kuttner, Robert. *The End of Laissez-Faire*. New York: Alfred A. Knopf, 1991.

Lake, David A. *Power, Protection and Free Trade: International Sources of U.S. Commercial Strategy, 1887-1939*. Ithaca, N.Y.: Cornell University Press, 1988.

———. "The State and American Trade Strategy in the Pre-Hegemonic Era." *International Organization*, Vol. 42, No. 1 (Winter 1988), pp. 33-58.

Lamborn, Alan C. "Risk and Foreign Policy Choice." *International Studies Quarterly*. Vol 29 (1985), pp. 385-410.

———. "Power and the Politics of Extraction." *International Studies Quarterly*, Vol. 27 (1983), pp. 125-46.

Lamborn, Alan C., and Stephen P. Mumme. *Statecraft, Domestic Politics and Foreign Policy Making: The El Chazimal Dispute*. Boulder, Colo.: Westview Press, 1988.

Langille, Howard Peter. *Changing the Guard: Canada's Defense in a World of Transition*. Toronto: University of Toronto Press, 1990.

Larson, Deborah Welch. *The Origins of Containment: A Psychological Explanation* Princeton, N.J.: Princeton University Press, 1985.

Latham, Earl. *The Group Basis of Politics*. Ithaca, N.Y.: Cornell University Press, 1952.

Lauren, Paul G., ed. *Diplomacy: New Approaches in History, Theory and Policy*. New York: Free Press, 1979.

Laux, Jeanne Kirk. "Limits to Liberalism." *International Journal*, Vol. 46 (Winter 1990-91), p. 113-36.

———. "Expanding the State: The International Relations of State-Owned Enterprises in Canada." *Polity*, Vol. 15, No. 3 (Spring 1983), pp. 329-50.

Lawrence, Robert Z., and Charles S. Schultze, eds. *An American Trade Strategy: Options for the 1990s*. Washington, D.C.: Brookings Institution, 1990.

Leech, David P. "Conversion, Integration, and Foreign Dependency: Prelude to a New U.S. Economic Security Strategy," Unpublished Manuscript, May 1993.

Lembo, Lois. *Foreign Vulnerability of Critical Industries*. Arlington, Va.: Analytical Sciences Corporation, March 1990.

Lepgold, Joseph. *The Declining Hegemon: The United States and European Defense, 1960-1990*. New York: Praeger, 1990.

Levin, Richard C. "The Semiconductor Industry." In Richard Nelson, ed. *Governments and Technical Progress*. New York: Pergamon Press,1982.

Levy, Jack S. "Learning and Foreign Policy: Sweeping a Conceptual Minefield." *International Organization*, Vol. 48, No. 2 (1994), pp. 279-312.

Lewis, Craig Anderson. "Waiting for the Big One: Principle, Policy, and the Restriction of Imports Under Section 232." *Law and Policy in International Business*, Vol. 22, No.

2 (1991), pp. 357-408.

Libicki, Martin C. *What Makes Industries Strategic?* Washington, D.C.: Institute for National Strategic Studies, 1989.

———. *Industrial Strength Defense: A Disquisition on Manufacturing, Surge and War.* Washington, D.C.: National Defense University Press, 1988.

Libicki, Martin C., Jack Nunn, and Bill Taylor, *U.S. Industrial Base Dependence/ Vulnerability: Phase II-Analysis.* Mobilization Concepts Development Center, Washington, D.C. National Defense University, September 1987.

Light, Paul C. *The President's Agenda.* Baltimore, Md.: Johns Hopkins University Press, 1982.

Lijphart, Arend. *Democracies: Patterns of Majoritarian and Consensus Government in Twenty-One Countries.* New Haven, Conn.: Yale University Press, 1984.

———. "The Comparable Case Strategy in Comparative Research." *Comparative Political Studies*, Vol. 8 (July 1975), pp. 158-77.

———. "Comparative Politics and the Comparative Method." *American Political Science Review*, Vol. 65, No. 3 (September 1971), pp. 682-93.

Lindsay, Alvin F. "Tuning into HDTV: Can Production Joint Ventures Improve America's High-Tech Picture?." *University of Miami Law Review*, Vol. 44 (1990), pp. 1159-1208.

Lipset, Seymour Martin. *Continental Divide: The Values and Institutions of the United States and Canada.* New York: Routledge, 1990.

Lodge, George C. *Comparative Business-Government Relations.* Englewood Cliffs, N.J.: Prentice-Hall, 1990a.

———. *Perestroika for America.* Boston: Harvard Business School Press, 1990b.

Lodge, George C., and Ezra F. Vogel, eds. *Ideology and National Competitiveness.* Boston: Harvard Business School Press, 1987.

Lowi, Theodore J. The End of Liberalism. 2d ed. New York: W.W. Norton, 1979.

"Machine Tools: Will the Cornerstone Erode?" *Industry Week*, Vol. 224, No. 8 (April 30, 1984), p. 75-80.

Magaziner, Ira, and Robert Reich. *Minding America's Business.* New York: Vintage, 1982.

March, James G., and Johan P. Olsen. *Rediscovering Institutions: The Organizational Basis of Politics.* New York: Free Press, 1989.

———. "The New Institutionalism: Organizational Factors in Political Life." *American Political Science Review*, Vol. 78 (1984), pp. 734-49.

Manufacturing Studies Board, National Research Council. *Industrial Preparedness: National Resource and Deterrent to War.* Washington, D.C.: National Academy Press, 1990.

Mastanduno, Michael. "Do Relative Gains Matter?: America's Response to Japanese Industrial Policy." *International Security*, Vol. 16, No. 1 (Summer 1991), pp. 73-113.

———. "The United States Defiant: Export Controls in the Postwar Era." *Daedalus*, Vol. 120, No. 4 (Fall 1991), pp. 91-112

———. "Trade as a Strategic Weapon: American and Alliance Export Control Policy in the Early Postwar Period." *International Organization*, Vol. 42, No. 1 (Winter 1988), pp. 121-50.

Mastanduno, Michael, David A. Lake, and G. John Ikenberry. "Toward a Realist Theory of State Action." *International Studies Quarterly*, Vol. 33 (1989), pp. 457-74.

Mayer, Kenneth R. "Problem? What Problem? Congressional Micromanagement of the Department of Defense." Paper prepared for delivery at the 1991 Annual Meeting of the American Political Science Association, Washington, D.C., August 29-September 1, 1991,

Mayhew, David. *Congress: The Electoral Connection.* New Haven, Conn.: Yale University Press, 1974.

McCain, John. "The Self-Destruction of America's Defense Industrial Base." *Armed Forces Journal International,* June 1990, pp. 40-46.

McLoughlin, Glenn J. *SEMATECH: Issues in Evaluation and Assessment.* Washington, D.C.: Congressional Research Service, October 1, 1992.

McLoughlin, Glenn J., and Nancy R. Miller. *The U.S. Semiconductor Industry and the Sematech Proposal.* CRS Report 87-354SPR, Washington, D.C.: Congressional Research Service, April 23, 1987.

McNaugher, Thomas L. *New Weapons, Old Politics.* Washington, D.C.: Brookings Institution, 1989.

Merritt, Hardy L., and Luther F. Carter. *Mobilization and the National Defense.* Washington, D.C.: National Defense University Press, 1985.

Middlemiss, Dan. "Canada and Defence Industrial Preparedness: A Return to Basics?" *International Journal,* Vol. 42 (Autumn 1987), pp. 707-30.

Miliband, Ralph. *Marxism and Politics.* Oxford: Oxford University Press, 1977.

Milner, Helen V. "Resisting the Protectionist Temptation: Industry and the Making of Trade Policy in France and the United States During the 1970s." *International Organization,* Vol. 41, No. 4 (Autumn 1987), pp. 639-66.

Milner, Helen V., and David B. Yoffie. "Between Free Trade and Protectionism: Strategic Trade Theory and a Theory of Corporate Trade Demands." *International Organization,* Vol. 43, No. 2 (Spring 1989), pp. 239-72.

Milward, Alan S. "Restriction of Supply as a Strategic Choice." In Gordon H. McCormick and Richard E. Bissell, eds. *Strategic Dimensions of Economic Behavior.* New York: Praeger, 1984, pp. 44-58.

Mitchell, Timothy. "The Limits of the State: Beyond Statist Approaches and Their Critics." *American Political Science Review,* Vol. 85, No. 1 (March 1991), pp. 77-96.

Moe, Terry M. "Control and Feedback in Economic Regulation: The Case of the NLRB," *American Political Science Review,* Vol. 79 (1985), pp. 1094-1116.

Mogee, Mary Ellen. *Technology Policy and Critical Technologies: A Summary of Recent Reports.* Discussion Paper Number 3 of the Manufacturing Forum. Washington, D.C.: National Academy Press, December 1991.

Moltz, James Clay. "Divergent Learning and the Failed Politics of Soviet Economic Reform." *World Politics,* Vol. 45 (January 1993), pp. 301-25.

Moore, Mark H. "What Makes Public Ideas Powerful?" In Robert B. Reich, ed. *The Power of Public Ideas.* Cambridge, Mass.: Ballinger, 1987.

Moran, Theodore H. *American Economic Policy and National Security.* New York: Council on Foreign Relations Press, 1993.

————. "The Globalization of America's Defense Industries: Managing the Threat of Foreign Dependence." *International Security,* Vol. 15, No. 1 (Summer 1990), pp. 57-99.

Moravcsik, Andrew. "Arms and Autarky in Modern European History." *Daedalus,* Vol. 120, No. 4 (Fall 1991), pp. 23-46.

————. "The European Armaments Industry at the Crossroads." *Survival,* Vol. 32, No. 1 (January/February 1990), pp. 65-85.

Morici, Peter, ed. *Making Free Trade Work.* New York: Council on Foreign Relations Press, 1990.

Morita, Akio, and Shintaro Ishihara. *The Japan That Can Say No,* Washington, D.C.: U.S.

government translation, 1989.

Moteff, John D. "The Commercial Implications of Exporting and Importing Military Technology: A Review of the Issues." Report No. 90-409. Washington, D.C.: Congressional Research Service, August 24, 1990.

Mowery, David C., and Nathan Rosenberg. "New Developments in U.S. Technology Policy: Implications for Competitiveness and International Trade Policy." *California Management Review*, Vol. 32, No. 1 (Fall 1989), pp. 107-24.

Murray, Douglas J., and Paul R. Viotti. *The Defense Policies of Nations: A Comparative Study*. 2d ed. Baltimore, Md.: Johns Hopkins University Press, 1989.

National Academy of Engineering. *National Interests in an Age of Global Technology*. Washington, D.C.: National Academy Press, 1991.

National Advisory Committee on Semiconductors. *A Strategic Industry at Risk. A Report to the President and the Congress*. Washington, D.C.: NACS, November 1989.

"National Center for Manufacturing Sciences Gains Corporate Sponsors, Looks for Site." *American Machinist*, November 1986, p. 47.

National Research Council, Committee on Electonic Components. *Foreign Production of Electronic Components and Army System Vulnerabilities*. Washington, D.C.: National Academy Press, 1985.

National Research Council, Committee on the Machine Tool Industry. *The Machine Tool Industry and the Defense Industrial Base*. Washington, D.C.: National Academy Press, November 21, 1983.

Nau, Henry R. *The Myth of America's Decline: Leading the World Economy into the 1990s*. Oxford: Oxford University Press, 1990.

Nelson, Barbara J. *Making an Issue of Child Abuse: Political Agenda Setting for Social Problems*. Chicago: University of Chicago Press, 1984.

Nelson, Douglas. "Domestic Political Preconditions of U.S. Trade Policy: Liberal Structure and Protectionist Dynamics." *Journal of Public Policy*, Vol. 9, No. 1 (1989), pp. 83-108.

Nelson, Richard R., ed. *National Innovation Systems: A Comparative Analysis*. New York: Oxford University Press, 1993.

———. *High Technology Policies: A Five-Nation Comparison*. Washington, D.C.: American Enterprise Institute, 1984.

———. "Government Stimulus of Technological Progress: Lessons from American History." In Richard R. Nelson, ed., *Government and Technical Progress: A Cross-Industry Analysis*. New York: Pergamon Press, 1982, pp. 451-82.

Nettl, J. P. "The State as a Conceptual Variable." *World Politics*, Vol. 20 (1968), pp. 559-92.

Nimmo, Dan D., and Keith R. Sanders, eds. *Handbook of Political Communication*, Beverly Hills, Calif.: Sage, 1981.

Nivola, Pietro S. *Regulating Unfair Trade*. Washington, D.C.: Brookings Institution, 1993.

———. "More Like Them?: The Political Feasibility of Strategic Trade Policy." *Brookings Review*, Spring 1991, pp. 14-21.

Nordlinger, Eric A. *On the Autonomy of the Democratic State*. Cambridge, Mass.: Harvard University Press, 1981.

North American Defense Industrial Base Organization (NADIBO). *Continental Preparedness: Strengthening the NADIB Alliance*. Alexandria, Va.: NADIBO, 1988.

———. *The NADIB and Industry: Responsibilities and Opportunities*. Alexandria, Va.: NADIBO, 1988.

———. The North American Defense Industrial Base: A Half-Century of Defense

Industrial Cooperation. Alexandria, Va.: NADIBO, 1988.

————. *North American Defense Industrial Preparedness Planning.* Alexandria, Va.: NADIBO, 1988.

Nye, Joseph S., Jr. *Bound to Lead: The Changing Nature of American Power.* New York: Basic Books, 1990.

————. "Nuclear Learning and U.S.-Soviet Security Regimes." *International Organization,* Vol. 41, No. 1 (1988).

Nye, Joseph S., Jr., and Sean Lynn-Jones. "International Security Studies: A Report of a Conference on the State of the Field." *International Security,* Vol. 12 (Spring 1988), pp. 5-27.

Odell, John S. *U.S. International Monetary Policy: Markets, Power and Ideas as Sources of Change.* Princeton, N.J.: Princeton University Press, 1982.

Okimoto, Daniel J. *Between MITI and the Market.* Stanford, Calif.: Stanford University Press, 1991.

Okimoto, Daniel J., T. Sugano, and F. Weinstein, eds. *Competitive Edge: The Semiconductor Industry in the U.S. and Japan.* Stanford, Calif.: Stanford University Press, 1985.

Olsen, Edward A. "A Case for Strategic Protectionism." *Strategic Review,* Vol. 15, No. 4 (Fall 1987), pp. 63-69.

Olson, Mancur. *The Logic of Collective Action.* Cambridge, Mass.: Harvard University Press, 1965.

Oye, Kenneth A., ed. *Cooperation Under Anarchy.* Princeton, N.J.: Princeton University Press, 1986.

Pages, Erik R. "The Future of the American Defense Industry: Smaller Markets, Bigger Companies, and Closed Doors," *SAIS Review,* Vol. 15, No. 1 (Winter/Spring 1995), pp. 135-151.

————. "Coming to Terms with Foreign Dependence: Proactive Alternatives to Cold War Trade Laws." Washington, D.C.: Business Executives for National Security, July 1993.

Palmer, Glenn. "Alliance Politics and Issue Areas: Determinants of Defense Spending." *American Journal of Political Science,* Vol. 34, No. 1 (February 1990), pp. 190-211.

Paret, Peter, ed. *Makers of Modern Strategy.* Princeton, N.J.: Princeton University Press, 1986.

Park, Hongsuk. *American Politics and Foreign Economic Challenges.* New York: Garland, 1990.

Peterson, Donna J. S., Gerald T. Kelley and Myron G. Myers. *An Assessment of the Economic Status of the Antifriction Bearing Industry.* Bethesda, Md.: Logistics Management Institute, October 1991.

Peterson, Paul E. "The Rise and Fall of Special Interest Politics." *Political Science Quarterly,* Vol. 105, No. 4 (Winter 1990-91), pp. 539-56.

————. "The New Politics of Deficits." In John E. Chubb and Paul E. Peterson, eds. *The New Direction in American Politics.* Washington, D.C.: Brookings Institution, 1985, pp. 389-96.

Pierson, Paul. "When Effect Becomes Cause: Policy Feedback and Political Change." *World Politics,* Vol. 45, No. 3 (July 1993), pp. 595-628.

Pollard, Robert A. *Economic Security and the Origins of the Cold War, 1945-1950.* New York: Columbia University Press, 1985.

Polsby, Nelson W. *Community Power and Political Theory.* New Haven, Conn.: Yale University Press, 1963.

Porter, Michael E. *The Competitive Advantage of Nations.* New York: Free Press, 1990.

Potter, William C. "Issue Area and Foreign Policy Analysis." *International Organization,*

Vol. 43, No. 3 (Summer 1980), pp. 405-27.

Powell, Robert. "Absolute and Relative Gains in International Relations Theory." The *American Political Science Review*, Vol. 85 (1991), pp. 1303-20.

Prestowitz, Clyde. *Trading Places*. Paperback edition. New York: Basic Books, 1989.

Puttnam, Robert D. "Diplomacy and Domestic Politics: The Logic of Two-Level Games." *International Organization*, Vol. 42, No. 3 (Summer 1988), pp. 427-60.

Ratner, Jonathan, and Celia Thomas. "The Defence Industrial Base and Foreign Supply of Defence Goods." *Defence Economics*, Vol. 2 (1990), pp. 57-68.

Reich, Robert B. "The Stateless Manager." *Best of Business Quarterly*, Fall 1991, pp. 85-91.

Reich, Robert B. "Who is Us?" *Harvard Business Review*, January-February 1990, pp. 53-64.

"The Relative Gains Problem for International Cooperation." *American Political Science Review*, Vol. 87 (1993), pp. 729-43.

"Research Center Opens in Michigan." *American Machinist*, September 1987, pp. 138-39.

Rich, Michael, and Edmund Dews. *Improving the Military Acquisition Process: Lessons from RAND Research*. R-3373-AF/RC. Santa Monica, Calif.: RAND Corporation, February 1986.

Richardson, J. David. "The Political Economy of Strategic Trade Policy." *International Organization*, Vol. 44, No. 1 (Winter 1990), pp. 107-35.

Riche, Melvin. "Foreign Ownership, Control or Influence: The Implications for U.S. Companies Performing Defense Contracts." *Public Contract Law Journal*, Vol. 20, No. 2 (Winter 1991), pp. 143-87.

Richelson, Jeffrey. "PD-59, NSDD-13 and the Reagan Strategic Modernization Program." *Journal of Strategic Studies*, Vol. 6, No. 2 (June 1983), pp. 125-46.

Riddell, Tom. "Concentration and Inefficiency in the Defense Sector: Some Policy Options." *Journal of Economic Issues*, Vol. 19, No. 2 (June 1985), pp. 451-61.

Riker, William H. *The Art of Political Manipulation*. New Haven, Conn.: Yale University Press, 1986.

———. "Federalism." In Fred I. Greenstein and Nelson W. Polsby, eds. *Handbook of Political Science, Vol. 5, Governmental Institutions and Processes*. Reading, Mass.: Addison-Wesley, 1975.

Rockman, Bert A. "Minding the State-Or a State of Mind?: Issues in the Comparative Conceptualization of the State." *Comparative Political Studies*, Vol. 23, No. 1 (April 1990), pp. 25-55.

Rohatyn, Felix. "Restoring American Independence." *New York Review of Books*, February 18, 1988, pp. 8-10.

Roper, John, ed. *The Future of British Defense Policy*. London: Gower, 1985.

Rosati, Jerel A. *The Carter Administration's Quest for Global Community: Beliefs and their Impact on Behavior* Columbia, SC: University of South Carolina Press, 1987.

Rose, Richard and Ezra N. Suleiman, eds. *Presidents and Prime Ministers*. Washington, D.C.: American Enterprise Institute Press, 1980.

Rosenau, James N. "The State in an Era of Cascading Politics: Wavering Concept, Widening Competence, Withering Colossus or Weathering Change?" *Comparative Political Studies*, Vol. 21, No. 1 (April 1988), pp. 13-44.

Ruggie, John G. "Embedded Liberalism Revisited: Institutions and Progress in International Relations." In Emmanuel Adler and Beverly Crawford, eds. *Progress in Postwar International Relations*. New York: Columbia University Press, 1991.

Russett, Bruce. "Defense Expenditures and National Well-Being." *American Political Science Review*, Vol. 76, No. 4 (December 1982), pp. 767-77.

Sabatier, Paul A.. "Knowledge, Policy-Oriented Learning, and Policy Change," *Knowledge: Creation, Diffusion, Utilization.* Vol. 8 (1987), pp. 649-92.

Salvatore, Dominick, ed. *Protectionism and World Welfare.* Cambridge: Cambridge University Press, 1993.

Sartori, Giovanni, ed. *Social Science Concepts: A Systematic Analysis.* Beverly Hills, Calif.: Sage, 1989.

————. "Concept Misinformation in Comparative Politics." *American Political Science Review,* Vol. 64, No. 4 (December 1970), pp. 1033-53.

Sawyer, Herbert L., ed. *Business in the Contemporary World.* Lanham, Md.: University Press of America, 1988.

Schacht, Wendy H. *Technological Advancement and U.S. Industrial Competitiveness.* CRS Report No. 88-689 SPR. Washington, D.C.: U.S. Library of Congress, 1988.

Schattschneider, E. E. *The Semisovereign People.* New York: Holt, Rinehart and Winston, 1960.

————. *Politics, Pressures and the Tariff.* New York: Prentice Hall, 1935.

Schneider, William. "The Old Politics and the New World Order." In Kenneth Oye, Robert Lieber, and Donald Rothchild, *Eagle in a New World: American Grand Strategy in the Post-Cold War Era.* New York: Harper Collins, 1992.

Schulman, Paul R. "The Politics of 'Ideational Policy.'" *Journal of Politics,* Vol. 50, No.3 (1988), pp. 263-91.

Schultze, Charles L. "Industrial Policy: A Dissent." *Brookings Review,* Vol. 12, No. 1 (Fall 1983), pp. 3-12.

————. "Industrial Policy: A Solution in Search of a Problem." *California Management Review,* Vol. 24 (Summer 1983).

Schwartz, Bernard L. *Foreign Ownership of U.S. Defense Companies: Where Do We Draw the Line?* Washington, D.C.: Johns Hopkins University Foreign Policy Institute, 1989.

Scriberras, E., and B. Payne. *The UK Machine Tool Industry.* London: Technical Change Centre, 1987.

Seabury, Paul. "Industrial Policy and National Defense." *Journal of Contemporary Issues,* Vol. 6, No. 2 (1983), pp. 5-15.

Shafer, D. Michael. *Deadly Paradigms: The Failure of U.S. Counterinsurgency Policy.* Princeton, N.J.: Princeton University Press, 1988.

Shepsle, Kenneth A., and Barry R. Weingast, "When Do Rules of Procedure Matter?" *Journal of Politics,* Vol. 46, No. 1 (1984), pp. 206-21.

Sikkink, Kathryn. *Ideas and Institutions: Developmentalism in Brazil and Argentina.* Ithaca, N.Y.: Cornell University Press, 1991.

Skidmore, David, and Valerie M. Hudson, eds. *The Limits of State Autonomy.* Boulder, Colo.: Westview Press, 1993.

Skocpol, Theda. *Protecting Soldiers and Mothers.* Cambridge, Mass.: Harvard University Press, 1993.

————. *States and Social Revolutions.* Cambridge: Cambridge University Press, 1979.

Skocpol, Theda, and Kenneth Finegold. "State Capacity and Economic Intervention in the Early New Deal." *Political Science Quarterly,* Vol. 97, No. 2 (Summer 1982), pp. 255-78.

Slomovic, Anna. *An Analysis of Military and Commercial Microelectronics: Has DoD's R&D Funding Had the Desired Effect?* RAND Graduate School Dissertation. Santa Monica, Calif.: RAND Corporation, 1991.

Smith, Bruce L. R. *American Science Policy Since WWII.* Washington, D.C.: Brookings

Institution, 1990.

Snidal, Duncan. "Relative Gains and the Pattern of International Cooperation." *American Political Science Review*, Vol. 85 (1991), pp. 701-26.

————. "Public Goods, Property Rights, and Political Organizations." *International Studies Quarterly*, Vol. 23, No. 4 (December 1979), pp. 532-67.

Spencer, Linda M. *High Technology Acquisitions: Summary Charts*. Washington, D.C.: Economic Strategy Institute, May 1992.

Stegemann, Klaus. "Policy Rivalry Among Industrialized States: What Can We Learn from Models of Strategic Trade Policy?" *International Organization*,   Vol. 43, No. 1 (Winter 1989), pp. 73-100.

Stepan, Alfred. *The State and Society: Peru in Comparative Perspective*. Princeton, N.J.: Princeton University Press, 1978.

Sternberg, Ernest. *Photonic Technology and Industrial Policy*. Albany: State University of New York Press, 1992.

Stockholm International Peace Research Institute (SIPRI). *SIPRI Yearbook 1990: World Armaments and Disarmament*. New York: Oxford University Press, 1990.

Stone, Deborah A. "Causal Stories and the Formation of Policy Agendas." *Political Science Quarterly*, Vol. 104, No. 2 (1989), pp. 281-300.

Stowsky, Jay. "From Spin-Off to Spin-On: Redefining the Military's Role in American Technology Development." In Wayne Sandholtz et al., *The Highest Stakes: The Economic Foundations of the Next Security System*. New York: Oxford University Press, 1992, pp. 114-40.

Strange, Susan. "The Persistent Myth of Lost Hegemony." *International Organization*, Vol. 41, No. 4 (Autumn 1987), pp. 565-71.

Suleiman, Ezra N. "State Structure and Clientelism: The French State Versus the Notaires." *British Journal of Political Science*, Vol. 17, No. 4 (July 1987), pp. 257-79.

"Super Television: The High Promise-and High Risks-of High-Definition TV." *Business Week*, January 30, 1989, pp. 56-63.

Tansey, Kevin, and Rosa Johnson. "The Pentagon's Dependence on Foreign Sources." *GAO Journal*. No. 14 (Winter 1991-92), pp. 28-33.

Taylor, Phillip. "Weapons Standardization in NATO: Collaborative Security or Economic Competition?" *International Organization*, vol. 36, no. 1 (1982), pp. 95-112

Taylor, Trevor. "Defence Industries in International Relations." *Review of International Studies*, Vol. 16 (1990), pp. 59-73.

————. *Defence, Technology, and International Integration*. New York: St. Martin's Press, 1982.

Taylor, Trevor, and Keith Hayward. *The UK Defence Industrial Base: Development and Future Policy Options*. London: Brassey's, 1989.

Thompson, Loren. "The Defense Industrial Base: Going, Going . . ." *International Security Review*, Vol. 6, No. 2 (Summer 1981), pp. 237-72

Thurow, Lester C. *The Case For Industrial Policies*. Washington, D.C.: Center for National Policy, 1984.

Tilly, Charles, ed. *The Formation of National States in Western Europe*. Princeton, N.J.: Princeton University Press, 1975.

Todd, Daniel. *Defence Industries: A Global Perspective*. London: Routledge, 1988.

Tolchin, Martin, and Susan J. Tolchin. *Selling our Security: The Erosion of American Assets*. New York: Alfred A. Knopf, 1992.

Tolchin, Susan J. "The Impact of the LTV-Thomson Sale on U.S. National Security and Competitiveness," Testimony before the Subcommittee on Defense Industry and

Technology, Committee on Armed Services, U.S. Senate, April 30, 1992.

"Toolbuilders Seek Uncle Sam's Aid." *Industry Week*, November 29, 1982, p. 22.

Trebilcock, Michael J., Marsha Chandler, and Robert Howse. *Trade and Transitions: A Comparative Analysis of Adjustment Policies.* London: Routledge, 1990.

Treddenick, John M. "The Arms Race and Military Keynesianism." *Canadian Public Policy*, Vol. 11, No. 1 (1984), pp. 77-92.

Truman, David. *The Governmental Process: Political Interests and Public Opinion.* New York: Alfred A. Knopf, 1951.

Tucker, Jonathan B. "Partners and Rivals: A Model of International Collaboration in Advanced Technology." *International Organization*, Vol. 45, No. 1 (Winter 1991), pp. 84-120.

Tyson, Laura D'Andrea. *Who's Bashing Whom: Trade Conflict in High-Technology Industries.* Washington, D.C.: Institute for International Economics, 1992.

―――. "They Are Not Us: Why American Ownership Still Matters." *The American Prospect*, (Winter 1991), pp. 37-49.

U.S. Arms Control and Disarmament Agency. *World Military Expenditures and Arms Transfers 1987.* Washington, D.C.: GPO, 1988.

U.S. Congress, Congressional Budget Office. *The Technology Reinvestment Project: Integrating Military and Civilian Industries.* Washington, D.C.: CBO, July 1993.

―――. *Using R&D Consortia for Commercial Innovation.* Washington, D.C.: CBO, July 1990.

―――. *The Scope of the High-Definition Television Market and Its Implications for Competitiveness.* Washington, D.C.: CBO, July 1989.

―――. *The Benefits and Risks of Federal Funding for Sematech.* Washington, D.C.: CBO, September 1987.

―――. *Effects of Weapons Procurement Stretchouts on Costs and Schedules,* Washington, D.C.: U.S. Government Printing Office, 1987.

―――. *Defense Spending and the Economy.* Washington, D.C.: GPO, February 1983.

U.S. Congress, House Committee on Armed Services. *A Review of Defense Acquisition in France and Great Britain.* 101st Congress, 1st Session, August 16, 1989, Washington, D.C.: GPO, 1989.

―――. *Hearings on the National Defense Authorization Act for Fiscal Years 1988/1989: Research, Test, and Evaluation.* 100th Congress, 1st Session, February/March 1987.

―――. *The Ailing Defense Industrial Base: Unready for Crisis.* Defense Industrial Base Panel report. 96th Congress, 2d Session, (The "Ichord Panel Report"), Washington, D.C.: GPO, 1980.

U.S. Congress, House Committee on Armed Services, Defense Burdensharing Panel. *Measures of Defense Burdensharing and U.S. Proposals for Increasing Allied Burdensharing.* 100th Congress, 2d Session, May 10, 1988, Washington, D.C.: GPO, 1988.

U.S. Congress, House Committee on Armed Services, Special Subcommittee on RSI. *NATO Standardization, Interoperability and Readiness.* 95th Congress, 2d Session, Washington, D.C.: GPO, 1978.

U.S. Congress, House Committee on Armed Services, Subcommittee on Research and Development. *High Definition Television.* 101st Congress, 1st Session, May 10, 1989.

U.S. Congress, House Committtee on Banking, Finance, and Urban Affairs, Subcommittee on Economic Stabilization, *Reauthorization of the Defense Production Act and Possible Alternatives.* 101st Congress, Second Session, June 14, 1990.

―――. *Defense Production Act Amendments of 1989.* 101st Congress, First Session,

May 17, 18, 24 and June 20, 1989.

————. *New Industrial Base Initiative,* 100th Congress, First Session, July 8, 28, September 15, 16, 23, 29, 30, 1987.

U.S. Congress, House Committee on Energy and Commerce. *High Definition Television (Part 2).* 101st Congress, 1st Session, September 13, 1989.

————. *High Definition Television.* 100th Congress, 1st Session, March 8-9, 1989.

————. *Trade and Competitiveness (Part 2).* 100th Congress, 1st Session, March 5, 10, 11, 1987.

————. Subcommittee on Commerce, Consumer Protection, and Competitiveness. *Competitiveness of the U.S. Semiconductor Industry.* 100th Congress, 1st Session, June 9, 1987.

————. Subcommittee on Telecommunications and Finance. *Public Policy Implications of Advanced Television Systems.* 101st Congress, 1st Session, March 1989.

U.S. Congress, House Committee on Government Operations. *International Procurement and Waivers of the Buy American Act: U.S. Business at a Disadvantage.* 101st Congress, 2d Session, Washington, D.C.: GPO, November 29, 1990.

————. *Management of the Defense Industrial Base.* 101st Congress, 1st Session, July 18, 1989.

U.S. Congress, House Committee on Science, Space and Technology. *Federal Research Policy and the American Semiconductor Industry.* 101st Congress, 1st Session, November 8, 1989.

————. *The Role of Science and Technology in Competitiveness.* 100th Congress, 1st Session, April 28-30, 1987.

U.S. Congress, Joint Economic Committee. *High Technology Consortia: The Federal Role.* 101st Congress, 1st Session, June 8, 1989.

————. *The Machine Tool Industry and the Defense Industrial Base.* 98th Congress, 1st Session, June 7, 1983.

U.S. Congress, Office of Technology Assessment. *Redesigning Defense: Planning the Transition to the Future U.S. Defense Industrial Base.* OTA-ISC-500. Washington, D.C.: GPO, July 1991.

————. *Global Arms Trade.* Washington, D.C.: GPO, June 1991.

————. *Competing Economies: America, Europe, and the Pacific Rim.* Washington, D.C.: GPO, May 1991.

————. *Adjusting to a New Security Environment: The Defense Technology and Industrial Base Challenge-Background Paper.* OTA-BP-ISC-79. Washington, D.C.: GPO, February 1991.

————. *The Big Picture: HDTV and High-Resolution Systems.* OTA-BP-CIT-64. Washington, D.C.: GPO, June 1990.

————. Arming Our Allies: Cooperation and Competition in Defense Technology. OTA-ISC-449. Washington, D.C.: GPO, May 1990.

————. *Holding the Edge: Maintaining the Defense Technology Base.* OTA-ISC 420. Washington, D.C.: GPO, April 1989.

————. *The Defense Technology Base: Introduction and Overview-A Special Report.* OTA-ISC 374. Washington, D.C.: GPO, 1988.

————. *U.S. Industrial Competitiveness; A Comparison of Steel, Electronics and Automobiles.* Washington, D.C.: GPO, July 1981.

U.S. Congress, Senate Committee on Armed Services. *Manufacturing Programs Undertaken by the Department of Defense and the Department of Commerce.* 102nd Congress, 1st Session, Washington, D.C.: GPO, 1991.

———. *International Security Environment*. U.S. Senate, 101st Congress, 1st Session, April-June, 1989, Washington, D.C.: GPO, 1989.

———. *Manufacturing Capabilities of Key Second-Tier Defense Industries.* 100th Congress, 1st Session, July 23, 1987.

———. *Department of Defense Authorization for Appropriations for Fiscal Years 1988 and 1989.* 100th Congress, 1st Session, March 9, 1987.

U.S. Congress, Senate Committee on Banking, Finance and Urban Affairs. *Oversight Hearings on the Condition of the U.S. Financial and Industrial Base.* 101st Congress, 1st Session, July 11, 13, 19 and November 14 and 15, 1989.

U.S. Congress, Senate Committee on Commerce, Science, and Transportation. *Hearings on High Definition Television.* 101st Congress, 1st Session, May 16, 1989.

———. *High Definition Television,* 101st Congress, 1st Session, March 26, 1989.

U.S. Congress, Senate Committee on Foreign Relations. *U.S. Machine Tool Industry: Its Relation to National Security.* 98th Congress, 1st Session, November 1983.

U.S. Congress, Senate Committee on Governmental Affairs. *Prospects for Development of a U.S. HDTV Industry.* 100th Congress, 1st Session, August 1, 1989.

U.S. Congress, Senate Committee on Small Business. *Problems Confronting the Domestic Ball- and Roller-Bearing Industry.* 100th Congress, 2d Session, September 8, 1988.

U.S. Defense Science Board. *Foreign Ownership and Control of U.S. Industry*, Report to the Undersecretary of Defense for Acquisition. Washington, D.C.: DoD, June 1990.

U. S. Defense Science Board. *Report of the Defense Science Board Task Force on Semiconductor Technology.* Washington, D.C.: Office of the Undersecretary of Defense for Acquisition, February 1987.

U.S. Department of Commerce.. *Statistical Abstract of the United States.* various years.

U.S. Department of Commerce. *Petition Under the National Security Clause, Section 232 of the Trade Expansion Act of 1962 for Adjustment of Imports of Machine Tools.* Submitted by National Machine Tool Builders Association. March 10, 1983. ("NMTBA 232 Petition.")

U.S. Department of Commerce, Bureau of Export Administration, Office of Industrial Resource Administration. *The Effect of Imports of Ceramic Semiconductor Packages on the National Security.* Washington, D.C.: Department of Commerce, August 1993.

———. *National Security Assessment of the Antifriction Bearings Industry.* Washington, D.C.: Department of Commerce, February 1993.

———. *National Security Assessment of the Domestic and Foreign Contractor Base: A Study of Three U.S. Navy Systems.* Washington, D.C.: Department of Commerce, March 1992.

———. *Section 232 Investigations: The Effects of Imports on National Security.* Washington, DC: Department of Commerce, July 1989.

———. *The Effect of Imports of Anti-Friction Bearings on the National Security.* Washington, D.C.: Department of Commerce, July 1988. ("Bearings 232 Study.")

U.S. Department of Commerce, International Trade Administration. *A Competitive Assessment of the U.S. Ball and Roller Bearings Industry.* Washington, D.C.: Department of Commerce, February 1985. ("ITA Bearings Study.")

U.S. Department of Commerce, National Telecommunications and Information Administration. *Advanced Television, Related Technologies and the National Interest.* Washington, D.C.: NTIA, 1989.

U.S. Department of Commerce, Technology Administration. *Advanced Technology Program: A "How-To" Guide for Submitting Program Ideas.* Washington, D.C.:

Department of Commerce, October 1993.

———. *Emerging Technologies: A Survey of Technical and Engineering Opportunities.* Washington, D.C.: GPO, Spring 1990.

U.S. Department of Defense. *Report on the Bottom-Up Review.* Washington, D.C.: DoD, October 1993.

———. *Report to Congress on the Defense Industrial Base: Critical Industries Planning.* Washington, D.C.: DoD, October 1990.

———. Report to the U.S. Congress by the Secretary of Defense. *The Impact of Buy-American Restrictions Affecting Defense Procurement.* Washington, D.C.: DoD, July 1989.

———. *Enhancing Defense Standardization.* Report to the Secretary of Defense by the Under Secretary of Defense (Acquisition). Washington, D.C.: GPO, November 1988.

———. *Bolstering Defense Industrial Competitiveness.* Report to the Secretary of Defense by the Under Secretary of Defense for Acquisition. Washington, D.C.: GPO, July 1988. ("The Costello Report.")

———. *FY1984 Report of the Secretary of Defense.* Washington, D.C.: GPO, 1983.

U.S. Department of Defense, Joint Bearing Working Group. *Joint Logistics Commanders Bearing Study.* Washington, D.C.: JLC, June 18, 1986. ("JLC Bearing Study.")

U.S. Department of Defense, Office of the Inspector General. *Quick-Reaction Report on the Review of the Restrictive Contract Clause on Antifriction Bearings.* Report No. 92-067. Washington, D.C.: DoD, April 3, 1992.

U.S. General Accounting Office. *Industrial Base: Assessing the Risk of DoD's Foreign Dependence.* Washington, D.C.: GAO, April 1994.

———. *High Technology Competitiveness: Trends in U.S. and Foreign Performance.* Washington, D.C.: GAO, September, 1992.

———. *Federal Research: Sematech's Technological Progress and Proposed R&D Program.* Washington, D.C.: GAO, July 1992.

———. *Technology Transfer: Japanese Firms Involved in F-15 Coproduction and Civil Aircraft Programs.* Washington, D.C.: GAO, June 1992.

———. *International Procurement: NATO Allies' Implementation of Reciprocal Defense Agreements.* Washington, D.C.: GAO, March 1992.

———. *International Trade: U.S. Business Access to Certain Foreign State-of-the-Art Technology.* Washington, D.C.: GAO, September 1991.

———. *European Initiatives: Implications for U.S. Defense Trade and Cooperation.* Washington, D.C.:GAO, April 1991.

———. *Defense Procurement: DoD Purchases of Foreign-Made Machine Tools.* Washington, D.C.: GAO, February 1991.

———. *Industrial Base: Significance of DoD's Foreign Dependence.* Washington, D.C.: GAO, January 1991.

———. *Military Coproduction: U.S. Management of Programs Worldwide.* Washington, D.C.: GAO, 1989.

———. *Adequacy of Information on the U.S. Defense Industrial Base.* Washington, D.C.: GAO, November 15, 1989.

U.S. International Trade Commission. *Competitive Assessment of the U.S. Metalworking Machine Tool Industry.* USITC Publication 1428. September 1983.

Van Steenburg, Robert. "An Analysis of Canadian-American Defence Economic Cooperation: The History and Current Issues." In David G. Haglund, ed. *Canada's Defence Industrial Base.* Kingston, Ont.: Ronald Frye, 1988.

Vawter, Roderick L. *U.S. Industrial Base Dependence/ Vulnerability: Phase I-Survey of*

Literature. Washington, D.C. : National Defense University Press, 1986.

————. *Industrial Mobilization: The Relevant History.* Washington, D.C.: National Defense University Press, 1983.

Vogel, Stephen. "The Power Behind `Spin-Ons': The Military Implications of Japan's Commercial Technology." In Wayne Sandholtz et al., *The Highest Stakes: The Economic Foundations of the Next Security System.* New York: Oxford University Press, 1992, pp. 55-80.

Vollmer, C .D. "The Future Defense Industrial Environment." *Washington Quarterly,* Spring 1990, pp. 93-109.

Walker, Jack L., Jr. *Mobilizing Interest Groups in America.* Ann Arbor: University of Michigan Press, 1991.

Walker, William and Philip Gummett. "Britain and the European Arms Market." *International Affairs,* Vol. 65, No. 3 (Summer 1989), pp. 419-42.

Walker, Stephen G. "The Evolution of Operational Code Analysis." *Political Psychology,* Vol. 11, No. 2 (1990), pp. 403-18.

Walt, Stephen M. "The Renaissance of Security Studies." *International Studies Quarterly,* Vol. 35 (1991), p. 211-39.

Waltz, Kenneth N. "Reflections on *Theory of International Politics*: A Response to My Critics." In Robert O. Keohane, ed. *Neorealism and its Critics.* New York: Columbia University Press, 1986.

————. *Theory of International Politics.* New York: Random House, 1979.

————. *Man, the State and War.* New York: Columbia University Press, 1959.

Webb, Simon. *NATO and 1992: Defense Acquisition and Free Markets.* R-3758-FF. Santa Monica, Calif.: RAND Corporation, July 1989.

Weber, Max. *Economy and Society.* Edited by Guenther Roth and Claus Wittich. Berkeley: University of California Press, 1978.

Weidenbaum, Murray. *Small Wars, Big Defense: Paying for the Military after the Cold War.* New York: Oxford University Press, 1992.

Weiner, Myron, and Samuel Huntington, eds. *Understanding Political Development.* Boston: Little, Brown, 1987.

Weir, Margaret. "Innovation and Boundaries in American Employment Policy." *Political Science Quarterly,* Vol. 107, No. 2 (1992), pp. 256-57.

Wendt, Alexander E. "The Agent-Structure Problem in International Relations Theory." *International Organization,* Vol. 41, No. 3 (Summer 1987), pp. 335-70.

Williams, Roger. "UK Science and Technology: Policy, Controversy and Advice." *The Political Quarterly,* Vol. 59, No. 2 (1988), pp. 132-44.

Wilson, John S. "Collaboration in Research and Development: Selected Examples." In National Academy of Sciences, *The Government Role in Civilian Technology: Building a New Alliance.* Washington, D.C.: National Academy Press, 1992, pp. 131-51.

Wolfers, Arnold. "`National Security' as an Ambiguous Symbol." *Political Science Quarterly.* Vol. 67 (December 1952), pp. 481-502.

Yoffie, David B. "American Trade Policy: An Obsolete Bargain." In John Chubb and Paul Peterson, eds. *Can the Government Govern?* Washington, D.C.: Brookings Institution, 1989.

Ziegler, J. Nicholas. "Semiconductors." *Daedalus,* Vol. 120, No. 4 (Fall 1991), pp. 155-82.

Zweerts, Robert, with Kelly Campbell. "The Search for Integrated European Programme Management." In Jane Davis Drown, Clifford Drown, and Kelly Campbell, eds. *A Single European Arms Industry?* London: Brassey's, 1990, pp. 77-79.

Zycher, Benjamin, Kenneth A. Solomon, and Loren Yager. *An "Adequate Insurance" Approach to Critical Dependencies of the Department of Defense*. Santa Monica, Calif.: RAND Corporation, 1991.

Zysman, John. *Governments, Markets and Growth: Financial Systems and the Politics of Industrial Change*. Ithaca, N.Y.: Cornell University Press, 1983.

Zysman, John, and Laura D'Andrea Tyson, eds.   *American Industry in International Competition*. Ithaca, N.Y. : Cornell University Press, 1983.

Index

About the Author

ERIK R. PAGES is Deputy Vice President at Business Executives for National Security in Washington D.C. He previously served as Director of the Office of Economic Conversion Information at the U.S. Department of Commerce. His articles have appeared in *SAIS Review*, *Business & Society Review*, and *Defense Analysis*, among others.

ISBN 0-275-95313-0

EAN

9 780275 953133

HARDCOVER BAR CODE